ALSO BY UCADIA

Pactum De Singularis Caelum
Pactum De Singularis Christus
Pactum De Singularis Islam
Pactum De Singularis Spiritus

Maxims of Divine Law
Maxims of Natural Law
Maxims of Cognitive Law
Maxims of Bioethics Law
Maxims of Ecclesiastical Law
Maxims of Positive Law
Maxims of Sovereign Law
Maxims of Fiduciary Law
Maxims of Administrative Law
Maxims of Economic Law
Maxims of Monetary Law
Maxims of Civil Law
Maxims of Criminal Law
Maxims of Education Law
Maxims of Food & Drugs Law
Maxims of Urban Law
Maxims of Company Law
Maxims of Technology Law
Maxims of Trade & Intellectual Property Law
Maxims of Security Law
Maxims of Military Law
Maxims of International Law

MISSALE CHRISTUS

PRIMUS

Proper of Life and Mysteries

Official English First Edition

By

UCADIA

Published by Ucadia Books Company, a Delaware stock corporation (File Number 6779670)
901 N Market St #705 Wilmington Delaware 19801.
First edition.

ISBN 978-1-64419-066-1

Pactum De Singularis Caelum

Covenant of One Heaven

Article 134 (Supreme Sacred Gifts & Rites)

Supreme Sacred Gifts and Rites of Heaven shall be the customary rules, standards and procedures whereby the Thirty-Three (33) Sacred Gifts of Heaven are properly administered and dispensed by qualified and authorised persons, in accord with the most sacred Covenant.

"**Missal of Christ**" (*Missale Christus*) shall be the original and primary sacred text containing the necessary rubrics, canons, sacramentaries, votives, invocations, instructions and orders for the proper conduct and proceeding of Sacred Liturgy of the Universal Rites of One Christ. The conduct of all sacramentaries concerning the thirty-three Sacraments and Extra-Sacramental Rites and Rubrics of Heaven shall be in accord with the Missal of Christ (Missale Christus).

Pactum De Singularis Christus
Covenant of One Christ

Article 14 (Missale Christus)

Universal Ecclesia of One Christ shall fulfil its sanctifying function through the Sacred Liturgy, being the rightful exercise of the presbyterial function entrusted to it by Christ. Within the Sacred Liturgy, the sanctification of humanity is perfected through visible signs and effected in a competent manner proper to each sign. Through the Sacred Liturgy, the worship of God and the Divine Creator of Heaven and Earth is conducted by the united Members of the Living Body of One Christ.

In accord with Article 134 (*Supreme Sacred Gifts and Rites*) of the most sacred Covenant *Pactum De Singularis Caelum*, The Missal of Christ (*Missale Christus*) shall be the original and primary sacred text containing the necessary rubrics, canons, sacramentaries, votives, invocations, instructions and orders for the proper conduct and proceeding of Sacred Liturgy of the Universal Rites of One Christ.

The conduct of all Sacramentals and Extra-Sacramentals of Heaven is in accord with the Missal of Christ (*Missale Christus*).

The Missal of Christ (*Missale Christus*) shall be divided into three (3) sacred books:-

(i) Proper of Life & Mysteries; and

(ii) Proper of Days of Heroes & Saints; and

(iii) Proper of Sacraments, Rites & Prayers.

MISSALE CHRISTUS

PRIMUS

PROPER OF LIFE & MYSTERIES

CONTENTS

Title I – Divine Mission of Liturgy

I.I – DIVINE MISSION OF LITURGY

Divine Mission of Liturgy

1. A true Christian is not one that places the words of men and women above the Risen Christ, but one who gladly and willingly obeys the Magisterium of Christ, by bearing true witness to the Good News, through serving the real needs of others as a living embodiment of the Divine Word. There can be no doubt.

Verily, there is one commandment of faith above all others, whereby every Christian is called to testify, that: *Christ suffered and died for us; Christ is risen for us; Christ lives through us as his united living body.*

These are not mere words of some simple rote creed, or some ancient historic event to an authentic Christian, but a call to action, through the symbol of the cross: That God the Divine Creator of all Existence and all Heaven and Earth loves the Homo Sapien species and specifically each and every living and deceased member; and our history and struggles upon this beautiful planet have not been in vain, nor alone; and that God so loves us, that he brought forth a "singularity" of all human beings that have lived or will ever live, in the form of his flesh and blood, who chose to sacrifice himself, to end forever all forms of ritual blood sacrifice, to forgive the sins of our first forefathers as well as our future descendants, so that we might learn that the true nature of God and the Divine Creator is love and wisdom, not wrath and harsh judgement.

Indeed, in so many ways, the path of comprehending and living the deeper Revelations of the Good News of the Risen Christ mirror the journey of humanity in its own emancipation and enlightenment. We are a species proud of our technological achievements and scientific knowledge, yet still struggling to find a sustainable balance between nature and our own yearning to discover the deepest truths of the Universe. So too, Christians are awakening to a New Evangelisation through the simple, yet profoundly powerful messages found within Sacred Scripture and the capacity for sustainable and manifest change, when enough people choose to act as true Disciples of Christ.

People of all races, creeds and cultures have not lost the quest to find spiritual purpose, nor has the message or relevancy of the Universal Ecclesia weakened, but instead has been greatly strengthened by real and continued concrete acts of mercy, leadership and courage.

Through the miracle of the Resurrection, Christ did prove that death is not a finality and that all men and women have the capacity to eternal life and redemption; and that we should live in our hearts and act in accordance with the authentic Christian values as the Universal values of Divine maxims of Law: That all are equal before the same laws, and that no man or woman be enslaved, or bound against their will; and to make our promises and words be our bond; and that we live according to the Christian Virtues of respect, honesty, courage, enthusiasm, compassion, joy and discernment. This is the Divine Mission of Liturgy for all Christians.

Origin of the word Liturgy

2. Just as the ancient Greek composite word δημοκρᾰτῐᾱ (dēmokratíā) represents the public rules of the people (from demos meaning "people" and krateo meaning "rules or command"), there is no question that the composite word **Liturgy** (from *laos* meaning "faithful/religious people" and *ergon* meaning "actions, rituals, work or tasks") is firmly bound to describing the formula of purposeful religious worship from at least the time of Christ; and in particular the history of proper Christian worship.

Whilst it is a self evident truth that all forms of organised religious worship share the similar notions to "public duty" and "public service", it is a gross error to conclude that the term "liturgy" may be intermingled between public and ecclesiastical actions. Instead, all proper liturgy is first and foremost spiritual in character, before any public application; whereas numerous public acts may be without the necessary ethical and religious character to be considered "liturgical".

Thus, in a Christian and Jewish sense, the term Liturgy means the complete set of formal and official rites and services of the Universal Ecclesia of Christ. The term is also used as a permitted dignity of Customary and Traditional Christian Rites that have bound themselves in unity to the one true apostolic Universal Ecclesia of Christ.

Origin and Source of Christian Liturgy

3. A fundamental tenet of faith of all Christians is the immutable truth that the ultimate source and origin of all proper Christian Liturgy begins with the purposeful actions, rituals, works and tasks of our Lord and saviour Jesus Christ. To deny such reasoning is to deny the centrality of the blessed Eucharist in Christian worship and therefore to effectively deny Christian faith itself.

Through the Good News of the most sacred New Testament, a Christian finds his or her heart, calling and way of life, whether such Revelation is then applied personally, or collectively in purposeful religious worship as Liturgy.

There is no question that over the accumulation of time, the interpretation of the purposeful actions, rituals, works and tasks of the Crucified and Risen Christ, has given rise to great diversity, complexity and sometimes discord. Yet, no matter how complex or diverse the great body of Christian customs and traditions have become, there should be no uncertainty or disunity as to the ultimate source and origin of all proper Christian Liturgy.

Christ and Divine Mission of Liturgy

4. Christ himself was unequivocal and precise on the subject of organised worship as Liturgy. Such rites, prayers, rituals and services are the direct links between the minds and spirits of the people upon the Earth and our Heavenly Father and all the angels, saints and ancestors in Heaven. Secondly, that the intention, knowledge and heart behind such rites, prayers, rituals and services is as essential as the proper forms themselves. Finally, that an authentic rite, prayer, ritual or service is distinguished from hollow or "false actions" when it is inclusive, respectful, open and merciful. These teachings are at the heart of the Magisterium of Christ himself in expressing the Divine Mission of Liturgy.

In contrast, Jesus repeatedly condemned elaborate and hollow rituals, without proper intention, or designed to exclude or curse others as an abomination against all Heaven and Earth. Throughout his Ministry, he expressed his disappointment and even contempt for those who position themselves and claim to be interpreters of the Will of the Divine, yet demonstrate none of the qualities or competencies for an authentic clerical vocation.

Dead Liturgy of the Doctrines of Men

5. Despite the best of intentions and genuine faith of leaders of the past, the Liturgy of the Church has not stayed in perfect congruence with the Divine Mission given to it by Christ. In seeking to honour and protect the Divine Revelations and Divine Words of God, the Church created procedural norms and barriers and rules. Over time, these protections have become so overwhelming, so self consuming that a few in each generation of Christian leaders have fallen prey to the worship of clericalism as a false idol, rather than the true Words of Christ.

This is not the first time civilisation has witnessed this kind of phenomena. The city of Ur, the birthplace of Abraham was once a vibrant and living city. As centuries past, it became known as a place of the highest honour for the burial of notable kings, queens, priests and scholars. Six hundred years before the first arrival of Christ, Ur had become the most famous Necropolis of the ancient world – the city of the dead and a museum of the past maintained by a priest class obsessed in the false idol of clericalism and doctrinal purity. It mattered not to these priests that the very doctrines they worshipped as a form of god were written by men. Instead, they jealously guarded them, like infernal hounds, lest anyone question their authenticity to Divine Law.

The church itself faces such a crossroad. After centuries, many of its churches literally have become museums and mausoleums of death. Rites and rituals have become so chained by the worship of doctrinal rules made by men, that there is scarcely any space for the Holy Spirit to find light to breathe.

Any appearance of a decline of Christianity across western nations is not primarily due to external influences, but internal influences, fixed on a belligerent, obsessive and false doctrinal worship of a liturgy of death – in complete contradiction to the true teachings of Christ. A dead liturgy is not the liturgy of Christ. It is the liturgy of nihilists who believe in nothing but their own power and their doctrinal legacy.

6. When Christ first empowered his Disciples on a Divine Mission of Evangelisation through the Holy Spirit, it was an act of succession as an act of rebirth and renewal of a new apostolic generation. This understanding is in fact at the very heart and mission of bishops of the Universal Ecclesia as direct apostolic successors to the authority and powers of the first disciples of Christ. Such rebirth and renewal can only exist as a continual Divine act of creation and life.

Living Liturgy of Christ

When Christ called upon his disciples and successors to bear witness to the Good News, it was to lead by example not only by deed but by words. Thus, the blood of many thousands of martyrs over the centuries have been a source of constant renewal, precisely because of the courage and example of their lives. Yet it is also their Divinely inspired words that should rightly be considered an integral part of a Living Liturgy. With the inclusion of such words and teachings within a Living Liturgy, precisely to the instructions of Christ himself, the sacrifices of so many heroes of faith are manifestly more powerful and profound.

Thus, the Living Liturgy of Christ must continue to evolve and adapt. It must recognise the need to be respectful and inclusive of different cultures and peoples, as well as the history of different denominations of the Universal Ecclesia.

7. No matter how old a rite, or ritual or practice is claimed; if it is contradictory to the Magisterium of the Risen Christ, then it is contradictory to the Divine Mission of Christian Liturgy.

Restoring the true Liturgy of Christ

Thus, with the inspiration and assistance of our collective Divine Father, through the presence of the Risen Christ and the strength of the Holy Spirit, *Missale Christus* makes it entirely possible to redeem and restore the authentic Christian Liturgy to be fully compliant with the Good News of our Lord Jesus Christ.

I.II – UNIVERSAL ECCLESIA OF ONE CHRIST

1. The most sacred *Universal Ecclesia of One Christ*, also known as the *One Holy Apostolic Universal Ecclesia*, also known as the *Sol Ecclesia*, also known as the *Authentic Body of Christ*, is the first, highest and supreme association, aggregate, fraternity, body, entity and society of Members sharing spiritual heritage associated with all forms of Christian and Jewish faiths.

Universal Ecclesia of One Christ

In accord with Article 4 (*Authority and Power*) of the sacred Covenant *Pactum De Singularis Christus* and Article 92 (*One Christ*) of the most sacred Covenant *Pactum De Singularis Caelum*, no Christian or Jewish person, association, aggregate, institute, body, entity or society may assert or claim higher jurisdiction or authority than the Universal Ecclesia of One Christ.

All living Higher Life Forms who profess to be Christian or Jewish are *ipso facto* (as a matter of fact) subject first to the laws of One Heaven and second to the laws of the Universal Body of Christ above any other lesser society, association, aggregate, institute, fraternity, society, entity or body.

Furthermore, every and all ordained, acknowledged, commissioned or certified clergy of any Christian or Jewish body are also officers of One Christ; and subject to the laws and obligations of One Christ first above any other lesser society, association, aggregate, institute, fraternity, society, entity or body.

2. The Universal Ecclesia of One Christ as the *Sol Ecclesia* is a Supernatural and Spiritual entity registered and recognised in accord with the Great Ledger and Public Record of One Heaven as a *Divine Person* and *Divine Trust* possessing certain Divine Rights of Use and Purpose.

Trust & Personality of Sol Ecclesia

Sol Ecclesia symbolises the eternal forgiveness, mercy and redemption of all Christians and Jews that have physically departed; and the truth and fulfilment of the Divine Promise that the faithfully departed continue to live on in true spirit in the presence of the Divine Creator of all existence and the glory and joy of One Heaven.

As a Divine Person and Divine Trust, the Universal Ecclesia of One Christ as the *Sol Ecclesia* signifies the permanent and perfect presence of the *Holy Spirit* bound in sacred matrimony to the Universal Ecclesia. Thus, the permanent, perfect and irrevocable presence of the Holy Spirit personified as the Sol Ecclesia of the Universal Ecclesia signifies an eternal and complete communion between the Universal Ecclesia of One Christ and with God and the Divine Creator of all

Existence and all Heaven and Earth.

3. The Universal Ecclesia of One Christ as the Authentic Living Body of Christ is a Living and Universal entity registered and recognised in accord with the Great Ledger and Public Record of One Heaven as a True Person and *Universal True Trust* possessing certain Natural Rights of Use and Purpose. Trust & Personality of Authentic Living Body of Christ

The Authentic Living Body of Christ symbolises all Living Members as being incorporated into the true Living Body of Christ as one united family; and the fulfilment of Sacred Scripture in the return and permanent presence of Christ Redeemed.

As a Universal True Trust, the Universal Ecclesia of One Christ possesses a True Personality based upon its Divine Personality guided by its True Mind and Intent being the Covenant of One Christ. The Society of One Christ shall have mortal life for one (1) complete Era of three thousand two hundred ten (3210) years until its physical death.

Upon its physical death, the people of the Earth may choose for the Society to be reborn for another Era, or for a new named Society to be created in accord with the canons and laws of One Heaven.

I.III – DIVINE MISSION OF LITURGY OF UNIVERSAL ECCLESIA

1. The Universal Ecclesia of One Christ is solely authorised and empowered by God and the Divine Creator of all Existence, through Jesus Christ with the Holy Spirit, to protect, prescribe and promote the rightful exercise of the presbyterial function entrusted to it by Christ. Divine Mission of Liturgy of Universal Ecclesia of One Christ

The Universal Ecclesia of One Christ is solely entrusted to take full custody, responsibility and administration of the original and primary sacred text containing the necessary rubrics, canons, votives, invocations, instructions and orders for the proper conduct and proceeding of Sacred Liturgy of the Universal Rites of the Crucified and Risen Christ.

2. Within the Sacred Liturgy, the sanctification of humanity is perfected through visible signs and effected in a competent manner proper to each sign. Through the Sacred Liturgy, the worship of God and the Divine Creator of Heaven and Earth is conducted by the united Members of the Living Body of One Christ. Sacred Liturgy and Living Body of One Christ

3. The Missal of the Crucified and Risen Christ (*Missale Christus*) is the original and primary sacred text containing the necessary rubrics, canons, votives, invocations, instructions and orders for the proper conduct and proceeding of Sacred Liturgy of the Universal Rites of Missale Christus as fulfilment of Divine Mission

One Christ. The conduct of all rites concerning the thirty three Sacraments of Heaven is in accord with the Missal of Christ (Missale Christus).

I.IV – AMENDMENT & REVISION OF LITURGY OF UNIVERSAL ECCLESIA

Amendment & Revision of Liturgy of Universal Ecclesia

1. As Christ himself emphatically expressed, the Universal Ecclesia may be compared to a living vine with many branches as the living body of Christ. The expression and celebration therefore of sacred liturgy through sacred scripture, rubrics, canons, rites, votives, invocations, instructions and orders must reflect this living reality.

   Thus any church that encloses and seals its doctrines is like a "dead branch" as described by Christ, that cuts itself off from a living and vibrant faith that necessarily must undergo periods of renewal, pruning, cleansing and reaffirmation of its founding values to the Good News and the commandments of God the Father of all Creation and Existence.

   The careful management of necessary renewal, while preserving the intrinsic nature of faith is a delicate balance that necessitates a certain formality as given, for example, by God through the wonder of the seasons and nature.

   It is expected therefore, that change and renewal of Sacred Liturgy as with Sacred Doctrines will be a feature of each and every generation and that such change and renewal, whilst at times painful, shall continue to yield good fruit, without threatening the very existence of the vine.

   The Missal of the Crucified and Risen Christ (*Missale Christus*) shall be permitted to be amended and revised from time to time, in accord with the strict interpretation of the present section, according to the classifications of *Technical, Special* and *Universal*:

   (i) A *Technical Amendment* is where a specific clause contained within the Sacred Liturgy and Rites is approved for a minor amendment either through the complete replacement of the words contained within a clause, or minor word alteration, due to an error of presentation or translation, or grammar by a properly constituted and authorised Body; and

   (ii) A *Special Amendment* is where a new clause or enhanced meaning to a clause is proposed and added to the Sacred Liturgy and Rites by a properly constituted and authorised Body of an Ecumenical Council; and

(iii) A *Universal Amendment* is where significant new clauses or changes to clauses are proposed and added to the Sacred Liturgy and Rites by a properly constituted and authorised Ecumenical Council.

2. A *Technical Amendment* is where a specific clause contained within the present Sacred Liturgy and Rites is approved for a minor amendment either through the complete replacement of all the words contained within the clause, or minor word alteration. Technical Amendment

A Standing Body shall be formed to facilitate the management of proposed Technical Amendments, with the authority to issue an amended publication no more than once every five years.

A Technical Amendment is permitted to occur under one (1) or more of the following conditions:

(i) That the clause contains a style, typographical or simple grammatical error which will be corrected through the proposed amendment; or

(ii) That the clause contains a significant grammatical or semantic error that renders any true intention of the clause impossible and that the proposed amendment will correct this error to the original intent; or

(iii) That the clause contains a significant error contradicting one (1) or more other clauses of the Sacred Liturgy and Rites and that the proposed amendment will correct this error to the original intent.

3. A *Special Amendment* is where a new clause or enhanced meaning to a clause is proposed and added to the Sacred Liturgy and Rites other than in relation to a Technical Amendment. Special Amendment

A Body opened in session as part of an Ecumenical Council shall be constituted to facilitate the management of proposed Special and Technical Amendments, with the authority to issue a new authorised publication no more than once every ten years.

A Special Amendment is permitted to occur under one (1) or more of the following conditions:

(i) That the proposed Amendment does not in any way contradict a major tenet or principle of the present Sacred Liturgy and Rites; and

(ii) That the proposed Amendment significantly and materially enhances the living faith and times; and

(iii) That two thirds of the official delegates of the Ecumenical Council approve the proposed Amendment.

Universal Amendment

4. A *Universal Amendment* is where significant new clauses or changes to clauses are proposed and added to the Sacred Liturgy and Rites other than in relation to a Special Amendment.

Universal Amendments open the possibility for the greatest renewal and revitalisation of the Living Body of Christ, by re-affirming fundamental values, sacred scriptures, new revelations, doctrines and practices and enable the whole body and its parts an opportunity to undergo a New Evangelisation at least once every one hundred years.

A Body opened in session as part of an Great Ecumenical Council shall be constituted to facilitate the management of proposed Universal, Special and Technical Amendments, with the authority to issue a new authorised publication no more than once every one hundred years.

A Universal Amendment is permitted to occur under one (1) or more of the following conditions:

(i) That the proposed Amendment does not in any way contradict Divine Law, nor the highest principles and ethical values of Universal Faith, even if major tenets or principles are renewed or revised; and

(ii) That the proposed Amendment significantly and materially enhances the knowledge and discernment of the living faith and times; and

(iii) That two thirds of the official delegates of the Great Ecumenical Council approve the proposed Amendment.

Title II – Seven Mysteries of Christ

II.I – SEVEN MYSTERIES OF CHRIST

1. Authentic Mysteries of the Life of the Crucified and Risen Christ have always been the primary source of true Liturgy. Thus, it is without question that the fundamental professions of Christian faith are a true reflection of the mystery of the Life, Death and Resurrection of Christ being: Christ is the personification and embodiment of every human being that has lived or will ever live as a "singularity" of humanity and Divinity and the only son of God; and Christ was borne into this world as a flesh and blood being; and Christ did live and grow up in a family and face all the challenges of average human life; and Christ did willingly accept his ministry and did choose to suffer and die so that all our faults and transgressions may be forgiven; and Christ did transcend death and did return to new life in flesh; and Christ did call upon all his disciples to follow his teachings of humility, mercy and justice; and Those that follow Christ and his teachings can never die and are redeemed, as exemplified by our blessed Mother Mary.

Seven Mysteries of Christ and Liturgy

Therefore, it is irrefutable that proper Christian Liturgy must reflect the Christian faith through the elemental mysteries of the Life of the Crucified and Risen Christ.

2. It is self-evident in Christian tradition, that historic Christian Liturgy recognises more than one mystery associated with the life, death and resurrection of Christ, most notably the Mystery of Advent and Christmastide and the Mystery of Lent and Eastertide. It is appropriate that these two periods of reflection and worship are viewed as the most significant, with the celebration of the Mystery of Lent and Eastertide, followed by the Mystery of Advent and Christmastide being the highest standing.

The existence of more than one Mystery

It is clear then that Christian tradition and custom acknowledges the existence of more than two mysteries associated with the life, death and resurrection of Christ, even if the various Christian churches may not have formalised such recognition into a cohesive, complete and clear formal Liturgy.

It is therefore imperative that in celebrating the mysteries of the life, death and resurrection of Christ, that the Universal Ecclesia of Christ, representing the authentic and united body of all Christians and Jews, ensure the fullest and clearest possible description and liturgical rites in respect of the Mysteries of Christ.

3. To all Christians, the first and most significant Day of the Week is Sunday. In name (sun-day) it refers most strongly to the Illumination and Transcendence of the Risen Christ, yet by tradition and custom

Restoration of the Sacred Obligation of

since the beginning of Christianity, Sunday has always been seen as a day of solemn worship and obligation of attendance, free from the distractions and duties of the ordinary week.

every Sunday

In honour of the sacredness of each and every Sunday; and to aid in the restoration of its sanctity, each and every Sunday is recognised as a unique feast day and authentic Holiday within a particular Liturgical Season. Therefore, within societies owing to a Christian heritage, each and every such Holiday must be properly observed so that the faithful are not impeded by their own free will from exercising their choice of witness to faith.

Seven Mysteries of Christ

4. The Universal Ecclesia of One Christ recognises seven primary Mysteries of Christ (comprising the complete Liturgical Cycle of One Year and maximum of sixty-six primary Universal Feasts), being *Immanent, Filial, Eucharistic, Transcendent, Sacred Heart, Redemption* and *Apostolic*:-

(i) *Immanent Mystery* is a variable liturgical season of approximately 41 to 47 days and a maximum of 11 holy feast days, beginning on the *Feast of the Divine Light of the World* (1st Sunday after Mission Sunday), then rising to the solemnity of *Holy Nativity Day*, also known as *Christmas Day* (25th December); and concluding on the solemnity of *New Years Day* (1st January) as a time of expectant waiting, preparation and then celebration of the coming of Christ in flesh; and

(ii) *Filial Mystery* is a variable liturgical season of approximately 36 to 44 days and a maximum of 7 holy feast days, beginning on the *Feast of the Holy Exodus* (first Sunday of January after New Years Day), then rising to the solemnity of *Holy Baptism Day* (third Sunday after feast of the Holy Exodus); and concluding on the solemnity of *Holy Confirmation Sunday* (mid -February and Sunday before Ash Wednesday); and

(iii) *Eucharistic Mystery* is a fixed liturgical season of 40 days and a maximum of 12 holy feast days, beginning on the *Feast of Divine Humility,* also known as *Ash Wednesday* (at mid February), then rising to the solemnity of *Good Friday* (1st Friday after or upon Spring Equinox) and concluding on the solemnity of *Easter Sunday* (First Sunday after Good Friday at end of March); and

(iv) *Transcendent Mystery* is a fixed liturgical season of 44 days and a maximum of 8 holy feast days, beginning on the vigil for the *Feast of Authentic Revelation* (first Sunday after Easter Sunday), then rising to the solemnity of *Ascension Day* (first

Thursday 40 days since Easter Sunday); and concluding on the solemnity of *Pentecost Sunday* (First Sunday 50 days since Easter Sunday (end of May); and

(v) *Sacred Heart Mystery* is a fixed liturgical season of 44 days and a maximum of 7 holy feast days, beginning on the vigil for the *Feast of the Living Body of Christ,* also known as *Corpus Christi Sunday* (first Sunday after Pentecost Sunday), then rising to the solemnity of *Holy Matrimony Day (*4th Sunday after Corpus Christi*);* and concluding on the solemnity of *Sacred Heart Sunday* (last Sunday of June); and

(vi) *Mercy & Redemption Mystery* is a fixed liturgical season of 44 days and a maximum of 8 holy feast days, beginning on the vigil for the *Feast of Divine Mercy* (first Sunday after *Sacred Heart Sunday*), then rising to the solemnity of *Assumption Day* (August 15th); and concluding on the solemnity of *Redemption Sunday* (first Sunday after Assumption Day near end of August); and

(vii) *Apostolic Mystery* is a variable liturgical season approximately 78 to 85 days and a maximum of 13 holy feast days, beginning on the *Feast of the One True Apostolic Universal Ecclesia of Christ*, also known as *Ecumenical Sunday* (first Sunday after Redemption Sunday), then rising to the solemnity of *All Saints Day (*1st November*);* and concluding on the solemnity of *Mission Sunday (*2nd Sunday after All Saints Day).

II.II – IMMANENT MYSTERY OF CHRIST

Immanent Mystery of Christ

1. The most *Sacred Immanent Mystery of Christ*, also known as *Advent* and *Christmastide*, is a variable liturgical season of approximately 41 to 47 days and a maximum of 11 holy feast days, beginning on the *Feast of the Divine Light of the World* (1st Sunday after *Mission Sunday*), then rising to the solemnity of *Holy Nativity Day*, also known as *Christmas Day* (25th December); and concluding on the solemnity of *New Years Day* (1st January).

The liturgical season of the *Immanent Mystery of Christ* exists as a time of preparation and anticipation for the coming of Christ and the necessary and constant need for person and community renewal, rebirth and rejuvenation.

The term "Immanent" encompasses both Advent and Christmastide as elements of the liturgical season and is chosen as the core theme of the mystery of the Singularity of Christ choosing to become flesh and to experience the pains and trials of human life.

2. The Sacred Colour for the liturgical season of the *Immanent Mystery of Christ* is **purple**, representing the Divine Imperial Authority of Christ as the Singularity of all Humanity. All Vestments used in relation to all feast days of the liturgical season and all dressings and fabrics used throughout the church during this period, should adhere to the colour of purple.

Sacred Colour of Season and Vestments

3. The Eleven (11) Holy Feast Days for the liturgical season of the *Immanent Mystery of Christ* are:

Eleven Holy Feast Days

(i) *Feast of the Divine Light of the World* (first Sunday after Mission Sunday), being the opening Feast of the liturgical season; and

(ii) *Feast of the Annunciation of Blessed Mary*, also known as *Annunciation Sunday* (first Sunday after the Feast of the Divine Light of the World); and

(iii) *Feast of St Joseph*, also known as *St Joseph Sunday* (second Sunday after the Feast of the Divine Light of the World); and

(iv) *Feast of the Magnificat of Mary Mother of Mankind*, also known as *Magnificat Sunday* Mother of all (third Sunday after the Feast of the Divine Light of the World); and

(v) *Feast of the Nativity of John the Baptist*, also known as *St. John the Baptist Sunday* (fourth Sunday after the Feast of the Divine Light of the World); and

(vi) *Feast of Emmanuel*, also known as *Emmanuel Sunday* (Sunday before Christmas Day) as the fifth Sunday of the liturgical season when Christmas Day falls on a Wednesday, Thursday, Monday or Tuesday; and

(vii) *Christmas Vigil* (December 24th) as the night before Christmas; and

(viii) *Christmas Midnight* (December 25th); and

(ix) *Holy Nativity Day*, also known as *Christmas Day* (December 25th); and

(x) *Feast of Holy Testamen*t, also known as *Testament Sunday* as the Sunday before New Years Day, when Christmas Day falls on a Wednesday, Thursday, Friday, Monday or Tuesday; and

(xi) *New Years Day* (1st January).

4. *Annunciation Sunday*, also known as the Annunciation to Blessed Mary, is the Universal Solemnity of the first Sunday of Advent following the beginning of the Immanent Mystery of Christ and the Period of Advent with the Feast of the Divine Light of the World upon the previous Sunday.

Annunciation Sunday

Annunciation Sunday heralds the announcement by the Archangel Gabriel to Mary and the arrival of the Holy Spirit within her. It also signifies the most Holy Apostolic Life Sacrament of Annunciation and the blessing and sacredness of all unborn human life.

The solemnity was originally celebrated by the various churches around the end of March in a literal replication of the time associated with human pregnancy (9 months) before the following Christmas. However, sacred scripture makes frequent use of units of time in different contexts to condense time frames or express long time frames with the use of days to mean weeks, or even years. Thus, the necessity to confirm to such simplistic representation of time, contrary to the revelation and use of time within scripture is unnecessary. Furthermore, the solemnity of the Annunciation did also cause a diminishing of the most sacred season of Lent and the Paschal Mystery when such times did fall within the same period. Thus, the sanctity and meaning to our Blessed Lady and Divine Purpose has been restored as intended, by placing it within the season of proper Mystery of the Immanent Christ.

II.III – FILIAL MYSTERY OF CHRIST

1. The most *Sacred Filial Mystery of Christ*, is a variable liturgical season of approximately 36 to 44 days and a maximum of 7 holy feast days, beginning on the *Feast of the Holy Exodus* (the first Sunday of January after New Years Day), then rising to the solemnity of Holy Baptism Day (3rd Sunday after feast of the Holy Exodus); and concluding on the solemnity of *Confirmation Sunday* (mid-February and Sunday before Ash Wednesday).

Filial Mystery of Christ

The liturgical season of the *Filial Mystery of Christ* exists as a time of family, learning, initiation, tolerance, communication and commitment as necessary qualities of family life and the transition from infant to child, from child to youth and from youth to adulthood.

2. The Sacred Colour for the liturgical season of the *Filial Mystery of Christ* is **blue**, representing the eternal trust and covenant between the Divine Creator and all Humanity. All Vestments used in relation to all feast days of the liturgical season and all dressings and fabrics used throughout the church during this period, should adhere to the colour

Sacred Colour of Season and Vestments

of blue.

3. The Seven (7) Holy Feast Days for the liturgical season of the *Filial Mystery of Christ* are: Seven Holy Feast Days

(i) *Feast of the Holy Exodus,* also known as *Exodus Sunday* and *Refugee Sunday* (first Sunday after New Years Day); and

(ii) *Feast of the Holy Innocents,* also known as *Children Sunday* (first Sunday after feast of the Holy Exodus); and

(iii) *Feast of the Epiphany of Christ*, also known as *Epiphany Sunday* (second Sunday after feast of the Holy Exodus); and

(iv) *Feast of the Holy Baptism of Christ,* also known as *Holy Baptism Sunday* (third Sunday after feast of the Holy Exodus); and

(v) *Feast of the Apprentices*, also known as *Apprentice Sunday* (fourth Sunday after feast of the Holy Exodus); and

(vi) *Feast of the Teachers*, also known as *Teachers Sunday* (Sunday before Confirmation Day) as the fifth Sunday of the liturgical season after the Feast of the Holy Exodus when New Years Day falls on a Friday or Wednesday or Saturday; and

(vii) *Feast of Holy Confirmation*, also known as *Confirmation Day* (mid -February and Sunday before Ash Wednesday).

II.IV – EUCHARISTIC MYSTERY OF CHRIST

1. The most *Sacred Eucharistic Mystery of Christ*, also known as the Paschal Mystery and Lent and Eastertide, is a fixed liturgical season of 40 days and a maximum of 12 holy feast days, beginning on the *Feast of Divine Humility*, also known as *Ash Wednesday* (at mid February), then rising to the solemnity of *Good Friday* (1st Friday after or upon Spring Equinox) and concluding on the solemnity of *Easter Sunday* (First Sunday after Good Friday at the end of March). Eucharistic Mystery of Christ

The liturgical season of the *Eucharistic Mystery of Christ* exists as a most important time for personal austerity and abstinence, reflection, meditation on the sacrifice of Christ and all Heroes and Saints of the community, as well as the deeper meditation on the paradoxes of life and eternal life and death and resurrection.

The term "Eucharistic" is chosen in preference to Paschal and Lent and Eastertide as Lent and Eastertide remain elements of the Mystery, while the term "paschal" is better attributed to the days leading to

Good Friday than the entire liturgical season. Finally, to ensure the faithful adequately grasp the greater dimension of the Eucharist, the term seeks to make the season and the sacraments of the Mass united as clearly complimentary. In turn, this assists in education and protecting the integrity of the Eucharist celebration.

2. The Sacred Colour for the liturgical season of the *Eucharistic Mystery of Christ* is **red**, representing the ultimate sacrifice of Christ of his flesh and blood, his death and resurrection for the forgiveness of all the sins of humanity, of the past, now and forever. All Vestments used in relation to all feast days of the liturgical season and all dressings and fabrics used throughout the church during this period, should adhere to the colour of red.

Sacred Colour of Season and Vestments

3. The Twelve (12) Holy Feast Days for the liturgical season of the *Eucharistic Mystery of Christ* are:

Twelve Holy Feast Days

(i) *Feast of Divine Humility,* also known as *Ash Wednesday* (at mid February); and

(ii) *Feast of Holy Abstinence*, also known as *Abstinence Sunday* (first Sunday after Ash Wednesday); and

(iii) *Feast of the Golden Rule of Law*, also known as *Divine Law Sunday* (second Sunday after Ash Wednesday); and

(iv) *Feast of Divine Justice*, also known as *Justice Sunday* (third Sunday after Ash Wednesday); and

(v) *Feast of Divine Service*, also known as *Obligation Sunday* (fourth Sunday after Ash Wednesday); and

(vi) *Feast of the Divine New Covenant*, also known as *Pi Day* (always March 14th) and the Feast of the Last Blood Sacrifice; and

(vii) *Palm Sunday* (Sunday before Good Friday); and

(viii) *Holy Tuesday* (Tuesday before Good Friday); and

(ix) *Holy Wednesday* (Wednesday before Good Friday); and

(x) *Holy Thursday* (Day before Good Friday); and

(xi) *Good Friday*, (1st Friday after or upon Spring Equinox); and

(xii) *Easter Sunday*, also known as *Resurrection Day*.

II.V – TRANSCENDENT MYSTERY OF CHRIST

Transcendent Mystery of Christ

1. The most *Sacred Transcendent Mystery of Christ*, is a fixed liturgical season of 44 days and a maximum of 8 holy feast days, beginning on the *Feast of Authentic Revelation* (first Sunday after Easter Sunday), then rising to the solemnity of *Ascension Day* (First Thursday within 40 days since Easter Sunday); and concluding on the solemnity of *Pentecost Sunday* (First Sunday within 50 days since Easter Sunday (end of May).

   The liturgical season of the *Transcendent Mystery of Christ* exists as a time of deep learning and spiritual wisdom, courage and willingness to push beyond the boundaries of fear, prejudice, narrow judgement and selfishness to explore the supernatural mysteries of the transcendent Christ as the singularity of all human beings that have ever lived or will ever live, as the embodiment and personification of the Divine and son of the Divine and the extraordinary potential of all human beings.

Sacred Colour of Season and Vestments

2. The Sacred Colour for the liturgical season of the *Transcendent Mystery of Christ* is **gold**, representing the illumination of the Risen Christ with the gift of the Holy Spirit in the emancipation of the mind, spirit and body; and the renewal of the Universal Ecclesia. All Vestments used in relation to all feast days of the liturgical season and all dressings and fabrics used throughout the church during this period, should adhere to the colour of gold.

Eight Holy Feast Days

3. The Eight (8) Holy Feast Days for the liturgical season of the *Transcendent Mystery of Christ* are:

   (i) *Feast of Authentic Revelation*, also known as *Revelation Sunday* (first Sunday after Easter Sunday); and

   (ii) *Feast of the Archangels*, also known as *Angelic Sunday* (first Sunday after Revelation Sunday); and

   (iii) *Feast of the Apostles*, also known as *Apostolic Sunday* (second Sunday after Revelation Sunday); and

   (iv) *Feast of the Disciples* (third Sunday after Revelation Sunday); and

   (v) *Feast of St. Peter, Rock of Ages*, also known as *Foundation (Stone) Sunday* (fourth Sunday after Revelation Sunday); and

   (vi) *Feast of the Ascension of Christ*, also known as *Ascension Day* (Thursday approximately forty days after Easter Sunday); and

   (vii) *Feast of the New Evangelisation*, also known as *Evangelisation*

Sunday (Sunday before Pentecost); and

(viii) *Pentecost Sunday* (fifty days after Easter Sunday).

II.VI – SACRED HEART MYSTERY OF CHRIST

Sacred Heart Mystery of Christ

1. The most *Sacred Heart Mystery of Christ*, is a fixed liturgical season of 44 days and a maximum of seven holy feast days, beginning on the Feast of the *Living Body of Christ*, also known as *Corpus Christi Sunday* (first Sunday after Pentecost Sunday), then rising to the solemnity of *Holy Matrimony Day* (4th Sunday after Corpus Christi); and concluding on the solemnity of *Sacred Heart Sunday* (last Sunday of June).

   The liturgical season of the *Sacred Heart Mystery of Christ* exists as a time of celebration and joy at the abundance of love of the Divine and the institutions of the sacraments at the heart of our society, exemplified by the sacrament of Holy Matrimony between men and women.

Sacred Colour of Season and Vestments

2. The Sacred Colour for the liturgical season of the *Sacred Heart Mystery of Christ* is **pink**, representing the People of God as the Universal Ecclesia as the living flesh and living Body of Christ. All Vestments used in relation to all feast days of the liturgical season and all dressings and fabrics used throughout the church during this period, should adhere to the colour of pink.

Seven Holy Feast Days

3. The Seven (7) Holy Feast Days for the liturgical season of the *Sacred Heart Mystery of Christ* are:

   (i) *Feast of the Living Body of Christ*, also known as *Corpus Christi Sunday* (first Sunday after Pentecost Sunday); and

   (ii) *Feast of Divine Love* (first Sunday after Corpus Christi); and

   (iii) *Feast of Holy Union* (second Sunday after Corpus Christi); and

   (iv) *Feast of Authentic Fidelity*, also known as *Fidelity Sunday* (third Sunday after Corpus Christi); and

   (v) *Feast of Holy Matrimony*, also known as *Matrimony Sunday* (fourth Sunday after Corpus Christi); and

   (vi) *Feast of Immaculate Heart of Mary*, also known as *Immaculate Heart Sunday* (Sunday before Feast of Sacred Heart); and

   (vii) *Feast of the Sacred Heart of Jesus*, also known as *Sacred Heart*

Sunday.

II.VII – MERCY & REDEMPTION MYSTERY OF CHRIST

1. The most *Sacred Mercy & Redemption Mystery of Christ*, is a fixed liturgical season of 44 days and a maximum of 8 holy feast days, beginning on the Feast of *Divine Mercy* (first Sunday after *Sacred Heart Sunday*), then rising to the solemnity of *Assumption Day* (August 15th); and concluding on the solemnity of *Redemption Sunday* (first Sunday after Assumption Day near end of August).

Mercy & Redemption Mystery of Christ

The liturgical season of the *Redemption Mystery of Christ* exists as a time of thanksgiving, penance, confession, blessing and reconciliation with God in knowing the Divine Mercy, Forgiveness and Redemption of each person and each institution and the entirety of the Christian and Jewish family.

2. The Sacred Colour for the liturgical season of the *Redemption Mystery of Christ* is **white**, representing the purification of sin, the absence of blemish of humanity in the mind and face of God and the authenticity of penance and reconciliation of all the people of God through faith in the Crucified and Risen Christ. All Vestments used in relation to all feast days of the liturgical season and all dressings and fabrics used throughout the church during this period, should adhere to the colour of white.

Sacred Colour of Season and Vestments

3. The Eight (8) Holy Feast Days for the liturgical season of the *Redemption Mystery of Christ* are:

Eight Holy Feast Days

(i) *Feast of Divine Mercy*, also known as *Divine Mercy Sunday* (first Sunday after Sacred Heart Sunday); and

(ii) *Feast of Sacred Animal Life*, also known as *Animals Day* (first Sunday after the Feast of Divine Mercy); and

(iii) *Feast of Divine Charity*, also known as *Benevolence Sunday* (second Sunday after the Feast of Divine Mercy); and

(iv) *Feast of Atonement*, also known as *Atonement Sunday* (third Sunday after the Feast of Divine Mercy); and

(v) *Feast of Divine Reconciliation*, also known as *Reconciliation Sunday* (fourth Sunday after the Feast of Divine Mercy); and

(vi) *Feast of Divine Illumination of Christ*, also known as *Sacred Fire Sunday or Bonfire Sunday* (fifth Sunday after the Feast of Divine Mercy); and

(vii) *Feast of the Assumption of Blessed Mary*, also known as *Assumption Day* (August 15th); and

(viii) *Feast of Divine Redemption*, also known as *Redemption Day* (first Sunday after Assumption Day).

II.VIII – APOSTOLIC MYSTERY OF CHRIST

1. The most *Sacred Apostolic Mystery of Christ*, is a variable liturgical season approximately 78 to 85 days and a maximum of 13 holy feast days, beginning on the *Feast of the One True Apostolic Universal Ecclesia of Christ*, also known as *Ecumenical Sunday* (first Sunday after Redemption Sunday), then rising to the solemnity of All Saints Day (1st November); and concluding on the solemnity of Mission Sunday (2nd Sunday after All Saints Day).

Apostolic Mystery of Christ

The liturgical season of the *Apostolic Mystery of Christ* exists as a time of promise, courage, strength, faith, oath and vow to the Christian Mission of living, demonstrating and proclaiming the Good News of the Risen Christ and the continual Revelation found through actions of people working together for common and ethical purposes and unifying as the living flesh of Christ.

2. The Sacred Colour for the liturgical season of the *Apostolic Mystery of Christ* is **green**, representing the fruitful and vibrant life of the community of the people of God and the Universal Ecclesia, the sacredness of life and the journey of Apostolic Life for all living and departed souls. All Vestments used in relation to all feast days of the liturgical season and all dressings and fabrics used throughout the church during this period, should adhere to the colour of green.

Sacred Colour of Season and Vestments

3. The Thirteen (13) Holy Feast Days for the liturgical season of the *Apostolic Mystery of Christ* are:

Thirteen Holy Feast Days

(i) *Feast of the One True Apostolic Universal Ecclesia of Christ*, also known as *Ecumenical Sunday* (first Sunday after Redemption Sunday); and

(ii) *Feast of New Kingdom of Heaven on Earth*, also known as *Kingdom Sunday* (first Sunday after Ecumenical Sunday); and

(iii) *Feast of the Professions*, also known as *Profession Sunday* (second Sunday after Ecumenical Sunday); and

(iv) *Feast of the Fiduciaries*, also known as *Fiduciary Sunday* (third Sunday after Ecumenical Sunday); and

(v) *Feast of the Vocations*, also known as *Vocation Sunday* (fourth

Sunday after Ecumenical Sunday); and

(vi) *Feast of the Guardians*, also known as *Guardian Sunday* (fifth Sunday after Ecumenical Sunday); and

(vii) *Feast of Divine Healing*, also known as *Healing Sunday* (sixth Sunday after Ecumenical Sunday); and

(viii) *Feast of Elders*, also known as *Elders Sunday* (seventh Sunday after Ecumenical Sunday); and

(ix) *Feast of Heroes and Martyrs*, also known as *Martyrs Day* (eighth Sunday after Ecumenical Sunday); and

(x) *Feast of Universal Peace*, also known as *Peace Day* (ninth Sunday after Ecumenical Sunday); and

(xi) *All Saints Day* (1st November); and

(xii) *Feast of the sacred Earth*, also known as *Earth Sunday* (Sunday before Mission Sunday); and

(xiii) *Feast of Christian Mission*, also known as *Mission Sunday*.

Title III – The Word and Sacred Liturgy

III.I – THE WORD AND SACRED LITURGY

The Word and Sacred Liturgy

1. As affirmed by all who hold trust in Christ, God the Divine Father of all Creation wills that all men and women be saved by coming to comprehend and discern the knowledge of the truth. Such truth is the knowledge of the existence, mind, nature and will of the Divine, as exemplified through Divine Law as the foundation stone of all civilised law. The transmission of such truth is known as Revelation, and simply as "the Word", as received through the testimonies of various heroes, saints and prophets since the beginning of Civilisation to the present moment.

Christians rightly view the Word of authentic Revelation as possessing a living presence, beyond the time and space of its first formation. It is an essential character of Christian virtue, that all genuine sacred scripture is respected, even if such texts are not canonical for Christians. Thus, Christians of different traditions and customs respect and revere a wide history of sacred texts and writings such as the testimonies and sacred texts of ancient Asian and Middle Eastern prophets and even kings.

Yet, there exists one set of sacred scripture that stands above all others, as the direct revelation of God through his singular personification in the form of the Crucified and Risen Christ. We call this the Good News of Christ, or the Gospels. Through his humanity, united in the person of the Word of God, Christians rightly regard the Good News of Christ as the key instrument of salvation.

Thus the Word of God in the form of the Good News of Christ was, is, and has always been a central focus of Sacred Christian Liturgy from the days of the Apostles; and why by tradition, a particular segment of Divine Liturgy and the Mass was called The Liturgy of the Word for the adoration and reading of canonical sacred scripture, especially the reading of the Gospels.

Authentic Revelation

2. While it is an essential act of faith in accepting the fact that Revelations of the Divine Creator never cease, Christians are careful to distinguish hallucinogenic, or psychic, or spiritual and supernatural experiences, or vivid dreams or even visions, from Authentic Revelation.

Authentic Revelation is seen as the communication and disclosure of some self-evident manifestation of Divine Illumination to a reasonable and rational being of sound mind, through means beyond the scope and ordinary course of the transmission of knowledge. In other words, genuine Revelation is regarded as being some self-evident manifestation of Divine Illumination, providing extraordinary enlightenment, clarity, perception, reason and knowledge, beyond the norm. Therefore, prediction and claimed psychic messages alone do not make for Authentic Revelation.

Seven essential elements for Christians are therefore seen as vital in distinguishing Authentic Revelation from other forms of experiences, being *Relevancy, Timely, Useful, Revelatory, Self-Evidential, Illuminative* and *Supernatural*:

(i) *Relevancy* means that Authentic Divine Revelation is always relevant to an age and time, or crisis or need, or pertinent to an important topic. Thus, the first test of distinguishing Authentic Divine Revelation is that it comes when it is most needed, not when it may be wanted; and

(ii) *Timely* means that Authentic Divine Revelation always comes at precisely the right time, even if such time is not always known by all who seek or pray for such Revelation. Thus, the second test of distinguishing Authentic Divine Revelation is that it meets time lines and promises previously made, even if such time lines were not fully understood; and

(iii) *Useful* means that Authentic Divine Revelation is above all useful and practical and helpful at the relevant time it comes. Thus, the third test of Authentic Divine Revelation is that the Divine does not send useless or stereotypical messages, but gives true gems of Divine Wisdom as Authentic Divine Revelation; and

(iv) *Revelatory* means that Authentic Divine Revelation "reveals" something new from what already "exists in plain sight"; and

(v) *Self-Evidential* means that Authentic Divine Revelation once revealed is "self-evidential" in that it manifests its own validation as Divine Truth. Thus, even if such a message is ignored, repudiated and rejected for being contrary to the established doctrine of some body, profound Wisdom that is Self-evident is far harder to concoct and fabricate as such knowledge carries its own character of authenticity; and

(vi) *Illuminative* means that Authentic Divine Revelation demonstrates extraordinary enlightenment, clarity, perception, reason and knowledge, beyond the norm. It does not mean cliché, or stereotypical, or self-reinforcing, or superficial, or simplistic doctrinal reinforcement. Genuine Divine Illumination does not necessarily mean occult and encoded meaning, nor such phrases and messages deliberately constructed to be confusing or to sound "profound". Instead, true Revelation is powerful in its own right; and

(vii) *Supernatural* means that Authentic Divine Revelation comes from a source and a circumstance clearly with the hallmarks of Divine intervention.

3. Allegory is the technique of using words or symbols to represent certain abstract and sometimes more complex principles. In one sense, all languages are an example of allegory whereby symbols (letters of an alphabet) are used to ascribe certain units of meaning. In some languages where words may have multiple meanings, or multiple words may have similar meanings, the potential for richer allegory is greater or lesser.

Allegory and Authentic Revelation

The first functional purpose of allegory is to be able to "shorten" and "simplify" what might otherwise be a complex and confusing description into the use of less words, by ensuring that such the words chosen and their arrangement transmits the intended meaning.

Thus, words that may describe a people, or place, or time, or lineage within sacred scripture may themselves be allegories to a much deeper message and not to be taken only literally.

A second vital function of allegory, is to use symbols of everyday life that transcend time, languages and history to the present day and into the future. Such symbols are an essential assistance to comprehending complex and sometimes abstract notions that human consciousness may find difficult at first to grasp such as life and death, sacrifice and resurrection, eternal life, mercy and forgiveness.

It is these two essential functions of compacting knowledge and preserving the intent of knowledge that means all Authentic Revelation is allegorical to some degree.

Verily, no Christian can dispute the immutable fact that the Crucified and Risen Christ speaks in allegory as evidenced by the very passages of the Good News when Christ testifies to this fact. Thus, any Christian, or Christian teacher that seeks to promote Authentic Revelation without acknowledging the allegorical nature of the Word, commits a grave error, contrary to the norms and commands of Christ himself.

4. By having a sound comprehension of Sacred Scripture, the nature and test of Authentic Revelation and the power of Allegory, the Christian Faith is able to commit with total confidence to the accuracy of Sacred Scripture expressed within the present Sacred Liturgy and Rites as being the true translation and transliteration of the Authentic

Confidence of accuracy of Sacred Scripture

Revelation of God the Divine Father.

In particular, all Christians united as the Living Body of Christ may be confident that the Sacred Scripture passages of the Good News of Christ reflect the true words and intentions of the Crucified and Risen Christ, without error or contradiction. Such confidence is possible in recognising accrued translation and transliteration issues that have arisen over time, that have diminished the allegorical authority of Authentic Revelation of God, to literal statements impeded by such choices of translation and transliteration.

Therefore, none should regard such clarity and restoration of the Word of God, unless such restoration of the law weakens positions, founded upon using such divisions, confusions or errors for advantages against the will of Heaven.

III.II – THE LITURGY OF THE GOOD NEWS OF CHRIST

1. To all Christians, the Good News that is the Testament of Jesus Christ is the highest revelation and teaching of God the Divine Creator of all Existence and all Heaven and Earth. It is why the Liturgy of the Word is honoured as the Liturgy of Christ, as the expression of the New Testament is to express the teachings and faith in the Risen Christ.

The Liturgy of the Good News of Christ

Yet, as central as the Good News is for all Christians, there exist certain fundamental discernments that are equally as vital as witnessing and hearing the true Revelations of God.

Thus, a clear distinction is hereby made whereby the Liturgy of the Word associated with Universal Feasts is now described as the Liturgy of the Good News compared to the Liturgy of the Testimony of Revelation of other Sacred Scripture.

The Liturgy of the Good News of Christ comprises two parts, being *Magisterium* and *Good News*:

(i) *Magisterium* is the teaching authority of Jesus Christ as expressed through certain passages of prophecy, miracles or parables; and

(ii) *Good News* is a formal speech as accounted within the Gospels pertaining to Christ, that helps put in context the Magisterium of Christ in accord with the theme of the Universal Feast as part of the Liturgical Year.

2. Except for the Universal Feasts of Holy Wednesday, Holy Thursday, Good Friday, Easter Vigil (Saturday), Easter Midnight Mass and Easter Sunday, the remaining sixty Universal Feasts all contain a

Good News and Universal Feasts

specific Magisterium of Christ and Good News of Christ as the foundation of the Liturgy of the Good News. All readings and testimonies pertaining to the Apostles, Saints and Heroes then are referred to in the Liturgy of the Testimony of Revelation celebrated through the Proper of Heroes and Saints:

(i) Holy Wednesday, Holy Thursday, Good Friday, Easter Vigil and Midnight Mass only recite a Magisterium without a Good News; and

(ii) Easter Sunday (Resurrection Day) only recites a Good News, without Magisterium as the resurrection of Christ is the highest proof of Magisterium in itself.

III.III – THE LITURGY OF THE TESTIMONY OF REVELATION

The Liturgy of the Testimony of Revelation

1. In the Liturgy of the Testimony of Revelation, the Living Body of Christ is nourished by the testimonies and accounts of the heroes, saints and prophets throughout the ages, written under the inspiration of the Holy Spirit. Such scripture is the foundation and thus the bedrock of the Proper of Heroes and Saints throughout the Liturgical Year.

The separation of the Liturgy of the Testimony of Revelation from the Liturgy of the Good News does not mean such scriptures, accounts and testimony is diminished in the eyes of the Universal Ecclesia, but so that it may contribute an even stronger support to the faithful in providing contemporary testimony to the challenges, the questions and the development of the faith of each present and future generation.

The Liturgy of the Testimony of Revelation comprises two parts, being *Revelation* and *Testimony*:

(i) *Revelation* is a term reserved for certain passages and scriptures of the prophets, the Old Testament and of John of Patmos and other canonical accounts of testimony of Revelation; and

(ii) *Testimony* is a term reserved for the writings of the Apostles, especially Paul, the subsequent Church Fathers and universally recognised canonical works that assist in the continuing catechises of a one true Apostolic Universal Ecclesia.

Teaching Imperative of Liturgy of Testimony

2. Whereas the Universal Feasts corresponding to the Seven Mysteries of Christ of the Liturgical Year provide a base and foundation of knowledge for Christian Faith, the Liturgy of the Testimony of

Revelation is the rich cultural history, traditions, customs and capacity of the living vine that is the united Christian Faith.

Thus, in Masses celebrating the Proper of Heroes and Saints, there is no reading from the Good News, but instead the readings and testimonies associated with the Liturgy of the Testimony of Revelation as exemplary witnesses to the Crucified and Risen Christ.

Title IV – Authentic Christian Calendar

IV.I – AUTHENTIC CHRISTIAN CALENDAR

1. The Authentic Christian Calendar is the formal system of the Universal Ecclesia of One Christ of calculating periods of time and for organising such units of time for ecclesiastical, social, legal, fiduciary, administrative and personal purposes. The one true apostolic Universal Ecclesia of One Christ possesses three formal Calendar Systems being *Ucadia*, *Gregorian* and *Liturgical*: Authentic Christian Calendar

   (i) *Ucadia Calendar* is purely reserved for Divine and Ecclesiastical Purposes and is the system whereby all forms of sacred-space-day-time is recorded and all sacred circumscribed space is duly recorded and entered; and

   (ii) *Gregorian Calendar* is the common Calendar used for ecclesiastical, social, legal, fiduciary, administrative and personal purposes; and

   (iii) *Liturgical Calendar*, also known as the *Cycle of Mysteries* and the *Authentic Memory of the Universal Ecclesia*, consists of the cycle of liturgical seasons in Christian worship over a single solar year.

2. There can be no doubt that Christ through his Divine Mission, intended the Christian Calendar to be *Solar* and not *Unisolar* (lunar with periodic re-alignment) or Lunar. The symbolism of light, the sun, the embodiment of the sun, new days and new time are overwhelming throughout the Good News accounts of his ministry. Solar Liturgical Calendar

   The historic issues arising from calculation of the Liturgical Calendar rise from the fact that many adherents and contributors to early planning were familiar and comfortable with the ancient systems of Lunar calculation, thereby causing anomalies to arise when major feast days and events were then calculated upon Lunar events rather than Solar events.

3. The *Liturgical Calendar*, also known as the *Cycle of Mysteries* and the *Authentic Memory of the Universal Ecclesia*, refers and applies to all Christian churches, bodies, associations, fraternities, orders, companies and entities as the first and primary calendar, with all other calendars being secondary. Liturgical Calendar and all Christian bodies

4. In reference to all scriptures, readings, prayers, celebrations, feasts, solemnities and rites, the Liturgical Calendar extends for one Solar Year only, corresponding to the celebration of the Seven Mysteries of Christ. Liturgical Calendar is one Solar Year

IV.II – LITURGICAL DAY

1. A ***Liturgical Day*** is a day that is sanctified by liturgical actions. As all days are consecrated by God and the Divine Creator as sacred, all days are Liturgical and subject to the jurisdiction of the Universal Ecclesia. There exists three forms of Liturgical Days being *Sundays, Weekdays* and *Feast days*: Liturgical Day

    (i) *Sundays* being any day of a particular year designated as that day of a seven day week dedicated to Christ and Christian worship as the first day of a new week. Every Sunday is properly considered a Solemnity; and

    (ii) *Weekdays* being any other day of a particular week of a year, except Sunday or a Feast Day (i.e. Monday, Tuesday, Wednesday, Thursday, Friday or Saturday) ; and

    (iii) *Feast days* being a day designated to the celebration of a day of special importance associated with the celebration of a Mystery of Christ, or the memorial of one or more saints.

2. All Feast days may be further categorised according to three types (in order of priority) being *Solemnity, Memorial* or *Ordinary*: Types of Feast Days

    (i) *Solemnity* is the highest rank of feast days, celebrating every Sunday of the Liturgical Year and other key events in the celebration of the Mysteries of the life, death and resurrection of Christ, blessed Mary, Queen of Heaven or an Apostle or Saint of great importance; and

    (ii) *Memorial* is the second highest rank of feast days in honour of a significant saint, or mystery or church or event; and

    (iii) *Ordinary* is the third highest rank of feast day in honour of a saint, or church or event of importance. All days not Memorial or Solemnity have been dedicated to one or more heroes or saints. Therefore, all other days are what is properly called "Ordinary Time".

3. All Feast days may be classed in relation to the authority granted to inscribe such an event being *Universal, Patriarchal, Apostolic* or *Episcopal*: Sub Classes of Feast Days

    (i) *Universal* is the highest sub class when a Feast day is granted and inscribed by the Supreme Patriarch and the competent authorities of the Universal Ecclesia. Universal Solemnities are therefore the highest forms of Feast days of the Christian Calendar. There exists sixty six Universal Feast days, representing every Sunday and Universal Solemnities for the Liturgical Year; and

(ii) *Patriarchal* is the second highest sub class when a Feast day applies to the nation or place of a Patriarchy. The celebration of a national day in honour of the patron saints of the nation is considered a Patriarchal Solemnity for that particular nation; and

(iii) *Apostolic* is the third highest sub class when a Feast day applies to a particular basilica, or cathedral, or religious order, body or traditional right. For example, the celebration of the feast day of the founder of a religious institute is considered a solemnity; and

(iv) *Episcopal* is the lowest form of sub class where a feast day applies to a particular church.

4. The sixteen Universal Solemnities of the Universal Ecclesia of One Christ (in authority and rank order) are: Universal Solemnities

(i) *Easter Sunday,* also known as *Resurrection Day* (First Sunday after Good Friday at the end of March); and

(ii) *Good Friday* (1st Friday on or after Spring Equinox); and

(iii) *Holy Thursday* (Thursday before Good Friday); and

(iv) *Nativity Day*, also known as *Christmas Day* (25th December); and

(v) *New Years Day* (1st January); and

(vi) *Holy Exodus* (1st Sunday after New Years Day); and

(vii) *Holy Confirmation Sunday* (mid-February and Sunday before Ash Wednesday); and

(viii) *New Covenant Day* (14th March); and

(ix) *Pentecost Sunday* (first Sunday within 50 days since Easter Sunday (end of May); and

(x) *Ascension Day* (first Thursday within 40 days since Easter Sunday); and

(xi) *Redemption Sunday* (first Sunday after Assumption Day near end of August); and

(xii) *Assumption Day* (August 15th); and

(xiii) *Sacred Heart Sunday* (last Sunday of June); and

(xiv) *Holy Matrimony Day (*fourth Sunday after Corpus Christi*)*; and

(xv) *Mission Sunday (*second Sunday after All Saints Day); and

(xvi) *All Saints Day (*1st November*)*.

IV.III – CALCULATION OF LITURGICAL FEASTS

Calculation of Liturgical Feasts

1. The Liturgical Calendar for a given year is calculated around the Universal Solemnities in priority order. Once the Paschal Triduum (Easter Sunday, Good Friday and Holy Thursday) are calculated against the Solar Spring Equinox, all other Solemnities may then be calculated.

Rules for Calculating Liturgical Feasts

2. These be the rules for Calculating Liturgical Feasts:

   (i) Locate the day expected for Spring Equinox. Usually this will be the 20th of March. Then determine if this day is a Friday or the closest day to the Spring Equinox moving forward that is a Friday. This Day shall therefore be consecrated as the Feast of Good Friday; and

   (ii) Having calculated the precise Friday for the Solemnity of the Feast of Good Friday, the Sunday that comes three days thereafter shall be Easer Sunday; and the Thursday that precedes Good Friday shall be Holy Thursday and the Sunday that precedes Holy Thursday shall be Palm Sunday; and

   (iii) From Easter Sunday, count forty days forward and the day should be a Thursday. This day shall then be consecrated as Ascension Day (Ascension Thursday); and

   (iv) From Easter Sunday, count fifty days forward and the day should also be a Sunday. This day shall then be consecrated as Pentecost Sunday; and

   (v) From Easter Sunday, count forty days backwards. This should be a Wednesday and the Feast of Divine Humility (Ash Wednesday) as the Liturgical Season of the Eucharist is always forty days; and

   (vi) The Sunday before Ash Wednesday is always called the Feast of Holy Confirmation and the conclusion of the Liturgical Season of the Filial Mystery of Christ; and

   (vii) Nativity Day always falls upon December 25th; and

(viii) New Years Day always falls upon January 1st; and

(ix) The First Sunday after New Years Day is always the Feast of the Holy Exodus and the beginning of the Liturgical Season of the Filial Mystery of Christ; and

(x) Feast of the Holy Assumption of Mary always falls upon August 15th; and

(xi) The Sunday after the Feast of the Holy Assumption is always the Feast of Divine Redemption and the conclusion of the Liturgical Season of the Mystery of Divine Mercy & Redemption of Christ; and

(xii) All Saints Day always falls on the 1st November; and

(xiii) The second Sunday after All Saints Day is always Mission Sunday and the conclusion of the Liturgical Season of the Apostolic Life of Christ; and

(xiv) The first Sunday after Mission Sunday is always the Feast of the Divine Light of the World and the beginning of the Liturgical Season of the Immanent Mystery of Christ.

3. As the celebration of certain Universal Solemnities may be movable, it is likely in any given year that certain lesser feasts conflict in terms of the same given days. Therefore, the following rules apply: Priority of Feasts

(i) Universal Solemnities always take priority over lesser sub classes of feasts and types of feasts; and

(ii) A Lesser Solemnity is permitted to be moved to the following day, providing it does not then clash with another Universal Solemnity or Solemnity of higher ranking.

Title V – Apostolic Life of the People of God

V.I – APOSTOLIC LIFE OF THE PEOPLE OF GOD

1. The People of God are the servants of God. Thus, the consecrated men and women in Christ are ultimately the servants of the People of God. The mission therefore given by God and Christ with the Holy Spirit to those men and women who have professed their Holy Orders as servants of the People of God, is to guide, guard, nurture and protect the full apostolic life of all the People of God.

Apostolic Life of the People of God

2 The Holy Sacraments and Sacred Liturgy are the blessed gifts from Heaven through the Crucified and Risen Christ to empower and enable the Brothers and Sisters of Consecrated Life to support the People of God. However, the Holy Sacraments and Sacred Liturgy are not an end in themselves, just as all who have professed their oaths and vows to serve Christ do so, by serving his people first and foremost.

Sacraments are Divinely Ordained

3. By definition, a full apostolic life in the celebration of Sacred Liturgy means the complete recognition of life from the point of conception and annunciation, to death and emancipation into eternal life. The Sacred Liturgy of the one true Apostolic Universal Ecclesia of Christ illuminates and supports the completeness of life, not merely one part.

Sacred Liturgy focus on the completeness of Life not merely one part

Those that may seek to focus on merely an aspect of the Mysteries of Christ, whether it be sacrifice alone, or the manner of death alone, or judgement alone, are in gross error for not viewing the entirety of the Mysteries of Sacred Liturgy reflecting the completeness of the Divine Life of the Crucified and Risen Christ. Therefore, Sacred Liturgy must always be seen, viewed and interpreted as a cohesive and complete whole and not simply in parts.

V.II – FORMATION & NOURISHMENT OF FAITH

1. In the first instance, a Celebrant seeks to call upon the assistance of Sacred Liturgy and Holy Sacraments for the formation and nourishment of faith of the community.

Formation & Nourishment of Faith

2. The People of God do not and cannot come to celebrate the Eucharist through the ceremony of Mass and Sacred Liturgy out of fear, or coercion or ignorance, but as a means of fulfilling a deeper need and satisfying a yearning hunger. God and the Divine Creator command through the Risen Christ, that such worship is an act of free will. Therefore, the reflection of the numbers of Christian faithful that attend and appear and wish to participate in Mass and Sacred Liturgy shall always be a measure of the degree that the Sacred Liturgy, the

Free will of the People of God to participate

Universal Ecclesia and its clerics and laity positively engage and meet the genuine needs of the community.

3. Popularity and appealing to the perceived wants of people is not the same as an authentic and lasting faith. It is true that the engagement of the People of God has changed over time, yet this does not mean the approach for Sacred Liturgy should then be calculated upon the premise of satisfying wants, lest the integrity of ancient and fundamental principles are trivialised.

Popularity vs. Authentic & Lasting Faith

Instead, an authentic and lasting faith requires a framework that assists in the formation of proper faith and then its continued nourishment. Therefore, Sacred Liturgy must reflect such necessary needs of formation and nourishment.

4. By definition, people of most societies are attracted to the celebration of life than of death. It follows then that the greatest centres of celebrating life usually attract the most people. Entertainment, Sports and Shopping precincts in recent years therefore replaced the traditional notion of the town square or common space. Yet such modern hives of activity cannot replace the extraordinary spiritual attraction of people to the Living Liturgy of Christ to return to their local Places of Worship.

Attraction of People to Living Liturgy of Christ

When Places of Worship are empowered to celebrating the Living Liturgy of Christ, such sacred places will not only be sites for celebrating christenings, weddings, first communion and funerals, but the full spectrum of life ages and ceremonies of each member and family of the community and their beloved departed. People will see that their lives and the lives of all who have passed in their family and community are an integral part of the liturgy and of the life of the Church.

When the faithful come to see the full power of the Living Liturgy of Christ, not only will they be nourished and educated throughout the year and the Seven Divine Mysteries of Christ, but through the living testimony and living gospel of saints and heroes of the community that have lived in recent decades and centuries. The local Place of Worship will once again become a crucial touchstone for every person and this will be reflected in the attraction and strength of the living congregation.

V.III – DISCERNMENT & WISE GUIDANCE OF CHRISTIAN VIRTUE

1. The completeness of the Holy Sacraments and Sacred Liturgy of the one true and apostolic Universal Ecclesia of Christ, gives rise to the ability to encourage, teach and train discernment and wise guidance of

Discernment & Wise Guidance of Christian Virtue

Christian Virtue among the life of the community.

Members of the community should and need to be familiar and competent in comprehending the purpose and function of rites, sacraments and ceremonies where they participate or witness. Ignorance of Sacred Liturgy and the Holy Sacraments is neither conducive to the health and well-being of a Christian Community, nor to the health and well-being of the souls of such a community.

Pastors must therefore strive to overcome the obstacles and challenges of communication, time, commitment and discernment so that each and every generation may become conscious of the rites, sacraments and ceremonies that provide strength and unity to their lives.

2. Most local Pastors face the reality of dependence in large part upon the level of vibrancy of their community and upon the charitable assistance of their congregation. Thus, as the levels of participation within a community may fall, such a negative change has a real affect on the ability of local Pastors to perform a number of duties.

Vibrancy of Community under Living Liturgy of Christ

The Revelation of Missale Christus demonstrates that Christ is not unaware of the plight of local churches or the extraordinary suffering, stress and sacrifices of faithful Pastors in trying to support their communities. It is why the Living Liturgy of Christ has come to help restore the vibrancy of local communities and enable the demands of parish life to be met by many opportunities for charitable support.

What Christ asks through his bishops and leaders is that, having discovered the discernment of suffering and real poverty, that the church forever remains vigilant to always remain poor in its internal allocation of resources for personal use, but generous and rich in its support of the genuine needs of the community.

3. Most local Pastors face the reality of dependence upon the charitable assistance of their congregation. Thus, as the levels of participation within a community may fall, such a negative change has a real affect on the ability of local Pastors to perform a number of duties.

No Money ever permitted to be exchanged during Liturgy

The Revelation of *Missale Christus* demonstrates that Christ is not unaware of the plight of local churches or the extraordinary suffering, stress and sacrifices of faithful Pastors in trying to support their communities. It is why the Living Liturgy of Christ has come to help restore the vibrancy of local communities and enable the demands of parish life to be met by many opportunities for charitable support.

What Christ asks through his bishops and leaders is that, having discovered the discernment of suffering and real poverty, that the church forever remains vigilant to always remain poor in its internal allocation of resources for personal use, but generous and rich in its support of the genuine needs of the community.

There is one action that Christ in all times expressly forbids. It is a forbidden action that so enraged God and the Divine Creator, that we witnessed in scripture a real anger and disgust against those who willingly defiled the sanctity of the House of the Lord. It is the forbiddence to collect or exchange money or any form of money during the service Liturgy.

The Living Liturgy of Christ will restore life to communities. Yet the poverty of the parish is no excuse to defy the express laws of God. Pastors and the leaders of the faithful are expressly and absolutely forbidden to use collection plates, boxes or any mechanism for donations or deposits from the congregation of any form of money or financial instruments.

V.IV – COMPASSIONATE CARE & AUTHENTIC RECONCILIATION

1. Our Heavenly Father and Creator, through his son Jesus Christ with the Holy Spirit are unequivocal, emphatic and consistent through authentic scripture that none who genuinely seek reconciliation through the sacrament of Penance are to be denied the grace and dignity of communion with the sacrament of the Holy Eucharist. Compassionate Care & Authentic Reconciliation

For men and women to deliberately or ignorantly insert themselves as obstacles and impediments to redemption and reconciliation with God, especially those who have taken Holy Oaths and Vows, is a most serious transgression of impiety. Therefore, all edicts, prescripts, decrees, canons, resolutions, sentences or arguments to the contrary are to be separately treated as evidence of over zealousness or error of interpretation and then subject to abrogation or suppression.

No matter how grave the transgressions of the penitent, it is a fundamental tenet of Christianity that all who openly and honestly confess their faults through the Sacrament of Penance; and seek to live honestly, respectfully and earnestly, therefore possess the right to partake in communion and receive the Holy Eucharist.

However, it follows that a lack of remorse or genuine contrition necessarily prevents a member of a Christian congregation from the grace of reconciliation by their own actions and therefore prevents them from participating in the Sacrament of Holy Eucharist.

Furthermore, it is absolutely forbidden for a person consecrated into the life of Christ through Holy Orders to then demand or determine extraordinary sanctions or punishments upon a penitent seeking authentic reconciliation with God and their wish to resume participation in Holy Communion.

2. The duty of compassionate care and the authentic reconciliation of all those consecrated into the life of Christ means that none may be denied the right to participate in the Sacrament of Holy Eucharist at the appropriate forms of Mass, where such communicants are properly baptised, confirmed and reconciled in Christ. However, a person may not demand to partake in the Eucharist where the form of Mass is Special or Ordinary or Extraordinary, unless by such form they possess such a participatory right.

Eucharist available to all baptised and reconciled in Christ

3. While the faults of the past in applying overzealous and strict moral codes in the administration of pastoral care of Christian congregations can be excused and even forgiven, in the light and revelation of the Risen Christ, such continuation of defending the indefensible is no excuse for belligerent or passive continuation of such error and impiety.

Defending the indefensible no excuse for continued injury and impiety

All Celebrants culpable of such errors must seek to redress their behaviours and attitudes, preferably through willing consent to comprehend more clearly such wise discernment in the manner and methods of defence of the sacraments and the necessary compassionate care and authentic reconciliation of the people of God. However, an obstinate or belligerent cleric, by his or her own actions, temporarily disqualifies themselves from possessing the authority and power to occupy any pastoral office and administer any Holy Sacraments.

Title VI – Purpose & Nature of the Eucharist & Mass

VI.I – PURPOSE & NATURE OF THE EUCHARIST

Purpose & Nature of the Eucharist

1. The history of humanity and its perception of the Divine is not without ages of great sadness. In the time of Christ, financial slavery did abound in almost every culture, whereby the value of human life was traded as a mere commodity. The price of life was considered cheap, as those with wealth were indifferent to others and gluttonous in their excesses, while children and women suffered. Most tragically, it was also a time of continued actual and simulated ritual blood sacrifice, whereby such rituals were considered a form of spiritual currency and power.

The oldest of these were the rituals surrounding the ancient "Day of Blood", also known as *Dies Sanguinis* upon the Mide (Middle) of Mars according to the ancient 28 day month cycle, being the 14th of Mars (14th March), or the 14th of Nisan to the Persians. It was upon this day, that the ancient religion of Mithra of the Persians and Mitra of the Roman Empire celebrated the birth and sacrificial death of the god Mithra. The eve of the day was called the Ides of Mars (13th March) to the Romans and to the Persians, the day was called the Passion. Thus, when Christ chose to willingly sacrifice himself, it was specifically, consciously and deliberately to end all forms of blood sacrifice forever more, by transforming what was once the ritual celebration of the flesh and blood of the victim, into the spiritual gifts of reconciliation and redemption with the Heavenly Father.

Thus, to ignore the true context of the Eucharist and to misinterpret the Last Supper from being the last ever Blood Sacrifice to Heaven, whereby every ritual blood sacrifice thereafter would be an abomination, is to completely misinterpret and misrepresent the most profound act of the saviour Jesus Christ in ending all forms of false ritual, false piety and blood worship.

The words of Jesus were absolutely clear for them to "remember" what he had done and to follow through action his teachings, not to repeatedly simulate his torture and death, nor treat the most sacred Eucharist as a simulated ceremony akin to the pagan god Mithra. Christ is Risen. Christ died once. The Eucharist in its fullest revelation is the celebration of eternal life, not death and ritual sacrifice.

Verily, the true Revelation of the commandment of Christ at the Last Supper is for every authentic Disciple of Christ to "remember" the selfless act of our Saviour and to offer their actions and lives as a worthy offering to a loving God. The entire ministry of Christ is devoted to the education that God and the Divine Creator of all Existence is a loving God, a logical God and a forgiving God.

Indeed, Christ himself sought to reinforce the true Revelation and meaning of the Last Supper and the Eucharist, when he called upon all those who claim to be true followers to "take up their cross". The path of a Christian throughout the ages is not easy, nor are the deeper symbols of the Mystery of the Crucified and Risen Christ without challenge.

The authentic celebration of the Eucharistic Mystery is the celebration of the offering made by the celebrant and all participants first and foremost; and then secondly the remembrance of the ultimate sacrifice already made by Christ for all of us; and third the miracle of the Divine Grace and Gift of the Sacrament of Sustentation.

Any image or action that contradicts this core message, diminishes the power and core message of Christ himself. Christ already died once to save all our sins now and forever more. He does not need to die again and again every time the Eucharist is celebrated. Thus, to mistakenly or deliberately simulate rituals associated with the Eucharist that emphasise and attempt the ritual sacrifice of Christ within every Mass, is wholly contradictory and incompatible with authentic Christian Revelation.

The Divine Mercy of the Holy Spirit forgives where such error has arisen out of a deep sense of devotion and longing to comprehend the Mysteries of Christ. This is one of the purposes of Missale Christus, to assist the faithful in being able to participate in the authentic and deeper mystery of the Eucharist as Christ intended.

The meaning of Mass

2. By definition, the term Mass in Latin means "bread, dough or sustenance". It is entirely consistent then to also find within the Holy Gospels the testimony of Christ referring to himself at times as the "bread of life". This metaphor is continually reinforced throughout the Ministry of Christ whilst in living flesh upon the Earth meaning a spiritual sustenance and not a continuation of past practices of ritual blood sacrifice.

Sacred Scripture recalls several episodes when Jesus did participate in meals possessing supernatural and sacred significance heralding a fundamental new covenant that ends blood sacrifice and a fearful and negative impression of God forever. The account of the miracle of the loaves and fishes bears striking resemblance to several other meals where the preparation of the food and wine, the prayers and intention and the symbolism of the breaking of bread, sharing of wine and other food herald deep liturgical importance.

Therefore, in the firmest and fullest sense, the celebration of Mass is the celebration of Christ as the "bread and fruits of eternal spiritual life" and the Holy Eucharist as examples of this immutable reality.

Indeed, there is one special ceremony and testimony that stands above all others being the last supper between Christ and his closest disciples where he unequivocally made the ceremony of the passover and the breaking and eating of unleavened bread and the pouring and consuming of wine the perpetual symbol of an extraordinary New Covenant between God and Man, whereby God made flesh chose to sacrifice himself, so that all men and women be forgiven, emancipated and enlightened to eternal life.

It is because the Eucharist represents the New Covenant between the Divine Creator of all existence and all humanity; and the extraordinary and unprecedented act of the Divine made flesh as a living singularity sacrificing himself upon the cross, dying and then rising from the dead, that the Eucharist is so central to the very notion of Mass and Divine Liturgy.

These true words and intentions of Christ are fully reflected in the recognition of the Sacrament of Sustentation at the heart of the Rite of Holy Eucharist.

Mystery of the Eucharist and Transubstantiation

3. In seeking to honour the clear message and ceremony of the Crucified Christ concerning the ultimate sacrifice of his own flesh and blood to save and awaken humanity to a New Covenant, the early Church Fathers adopted a deeply revered faith in the transformation of the symbols of bread and wine into the "bread and fruits of eternal spiritual life" as Christ himself had frequently used as his own description.

Yet, as with many of the mysteries concerning the authentic Revelation of Christ, debate ensued regarding the resolution of the spiritual dimension of the Eucharist and the physical representation of the bread and wine of the Eucharistic celebration. Some argued that the true interpretation rested in viewing the deeper purpose set forth by Jesus and that the bread and wine were but symbols.

Others argued rightly, that the message of Christ was unmistakable – that Jesus deliberately referred to the bread as his flesh and the wine as his blood as signs of a new Covenant, even though such flesh and blood had become a supernatural body since his complete ascension into Heaven.

Others still insisted on a literal and pedantic interpretation of the words of Jesus, much like ancient Pharisees and other doctors of the religious law, whereby the bread and wine are not symbols, or just supernatural objects but the actual flesh and blood of the body of Jesus "transformed", even if such a transformation cannot be seen by human eyes or mind. The term for this narrow, simplistic and literal interpretation of scripture was called "transubstantiation".

Thus, an ancient error against the true Revelations of Christ and the Divine Creator was introduced whereby the ritual transformation of bread and wine became worshipped as more important than the spiritual sustentation the Eucharist itself represents.

More disturbingly, over time the rite of most holy sacrament did corrupt to become for many a mere simulated ritual blood sacrifice of the body of Christ, in complete contradiction to the express intention of Jesus Christ to end all forms of ritual blood sacrifice. Even today, there are those who remain insistence in defying the teachings of Christ by defending and repeating such ancient errors.

4. For any Christian, there can be no equivocation in the words of Christ, nor any uncertainty that the bread and wine transformed through the sacrament and ceremony of the Eucharist becomes the true "bread and fruits of eternal spiritual life" as Christ promised. Nor should there be any doubt that the transformed Eucharistic offering be anything less than the supernatural body of the Risen Christ.

Authentic Mystery of Transfiguration of the Eucharist

However, to avoid the error of narrow, simplistic and literal interpretations of scripture that confuse and sometimes even contradict the notion of the Resurrection and the Ascension of Christ in body into Heaven, the word "Transfiguration" is used rather than "Transubstantiation" in the context of the Sacrament of Sustentation and Rite of Holy Eucharist.

VI.II – IMPORTANCE & DIGNITY OF MASS

1. Truly the forms of Mass as prescribed by the Revelation of God through the Holy Spirit, is Divine Liturgy and central to the life and future vitality of the Universal Ecclesia as the Living Body of Christ.

Importance of Mass

It is the path and way through the Liturgical Seasons and Mysteries to a greater knowledge of ourselves, of our family and community and of God our Divine Creator. It is the living rock of faith in our midst as testament to our community, well-being and unity of spirit and hearts. It is the deepest expression of the collective and personal emotions, compassion, forgiveness and healing of our community through the complete cycle of life, death and rebirth to eternal life. It is the highest point of worship and offering of our own sacrifices and willingness to be authentic Christians as we remember the sacrifice of Christ.

2. In as much as Mass is central to the life of every Christian, so then authentic dignity and genuine reverence comes, not from any close hearted intolerance to the joys and love of life, but the level of concrete

Dignity of Mass

engagement and true intention of those that attend and return to the Community of Christ and the open hearts and minds of those who are called to serve the People of God.

A ritual performed in ignorance has no power or meaning. Indeed, a Sacramental rite performed in a mechanical and closed mind manner is an affront to Heaven and all the angels and saints as well as to the Father, to Christ and the Holy Spirit.

It is true that all are called to come with due respect and sensitivity to the extraordinary supernatural and spiritual event that is an authentic Mass of Christ. Yet, the greatest obligation in respect of dignity is the right intention, mind and heart of the consecrated servants of the People of God.

VI.III – PARTICIPATION & EXPRESSION OF MASS

Participation & Expression of Mass

1. Participation in the celebration of Mass and the Eucharist is a fundamental element and purpose of Divine Liturgy. Yet, there is always a need for balance between the necessary formality of Liturgy and the authentic spontaneity of the congregation in expressing their individual and collective faith.

   On the one hand, the inclusion of greater amounts of words and formal responses of the congregation may appear to some as a kind of balance between necessary formality and participation. Yet, such interaction makes little allowance for the genuine expression of heart and instead promotes a kind of automated and desensitised response from the congregation, damaging the sanctity of Mass and injuring the Will and Trust of Christ.

   Therefore, congregation participation and expression in Mass must be one of genuine and precise meaning; and when called upon to be a deepest expression of faith, that it allows the most authentic of forms.

Movement and Posture of Celebrants, Assistants and Supplicants

2. The gestures and posture of the Celebrants, Assistants and Supplicants, as well as those of the Congregation, ought to contribute to making the entire celebration resplendent with beauty and noble simplicity, so that the true and full meaning of the different parts of the celebration is evident and that the participation of all is fostered. Therefore, attention should be paid to what is determined by these General Instructions and to what serves the common spiritual good of the People of God, rather than private inclination or arbitrary choice.

Vocal Expression of Texts

3. All sacred texts as part of the Order of Mass are to be spoken in a loud and clear voice, commensurate with the gravity and significance of the sacred words. Except in certain Extraordinary Masses, the attempt to sing the Liturgy of the Word is unnecessary and unhelpful, unless a

particular community be blessed with certain consecrated members, whose vocal abilities are a blessing and encouragement to the faithful.

4. Singing is a vital expression of unity and heart of the People of God and all Celebrants, Assistants and Supplicants. However, due consideration must always be given for the culture of the people, the abilities of the participants and the form of Mass. Expression of Singing

   In General forms of Mass, singing is preferable within Community Mass and Healing Mass. Similarly, in Special forms of Mass, appropriate singing is to be encouraged. However, in Ordinary Mass and Extraordinary Mass, singing should be held firmly through the actions of consecrated participants with the presence of choir, to uphold the highest beauty and function of such rites.

5. Silence expressed as Sacred Silence and witness by the Congregation in Ordinary and Extraordinary Masses is one of the most powerful forms of reverential participation, as are the moments of Sacred Silence within the proceeding of General and Special Masses. Expression of Silence

VI.IV – ESSENTIAL TRIPARTITE CHARACTER OF MASS

1. It is a firm and well established wisdom in understanding the Revelation of Christ and the Founding Fathers and Mothers of the Church, that the nature and character of Mass has always been "Tripartite". The word "Tripartite" literally meaning "in three parts" and relates to three distinct elements of one continuous celebration of liturgy being Liturgy of the Christian People, Liturgy of the Word and Liturgy of the Eucharist: Tripartite Nature & Character of Mass

   (i) *Liturgy of the Christian People*, also previously known as "Introductory Rites", is the celebration of the convocation and assembly of Christian People to worship and their preparation to receive the Authentic Revelations and teachings of God and then participate within the Liturgy of the Eucharist; and

   (ii) *Liturgy of the Word*, is the celebration not only of the Word of God and specifically the Magisterium of Christ in the form of the Good News, but the inspiration and revelations of the Holy Spirit as testament to the Christian faith throughout the ages; and

   (iii) *Liturgy of the Eucharist* is the penultimate and final element of Liturgy of the Trinity of Worship, whereupon in proper and genuine preparation, the opening of hearts and minds, the congregation assembled willingly unify themselves with God and the Divine Creator through the Crucified and Risen Christ in the sacrament of communion and the Holy Eucharist.

2. First and foremost, Mass is the celebration of the Christian People in their witness and participation in their faith. Thus, the first part of Mass is called the Liturgy of Christian People.

Liturgy of the Christian People

3. Liturgy of the Word in the form of the Liturgy of the Good News of Christ and the Liturgy of the Testimony of Revelation celebrates and recognises the words of Sacred Scripture in the context of the message of Christ, as well as those who have been prepared to stand witness to Christ. When true witness is given through authentic testimony in support of the recitation of Sacred Scriptures, then the actual and manifest presence of God and the Divine Creator of all Existence and all Heaven and Earth is resolutely self-evident.

Liturgy of the Word

4. The celebration of the Sacrament of Sustentation and the Rite of the Eucharist in the context as Christ intended, is the solemn and willing participation of the congregation and celebrant as the primary agent of offering, whilst remembering and honouring the previous sacrifice of the Crucified Christ. It is the love and mercy of God through the Risen Christ unified with the authentic offerings of the celebrant and congregation that transforms the simple symbols of the bread and wine into the "bread and fruits of eternal spiritual life" and the spiritual body of Jesus Christ providing spiritual sustenance to the People of God.

Liturgy of the Eucharist

5. In seeking to clarify, reform and unify liturgical practices many centuries past, the Synod Fathers of the Council of Trent reinforced this ancient tradition and custom, particularly in light of the deep call for firmer standards within liturgy. Unfortunately, the success of such reform over time cast its own shadow over the very reforms and clarity it sought to bring, when the standards of Mass defined by the Council of Trent came to be known as "Tridentine", rather than the primary term "Tripartite".

Tripartite vs. Tridentine

Since the heralding of a new age of illuminated and inspired thinking at the conclusion of the Second Vatican Ecumenical Council, there has continued to be unease by some in relation to the cessation of the label "Tridentine", whilst the Order of Mass continues to retain its Tripartite roots. Thus, Missale Christus seeks to redress these misconceptions and misunderstandings by ensuring the ancient custom of Tripartite Order of Mass is clearly comprehended and embraced by all Christians as their common heritage.

VI.V – AUTHENTIC NORMS OF MASS

1. There exists four Authentic Norms of Mass being General, Special,

Authentic

Ordinary and Extraordinary: Norms of Mass

(i) *General Mass*, pertains to the vital and regular events of a vibrant parish and Christian community life and the participation of the whole congregation or large elements of it with Holy Communion; and

(ii) *Special Mass*, pertains to the celebration of special events, personal events or important symbols of parish life, such as memorials, matrimony, funerary, family, youth and sacramental life where a distinct group of persons celebrate Holy Communion, while other members are witnesses to the event; and

(iii) *Ordinary Mass*, pertains to the exclusive participation only of the Celebrant or other consecrated clerical members in Holy Communion and any members of the congregation as silent witnesses only; and

(iv) *Extraordinary Mass*, pertains to a form of Mass similar in terms of Holy Communion to a Special Mass, but where certain charisms and sacraments are imparted during the formal Pentapartite format.

2. A ***General Mass*** is a celebration of Liturgy in a form that is vital and essential to the life of a Christian Community. There are only three forms of General Mass being *Customary* (Traditional), *Community* (Family) and *Consecratory* (Healing): General Mass

(i) *Customary* (Traditional) Mass is a General Mass dedicated to the entire Christian Community. There must be at least one Customary (Traditional) Mass offered each day in each functioning church; and

(ii) *Community* (Family) Mass is a General Mass dedicated to the Christian Family; and so seeks to encourage and promote the participation of the Family in the Liturgy; and

(iii) *Consecratory* (Healing) Mass is a General Mass dedicated to the healing, reconciliation of Christian members. There must be at least one Community or Consecratory Mass each day in each functioning church.

3. A ***Special Mass*** is a celebration of Liturgy dedicated for specific persons and members of a Christian Community. As the participation in the Eucharist is limited to such persons, such a Mass is called "Special" rather than "General" for the whole community. There are six forms of Special Mass being Memorial, Matrimonial, Apostolic, Special Mass

Funerary, Dedicatory and Pilgrim:

(i) *Memorial Mass* is a Special Mass dedicated to the memory and honour of one or more deceased persons, whereby filial or fraternal members of the deceased are invited to participate in the holy sacrament of the Eucharist, with remaining members of the congregation as witnesses to the event; and

(ii) *Matrimonial Mass* is a Special Mass dedicated to the consecration, honouring and celebration of the solemn vows of a man and woman entering into Holy Matrimony and participating exclusively in the holy sacrament of the Eucharist, with remaining members of the congregation as witnesses to the event; and

(iii) *Apostolic Mass* is a Special Mass dedicated to the initiation, consecration and blessing of members of the Community having qualified to participate in one of the Apostolic Life Rites such as *Annunciation, Baptism, Christening, First Communion, Majority, Maturity, Seniority or Elderity* whereby such members participate exclusively in the holy sacrament of the Eucharist, with remaining members of the congregation as witnesses to the event; and

(iv) *Funerary Mass* is a Special Mass dedicated to the consecration, blessing, emancipation and honouring of a departed member of the community, whereby family and friends participate exclusively in the holy sacrament of the Eucharist, with remaining members of the congregation as witnesses to the event; and

(v) *Dedicatory Mass* is a Special Mass dedicated to blessing, protecting and honouring one or more living members of the Christian community, particularly in association with the rite of Investiture, or the renewal of Oaths or Vows, whereby such persons participate exclusively in the holy sacrament of the Eucharist, with remaining members of the congregation as witnesses to the event; and

(vi) *Pilgrim Mass* is a Special Mass dedicated to the healing, reconciliation and blessing of Christian Pilgrims whilst they remain on their solemn Pilgrimage, whereby such persons participate exclusively in the holy sacrament of the Eucharist, with remaining members of the congregation as witnesses to the event.

4. An **Ordinary Mass** is a celebration of Liturgy by Clergy that Ordinary Mass consciously and deliberately excludes the congregation from participation, other than as solemn and silent witnesses. Only Ordinary Masses or High Masses of the extraordinary form may be recited in Latin. However, only Ordinary Masses may be said *Ad Orientem* and such custom is strictly forbidden in all other forms of Mass. There are only two forms of Ordinary Mass being Solitary and Fraternal:

(i) *Solitary Mass* is an Ordinary Mass dedicated whereby a single Celebrant vocalises and performs the Mass as if they are completely alone; and to the total exclusion of interaction with any members of the congregation or laity that may be present; and

(ii) *Fraternal Mass* is an Ordinary Mass of two or more Clergy, whereby the co-celebrants and clergy vocalise and perform Mass as if they are the sole community; and to the total exclusion of interaction with any members of the congregation or laity that may be present.

5. While the form of Tripartite is well established for ordinary, general and even special Masses, it is a long standing tradition and custom that Masses performed in relation to Universal Solemnities and major events at the highest level, demand a dignity that goes beyond the norm, to set apart the ideal and fulfil the highest possible expression of Christian faith.

Pentapartite Character of Extraordinary Masses

Missale Christus recognises that Extraordinary Masses possess a unique character whereby those sacraments and rites beyond the foundation of the Tripartite Order of Mass may be properly recognised in a form, that neither compromises the core heritage of the Mass, yet ensures a clear and distinct formula.

Extraordinary Masses are so by their very character and nature in adhering to the form of Pentapartite (meaning five parts) rather than simply Tripartite (three parts).

VI.VI – SACREDNESS OF COMMUNION PARTICIPATION

1. By definition, a Special Mass is a celebration of Liturgy dedicated to specific persons and members of a Christian Community. Therefore, the purpose of a Special Mass is to set apart one or more members of the community, in order for such events and celebrations to signify an important milestone in the journey of life and spirit; and as a manifest symbol of encouragement and support for the entire Community.

Special Mass and Participants

As sentient as well as sapient beings, all human beings by their innate nature, place greater emphasis upon those places, times and events of such spiritual, mental and physical significance. Therefore, the restoration and presence of such remembrances greatly assist each and every member of the Christian Community in more fully immersing and embracing their journey in life and the promise of a heavenly afterlife.

2. The full mystery and meaning of the Eucharist is revealed when seen not only from the celebration of General Mass, but Special Mass. The Christian Mission to live and act according to the Magisterium of Christ is most visually demonstrated in Liturgy when members of the community willingly and faithfully choose to participate in the Sacrament of the Holy Eucharist for special causes.

Special Mass and Congregation

The Sacrament of Holy Matrimony as a Special Mass becomes an opportunity to witness the mystery of the Eucharist as a wedding feast when the bride and groom choose through their sacred vows to sacrifice their individual selfish desires to choose to be united as one spirit recognised in Heaven and upon the Earth.

The celebration and consecration of Pilgrims as a Special Mass becomes an opportunity to see the Holy Eucharist as the greater events of the Mysteries and Life of Christ, when people of faith, choose to sacrifice their fears and constraints and take up their staff to follow Jesus.

The recognition and honouring of men and women of office and service, who keep and renew their oaths and vows to protect and serve the community is a further opportunity to witness the Holy Eucharist from the vocation and calling of Disciples not to abandon the world, but to live and work within communities, by harnessing their talents and sacrificing their worship of money as an end in itself, and any form of hardness of heart and lack of empathy, to devote their lives to making their communities a better place and that none are left behind.

3. The formal and traditional nature of Ordinary Mass whereby the Celebrant or Co-Celebrants offer the Mass to God, *in persona Christi* being “in the physical and manifest person of Christ” is a profound devotion that absolutely precludes the congregation and laity from participation other than as faithful witness to such sacred mystery.

The absolute exclusion of congregation and laity from Ordinary Mass

In proper recognition of ancient custom and tradition, Ordinary Mass is the purest form of imitation of the immanent and transcendent nature of the Crucified and Risen Christ. It serves as a vital channel between Heaven and Earth, for the health and well being of the Universal Ecclesia of Christ, especially in the relation to invoking the powers and systems of Heaven in answer to petitions and prayers of the community.

Therefore, the Ordinary form of Mass cannot usurp the General Form, just as the General form of Mass cannot usurp the Special form of Mass, as each form has specific function, purpose and place in the authentic living liturgy of Christ.

4. In strict honour to the purpose and function of the Ordinary form of Mass, the congregation and laity that may be present are absolutely excluded and forbidden to receive Holy Communion, nor participate in any vocalisation of the Liturgy of the Eucharist. Any clergy, or diocese, or traditional or customary rite that permits the congregation or laity present at an Ordinary Mass to receive Holy Communion is culpable of a grave delict against the sacraments of the Universal Ecclesia. However, the congregation and laity should always be welcome to observe in silent reverence at such sacred mystery.

The exclusion of congregation and laity from Communion in Ordinary Form

5. Ordinary Mass is the only form of Liturgy permitted to be performed *Ad Orientem*, meaning "to the east" in honour of the light and revelation of the Risen Christ and the unity of the one, true apostolic Universal Ecclesia as the fulfilment of prophecy as the authentic Living Body of Christ. Any claim or assertion of its use, as a rejection of authentic liturgy, or as a challenge to the true Magisterium of Christ is a gross error and falsity.

Ad Orientem

Ad Orientem is reserved exclusively for Ordinary Mass, precisely because of the profound and sacred purpose of the Ordinary form of Mass and not to diminish the significance of custom and tradition, nor such formality.

Title VII – Places & Objects of Sacred Liturgy

VII.I – PLACES & OBJECTS OF SACRED LITURGY

1. Sacred Places and Sacred Objects are those designated for divine worship, by dedication through the liturgical and sacramental rituals provided in accord with the most sacred covenants *Pactum De Singularis Caelum, Pactum De Singularis Christus* and approved liturgy. Places & Objects of Sacred Liturgy

The one true and holy apostolic authority, powers and functions of the Universal Ecclesia of One Christ are exercised to their fullest extent in dedicated sacred places.

2. Sacred Places are recognised, established, maintained and protected in character through the receiving and written memorial of the Cardinal *Sacrament of Sanctification* (Rite of Consecration) through a Dedicatory Rite forming Sacred Circumscribed Space. Sacred Places

Once a place is properly dedicated to sacred purpose, in accord with the most sacred Covenants *Pactum De Singularis Caelum, Pactum De Singularis Christus* and approved liturgy, its fundamental character and nature is permanently changed.

Only through the performance of the appropriate liturgical rite may a place or building be properly dedicated, consecrated or imparted with special significance and function. There exists no such power, capacity or effect as "secular dedication".

Thus, a building or place not properly consecrated through the appropriate liturgical rite, may have no special or sacred significance, whereas a place once properly made sacred, cannot be unmade.

However, the sanctity of a place may be impeded, from time to time, due to severe damage or destruction of the edifice, or deliberate conversion of its use for profane use, or the performance of some gravely injurious acts contrary to liturgical norms and the appropriate holiness and respect of sacred places.

During such a time of immediate impediment, a sacred place may temporarily lose its capacity or authority to be used as a place for certain liturgical works. The restoration of such a place and the removal of any impediments is recognised through the Rite of Restoration.

3. Only those things that serve the exercise or promotion of worship, piety or liturgy are permitted in a Sacred Place. Anything that is not consonant with the holiness of the place is forbidden, unless in individual cases the relevant clerical authority permits another use that is not contrary to the holiness of the Sacred Place. Permitted Actions within Sacred Places

4. Certain Liturgical Acts necessitate the availability and presence of an unimpeded dedicated Sacred Place. The ministration of the Cardinal and Apostolic Sacraments demand they are performed in Sacred Places. Similarly, certain Rites such as Ordination can only be performed in Sacred Places dedicated to Worship, Piety and proper Liturgy.

Actions that necessitate the presence of a Sacred Place

5. It is essential to understand that no properly dedicated Sacred Place can be made unholy; and any such notion to the contrary is against Divine Law, Natural Law and the teachings of the most sacred Covenants *Pactum De Singularis Caelum* and *Pactum De Singularis Christus*:-

Impediments to Sacred Places

(i) By its nature, an impediment inflicted upon a Sacred Place prevents its proper use for sacred purpose. It is a wholly logical consequence of one or more actions that grievously injure the edifice of the place itself, or blemish the record and history of proper and sacred Liturgical acts performed within it; and

(ii) A building or structure of a Sacred Place that is destroyed in large part, may for practical and safety purposes, prevents its proper use for Liturgical acts for a time. However, the accidental or deliberate damage to the edifice of a Sacred Place does not imply in anyway that such a place necessarily loses its state of holiness; and

(iii) A building or structure of a Sacred Place that may be deconsecrated and subsequently set aside for profane use does not diminish the legitimacy of its previous history, nor prevent it from being restored to sacred use sometime in the future according to the proper Rite of Restoration; and

(iv) A Sacred Place may be violated by gravely injurious actions done in them with scandal to the faithful, actions which, in the judgement of the appropriate clerical authority, are so grave and contrary to the holiness of the place that it is not permitted to carry on worship in them until the blemish is removed according to the norms of sacred liturgy.

VII.II – SACRED CIRCUMSCRIBED SPACE

1. ***Sacred Circumscribed Space*** is a uniquely recorded enclosure and dimension of Ucadia Sacred Space-Day-Time as prescribed by the most sacred Covenant *Pactum De Singularis Caelum*, associated covenants and charters and Ucadia Law. Only duly authorised Ucadian Bodies, Ucadian Societies, Ucadian States, Ucadian Persons and

Sacred Circumscribed Space

Ucadian Companies, or those bodies, persons or corporations granted limited Rights under Convention and Treaty are permitted to record, register, keep and maintain Sacred Circumscribed Space.

2. The Universal Ecclesia of One Christ having been granted certain Rights of Ecclesiastical and Sovereign Dominion by the Divine Creator of all Existence and all Heaven and Earth, hereby reserves its absolute Rights to assert, declare, affirm, avow, enforce and defend its Divine and Natural Rights to record, register, keep and maintain Sacred Circumscribed Space, by any and every lawful means necessary.

Authority of Ecclesia and Sacred Circumscribed Space

3. All proper, valid and legitimate Sacred Circumscribed Space is a clearly and uniquely named dimension of Ucadia Space-Day-Time, whereby:-

Elements of Valid Sacred Circumscribed Space

(i) Such Sacred Circumscribed Space is properly defined by character number and identifier, consistent with the most sacred Covenant *Pactum De Singularis Caelum* and *Pactum De Singularis Christus*; and

(ii) The specific Sacred Circumscribed Space is able to properly define its origin to a higher jurisdiction of Sacred Circumscribed Space, also identified by a proper character number and identifier; and

(iii) The specific Sacred Circumscribed Space was either formed in accord with the most sacred *Covenant Pactum De Singularis Caelum*, or associated Covenants and Charters, or by one or more properly dispensed sacraments of the thirty three *Summa Sacramenta*; and

(iv) The Sacred Circumscribed Space does not contradict or usurp any previous proper, valid and legitimate existing Sacred Circumscribed Space.

4. Any claimed space, close, place, region, zone, precinct or any other type of enclosure formed by edict, or statute or sacrament that is in conflict with the most sacred Covenants *Pactum De Singularis Caelum* and *Pactum De Singularis Christus* shall be invalid, illegitimate and null and void *ab initio* (from the beginning), having no force or effect or Rights in law.

Space created by falsity or error

VII.III – SACRED PLACES OF WORSHIP

1. A ***Sacred Place of Worship***, also known as a *Religious Place of Worship*, is a sacred building designated and duly consecrated for divine worship whereby Members of the Living Body of One Christ

Sacred Places of Worship

possess the right of entry for the exercise of such divine worship.

2. No Religious Place of Worship may be built or designated and consecrated without the express written consent of the appropriate Apostolic Bishop of a Customary and Traditional Rite or Diocesan Bishop:-

Construction of Sacred Places of Worship

(i) The appropriate authorised Bishop may not give consent to the construction of a new Sacred Place of Worship without first hearing from the representatives and clerics of any immediate neighbouring Sacred Places of Worship, providing for them the formal and procedural right of objection; and

(ii) Although religious institutes may have received from the appropriate authorised Bishop consent to establish a new house in the diocese or the city, they must also obtain his permission before building a Sacred Place of Worship in a certain and determined place; and

(iii) No consent may be given for the construction of a new Sacred Place of Worship if a more appropriate option is represented in the same general location by the proper restoration of a previous Sacred Place to dedicated religious use, than the commencement of a new building; and

(iv) In the building and repair of Sacred Places of Worship, the principles and norms of the liturgy and of sacred art are to be observed, after the advice of experts has been taken into account; and

(v) If the proposed construction of a new Sacred Place of Worship lacks at the time a sufficiently active community of faithful, or sufficient funds for construction or suitable clerical representation to serve the community, then consent cannot be given.

3. After construction or significant repair work has been completed properly, a new Sacred Place of Worship is to be dedicated as soon as possible with the laws of the sacred liturgy observed:-

Rite of Dedication and Sacred Places of Worship

(i) Each church as a Sacred Place of Worship is to have its own title that cannot be changed after the church has been dedicated; and

(ii) Churches, especially cathedrals and parish churches, are to be dedicated by the appropriate solemn Rite of Dedication.

4. Entry to a Sacred Place of Worship is to be otherwise free and gratuitous during the time of sacred celebrations, unless upon grounds

Entry into Sacred Places of

of health, security or the essential nature of the Rite prevent it. Worship

VII.IV – ORATORY

1. An ***Oratory*** is a Sacred Place for divine worship designated by permission of the relevant Diocesan Bishop or Apostolic Bishop for the benefit of some community or group of the faithful who gather in it and to which other members can also come with the consent of the competent superior. Oratory

The relevant Diocesan Bishop or Apostolic Bishop is not to grant the permission required to establish an oratory unless he has first visited the place destined for the oratory personally or through another and has found it properly prepared.

After permission has been given, however, an oratory cannot be converted to profane use without the authority of the same ordinary.

All sacred celebrations can be performed in legitimately established oratories except those which the law or a prescript of the local ordinary excludes or the liturgical norms prohibit.

It is fitting for oratories to be blessed according to the rite prescribed in the liturgical books. They must, however, be reserved for divine worship alone and free from all domestic uses.

VII.V – CHAPEL

1. A ***Chapel*** is a Sacred Place for divine worship designated by permission of the relevant Diocesan Bishop or Apostolic Bishop for the benefit of one or more physical persons holding Offices. Chapel

Bishops can establish a Personal Chapel for themselves that possesses the same rights as an oratory. However, the permission of the relevant Diocesan Bishop or Apostolic Bishop is required for Mass or other sacred celebrations to take place in any private chapel.

It is fitting for Personal Chapels to be blessed according to the rite prescribed in the liturgical books. They must, however, be reserved for divine worship alone and free from all domestic uses.

VII.VI – SHRINE

1. A ***Shrine*** is a Sacred Place dedicated and consecrated to Heaven and to one or more venerated deities, ancestors, heroes, martyrs, saints or spirits, where Living Ordinary Members make pilgrimage as a mark of respect and piety. Shrine

A Shrine may exist in a number of forms including (but not limited to) a sanctuary, or preserved location, or holy city, or temple, or church or altar. In all cases, a Shrine must be respected as a place of great sanctity and free from profane or sordid behaviours. Above all, a Shrine is a spiritual portal between Heaven and Earth, given to all people as a means of sustaining and edifying their faith and enlarging and strengthening their trust and knowledge in God and the Divine Creator of all Existence.

2. All Shrines may be defined by six characters being: Universal, Traditional, National, Historical, Communal or Familial, whereby a particular Shrine may qualify according to one or more characteristics: Forms of Shrine

(i) *Universal Shrine,* also known as Supreme Shrine, is a Sacred and Consecrated Place ordained by Heaven in unity and perpetual remembrance of the most sacred Covenant P*actum De Singularis Caelum*. There are eleven Sacred Cities and Sanctuaries representing supreme sacredness across all six Unions (Africa, Americas, Arabia, Asia, Europe and Oceania) being the Holy See, the Holy City of Jerusalem, the Holy City of Mecca, the Holy City of Istanbul (Constantinople), the Holy City of Bodh Gaya, the Holy City of Varanasi, the Holy City of Tunis (Carthage), the Holy City of London, the Holy City of Washington, the Holy City of Melbourne and the Holy Sovereign Sanctuary of One Ireland; and

(ii) *Traditional Shrine* is a Sacred and Consecrated Place ordained and worshipped by one or more Customary and Traditional Rites as a Sacred Place of the utmost significance; and

(iii) *National Shrine* is a Sacred and Consecrated Place ordained by approval of the Supreme See and the Bishops and Patriarch of the relevant University and nation; and

(iv) *Historical Shrine* is a Sacred and Consecrated Place approved by the Patriarch and Bishops of a University and Nation as a place of sanctity and importance, deserving of preservation and reverence; and

(v) *Communal Shrine* is a Sacred and Consecrated Place approved by the relevant Diocesan Bishop or Apostolic Bishop for a community; and

(vi) *Familial Shrine* is a Sacred and Consecrated Place within a building occupied by one or more households, approved by the relevant Diocesan Bishop or Apostolic Bishop for votive offerings and celebrations.

VII.VII – ALTAR

1. An ***Altar*** is any fixed or movable structure dedicated for the purpose of votive, or penitential or sacramental offerings. The most sacred ceremony upon a properly sanctified and dedicated altar is sacrament of Holy Eucharist. Altar

   Fixed altars must be dedicated, and movable altars must be dedicated or blessed, according to the rites prescribed in the liturgical books. An altar, whether fixed or movable, must be reserved for divine worship alone, to the absolute exclusion of any profane use. However, Altars, whether fixed or movable, do not lose their dedication or blessing if the church or other sacred place is relegated to profane uses.

   The Customary and Traditional Rite of placing relics of martyrs or other saints under a fixed Altar is permitted to be preserved within those Customary and Traditional Rites that deem such ancient tradition as absolutely necessary. However, in all other instances, no bones or relics or bodies are to be buried within or beneath Altars.

VII.VIII – VESTRY

1. A ***Vestry***, also known as a Sacristy, is a dedicated room within a Sacred Place of Worship for the secure storage of sacred vestments and liturgical objects; and the preparation and completion of Mass and other Rites; and the storage, or blessing or inspection of the rolls of the community; and the conducting of personal or small official liturgical meetings concerning the community. Vestry

VII.IX – REGISTRY

1. A ***Registry*** is a dedicated office for the safe storage, administration, inspection and conduct of transactions concerning the registers of the community. Registry
2. Register books shall be provided, maintained, and kept in accordance with the rules relating to registers in general and specifically to the forms of registers held. Registers

VII.X – OFFICE

1. An ***Office*** is a movable or immovable Sacred Circumscribed Space where are held certain rights, authorities, capacities and powers, conferred upon one who has pronounced one or more Oaths or Vows and Sacraments and preserved by their continued honour to the Office

fiduciary principles of good faith, good character and good conscience. One who holds an Office under such fiduciary capacity is called an Officer. An Agent can never legitimately hold an Office.

2. There are only four possible types of Office as defined and determined by the nature of their creation, their authority and powers and sacred and ecclesiastical superiority being *Divine, True, Superior* and *Inferior*: Types of Office

   (i) A *Divine Office* is an Office named and created in accord with the sacred Covenant *Pactum De Singularis Caelum* in which a spiritual member of One Heaven vows to personify such unique Office, as custodian and guardian spirit for a period not less than one thousand and eighty years. Some Divine Offices such as the *Supreme Patriarch of the Universal Ecclesia of Christ*, also known as the Holy Father, may be occupied by living flesh and blood carnated Members. Thus a Divine Office can never be dissolved, usurped, seized or surrendered; and

   (ii) A *True Office* is either the Office of Man or the Office of Woman as defined by the Divine Creator of all Existence and into which each and every flesh carnated Member is invested and commissioned from the time of their physical birth until their physical death. Therefore, a True Office can never be usurped, seized, sold or stolen; and

   (iii) A *Superior Office* is primarily associated with the performance of one or more Oaths or Vows in the creation of a sacred Fiduciary and Ecclesiastical Office and is sustained so long as such oaths or vows are honoured; and

   (iv) An *Inferior Office*, or "Pseudo Office" are all positions whereby a defective or inferior Oath or Vow has been offered, or no Oath provided or where the fiduciary obligations have been abrogated in favour of agent and commercial advantages.

3. As all rights and property are by definition sacred, all clerical and professional obligations and responsibilities in relation to the administration, transference and conveyance of any rights or property must be concluded in a valid Office. Any and every transaction or claimed transference or conveyance of property or rights must be concluded within the sacred space and place of a valid Office to have ecclesiastical, moral, lawful and legal force and effect. Conveyances and Transfers must be conducted in proper Office

4. By definition, the authority, rights and powers of a Divine Office is superior to any and all other forms of Office, regardless of title or claimed status. No Inferior Office possesses any power, force, Hierarchy of Authority of Office

authority, right or ability to abrogate or usurp the decisions or authority of a Divine Office. Similarly, no Superior Office or Inferior Office possesses any force, authority, right or ability to abrogate or usurp the authority of a True Office to exercise any of the Natural Rights granted to it, unless the occupant of a True Office wilfully and deliberately repudiates the Golden Rule of Law and all forms of logic, reason and sense.

VII.XI – CEMETERIES & CREMATORIUMS

Cemeteries & Crematoriums

1. A proper designated character of a ***Cemetery*** or ***Crematorium*** is by definition a sacred circumscribed space in accord with the norms of the liturgical books. There exists no spiritual impediment whether a deceased or their family chooses burial or cremation.

   Furthermore, there exists no spiritual impediment if a deceased is buried or cremated in a sacred circumscribed space that is not dedicated to the faith of One Christ. However, where possible and for the dignity of its Members, the Church is to have its own cemeteries or at least areas in civil cemeteries that are designated for the deceased members of the faithful and properly blessed.

   Parishes and religious institutes may have their own cemetery. Other juridic persons or families may also have a special cemetery or tomb, to be blessed according to the judgement of the local Diocesan or Apostolic Bishop.

   In respect to church burial, bodies are not to be buried or entombed within churches unless it is a matter of dignity of position to certain offices of clergy, or in relation to the dedication of a church also as a Shrine to a beloved and saintly life.

VII.XII – RELIGIOUS HOUSES

Religious Houses

1. Clerics and Ministers holding such sacred office (such as one of the Great Offices of State), must live in legitimately established Religious Houses, designated according to the norm of law of the Universal Ecclesia of One Christ. The erection of such Religious Houses shall take place with consideration for their advantage and proximity to Religious Institutes of the Universal Ecclesia of One Christ.

VII.XIII – SACRED VESTMENTS

1. ***Sacred Vestments*** are Liturgical and Clerical garments and articles that symbolise the manifest Divine, Natural and Ecclesiastical Rights, Powers and Authority of the one true apostolic Universal Ecclesia of One Christ. Vestments therefore represent the heritage of Divine Covenants as expressed through the Sacred Deposit of Faith, also known as *Authenticus Depositum Fidei*, as well as the distinct traditions and customs associated with Christian worship: Sacred Vestments

   (i) *Clerical Vestments* are distinct non liturgical clothing, worn exclusively by Clergy and consecrated persons; and

   (ii) *Liturgical Vestments* are special garments and clothing reserved specifically for liturgical service and the conferral of the sacraments.

2. The use of distinct, sacred and special garments in the worship of the Divine is an ancient tradition and custom that compliment the authentic heritage of the Divine Covenants of *Authenticus Depositum Fidei*. In this sense, the traditions and customs of Christian liturgy comes after many millennia of the use of distinct, sacred and special forms of liturgical garments. It also means that there exists some similarities within the forms of Sacred Vestments and these ancient forms. However, it is a gross error and falsity to therefore presume that the Sacred Vestments of the Universal Ecclesia of Christ are one and the same as such ancient traditions. Each and every liturgical garment and article approved and recognised for Divine Liturgy is distinct and separate in its purpose and function to any non-Christian rite, nor does authentic doctrine permit any "carry forward" or "inheritance" of non-Christian purposes and functions of liturgical garments into the use of Sacred Vestments of the Universal Ecclesia. Heritage and Origin of Sacred Vestments

3. The primary purpose and function of Sacred Vestments is to symbolise the manifest Divine, Natural and Ecclesiastical Rights, Powers and Authority of the one true apostolic Universal Ecclesia of One Christ; and secondly in the nature of Liturgical Vestments, the authority and powers of the Celebrant, or Assistant, or Supplicant of Liturgy or conferral of sacraments. As clear symbols, Liturgical Vestments are meant to positively contribute to the beauty of Liturgical Rites, without negatively distracting or impeding the minds and hearts of participants. Therefore, such Sacred Vestments encourage the use of rich symbolism, whilst also finding the correct balance that complements Sacred Liturgy. Purpose and Function of Sacred Vestments

4. Sacred Vestments do not in themselves impart any special Divine, Sacred Vestments and

Natural and Ecclesiastical Rights, Powers and Authority upon the one who holds them or adorns them. This is a resolute Divine Command through Authentic Revelation and never to be contradicted, nor usurped by permitting superstitions to cloud the clear source of real supernatural power through the sacraments. Instead, Sacred Vestments are an aid and an assistance to recognise the solemnity of Ecclesiastical Office and Divine Liturgy and to achieve and maintain the appropriate presence of mind and openness of heart when participating in the proper Rites of the Universal Ecclesia. Consecrated Powers

5. Religious Clerics are expected to wear suitable and modest Clerical Vestments according to the norms issued by their Association or Institute or Society and according to any associated Customary and Traditional Rite. Norms of Clerical Vestments

6. The Customary and Traditional Rites of the united body of Christ possess a wide array of Sacred Liturgical Vestments in keeping with their heritage. In addition, the Universal Ecclesia of Christ defines two specific classes of Liturgical Vestments as the norms, being Universal and Reserved:- Norms of Liturgical Vestments

(i) *Universal Liturgical Vestments* are those prescribed to Clerics and participants on association with the form of universally prescribed Divine Liturgy; and

(ii) *Reserved Liturgical Vestments* are those reserved to specific offices and dignities within the Universal Ecclesia, heralding certain rights or powers.

7. In the universal celebration of Mass, recognising the right of Customary and Traditional Rites to their prescribed Liturgical Vestments, there exists three primary Liturgical Vestments required of a Celebrant, being the *Alb*, the *Cinture* and the *Chasuble*: - Universal Liturgical Vestments for Celebrants

(i) The *Alb* is a long, white garment, which flows from shoulders to ankles, and has long sleeves extending to the wrists. The word alb means “white” and it signifies the pious intention, clarity and humble service of the Celebrant in performing their sacred duty; and

(ii) The *Cincture* is a long, thick cord with tassels at the ends that secures the alb around the waist. It may be white or may be the same liturgical colour as the other vestments. The Cinture represents the binding of service and remembrance of sacred oath and vows of consecrated life; and

(iii) The *Chasuble* is the outer garment worn over the alb and cinture. Derived from the Latin word *casula* meaning “house”.

It may be Gothic in form, draping from the shoulders, or Roman, broad at the front and back and narrow over the shoulders so as to leave the arms free. It is a symbol of Divine Authority of the Celebrant through their consecrated orders.

8. Outside of the celebration of Mass, there is but one Universal Liturgical Vestment that is mandated being the *Stole*. The Stole is a long cloth, about four inches wide that is worn around the neck by the Celebrant like a scarf. In this sense, the stole reminds the Celebrant not only of their authority and dignity through consecrated orders, but also of their duty to preach the *Word of God* with courage and conviction and to serve the needs of the faithful.

Universal Liturgical Vestment for Sacraments

VII.XIV – SACRED PERENNIAL OBJECTS

1. ***Sacred Perennial Objects*** are enduring, permanent and timeless Sacred Objects important to Divine Worship and the celebration of the Sacraments and Divine Liturgy.

Sacred Perennial Objects

There exists a wide array of Sacred Perennial Objects within the life of the Customary and Traditional Rites of the People of God. Some of these Sacred Objects are in the form of revered statues and paintings as well as objects of great historic and devotional importance, while other sacred perennial objects relate to the adornment and furniture within various places of sacred worship, or to the ceremony of Mass itself.

Sacred Perennial Objects are therefore categorised into four classes being *Devotional, Ornamental, Liturgical* and *Sacramental*:

(i) *Devotional Perennial Objects* are sacred objects of devotional importance including (but not limited to) crosses, statues, paintings, murals, relics and shrines; and

(ii) *Ornamental Perennial Objects* are important objects of furniture, or fixtures, or equipment or apparatus; and

(iii) *Liturgical Perennial Objects* are sacred objects essential to the function of Mass; and

(iv) *Sacramental Perennial Objects* are sacred objects vital to the conferral of certain sacraments, independent of Mass (such as a baptismal font).

2. In the universal celebration of Mass, recognising the right of Customary and Traditional Rites to their prescribed Sacred Perennial Objects, there exists seven primary Liturgical Objects required of a

Universal Sacred Perennial Objects for Mass

Celebrant, being:-

(i) The *Cross* in its purest form is the symbol of both the Crucified and Risen Christ and central to the celebration of Mass. Therefore, there must always be a simple and unobtrusive Cross present upon the Altar as a reminder of the Magisterium of Christ, the Sacrifice of Christ and the source of all authority and power; and

(ii) The *Chalice* is the sacred cup and vessel that holds the wine then consecrated during the celebration of the Eucharist. By tradition, it is usually of a precious metal with the inside plated with gold; and

(iii) The *Paten* is a plate of precious metal used to hold the major Host consecrated at Mass; and

(iv) The *Ciborium* is the large cup that holds the minor Hosts used for the communion of the congregation. It is of precious metal and has a cover of the same material; and

(v) The *Corporeal* is a linen cloth spread on the altar at the beginning of Mass on which stand the Sacred Host and the Chalice; and

(vi) The *Pall* is a small square of stiffened linen, or a square of card-board covered with linen, which covers the Chalice; and

(vii) The *Veil* is a cloth of the same colour and material as the Chasuble, used to cover the Chalice and Paten up to the Offertory and after the Communion.

VII.XV – SACRED SEASONAL OBJECTS

1. ***Sacred Seasonal Objects*** are sacred objects associated with the Liturgical seasons important to Divine Worship and Divine Liturgy. Sacred Seasonal Objects

Similar to Sacred Perennial Objects, there exists a wide variety of Sacred Seasonal Objects within the life of the Customary and Traditional Rites of the People of God. Some of these Sacred Objects are devotional and hold great importance during the year, whilst others pertain to the use of colour during the various seasons and mysteries of Christ, while others symbolise the community and the abundance and life of the community, especially in places that retain strong roots to the land and seasons of nature.

Sacred Seasonal Objects are therefore categorised into four classes being *Devotional, Ornamental, Liturgical* and *Providential:*

(i) *Devotional Seasonal Objects* are sacred objects of devotional importance including (but not limited to) crosses, statues, paintings, murals, relics and shrines; and

(ii) *Ornamental Seasonal Objects* are important objects of furniture, or fixtures, or equipment or apparatus; and

(iii) *Liturgical Seasonal Objects* are sacred objects essential to the function of Mass; and

(iv) *Providential Seasonal Objects* are sacred objects representing blessed and consecrated produce of the land or sea, the product of work and seasonal endeavours and the vital signs of nature and our dependence upon the earth as our home and provider.

2. Colour is an essential and vital element of Divine Worship, especially in the delineation between the Liturgical Seasons and Seven Mysteries of Christ.

Sacred Seasonal Colours

(i) *Purple* is the colour for the Liturgical Season of the *Immanent Mystery of Christ*; and

(ii) *Blue* is the colour for the Liturgical Season of the *Filial Mystery of Christ*; and

(iii) *Red* is the colour for the Liturgical Season of the *Eucharistic Mystery of Christ*; and

(iv) *Gold* is the colour for the Liturgical Season of the *Transcendent Mystery of Christ*; and

(v) *Pink* is the colour for the Liturgical Season of the *Sacred Heart Mystery of Christ*; and

(vi) *White* is the colour for the Liturgical Season of the *Redemption Mystery of Christ*; and

(vii) *Green* is the colour for the Liturgical Season of the *Apostolic Mystery of Christ.*

3. The physical, mental and spiritual health of a community can be gauged in one sense by the providence and good management of those natural resources and splendour granted to it by God and the Divine Creator. Thus in times of plenty, it is right and just to give thanks for the many blessings of abundance, as much as in times of hardship and difficulty.

Importance of Providential Sacred Seasonal Objects

The blessing and consecration of Providential Seasonal Objects is therefore an intimate and vital connection between the community of the People of God and with the Earth and Sea. Within reason, each community of the faithful should bear witness in a concrete manner during each season to these real connections with nature, with ecology, with the economy and positive productivity of the people.

VII.XVI – SACRED CONSUMABLE OBJECTS

1. ***Sacred Consumable Objects*** are sacred objects consumed during the celebration of Divine Liturgy or the conferral of Holy Sacraments. — Sacred Consumable Objects

   All Sacred Consumable Objects are consecrated and blessed in strict accordance with the Proper of Sacraments, Rites & Prayers. These include (but are not limited to) Unleavened Bread (or Wafer), Wine, Incense, Candles, Water and Oil.

2. *Holy Eucharist* of bread (host) is a sacred consumable object prepared only from wheat and recently made so there is no damage of spoiling; and wine is a sacred consumable object that must be natural from the fruit of the vine and not spoiled:- — Holy Eucharist

   (i) Consecrated hosts in a quantity sufficient for the needs of the faithful are to be kept in a pyx or small vessel; and are to be renewed frequently and the older hosts consumed properly; and

   (ii) The Most Holy Eucharist must be reserved in a tabernacle in a Sacred Place of Worship appropriately designated for the Rite of Holy Eucharist; and

   (iii) A special lamp which indicates and honours the presence of Christ is to shine continuously before a tabernacle in which the Most Holy Eucharist is reserved.

3. *Holy Water* is a sacred consumable object prepared for specific actions and rites in association with blessings, purifications, consecrations, healing and the conferral of certain holy sacraments and rites, especially Baptism. There are three forms of Holy Water, reserved for use in accord with proper Rites being *Ordinary*, *Special* and *Extraordinary*: — Holy Water

   (i) *(Ordinary) Holy Water* is prepared from pure water and sea salt, consecrated by a Presbyter or higher, for general use in Sacraments, Mass and personal devotion; and

   (ii) *(Special) Holy Water* is prepared from pure rosewater and gardenia flower extract, consecrated by a Bishop or Patriarch, for use in special blessings, consecrations, unctions, last rites and Special Masses; and

   (iii) (Extraordinary) Holy Water is prepared from pure rosewater and extract from the Holly Tree berries, consecrated by a Patriarch for use in holy orders, major consecrations and extraordinary Masses.

4. *Holy Oil* is a sacred consumable object prepared for specific actions and rites in association with blessings, purifications, consecrations, healing and the conferral of certain holy sacraments and rites, especially Baptism, First Communion, Ordination, Coronation, Unction and Reconciliation (Last Rites). There are three forms of Holy Oil, reserved for use in accord with proper Rites being *Ordinary*, *Special* and *Extraordinary*: Holy Oil

   (i) *(Ordinary) Holy Oil* is prepared from pure olive oil, consecrated by a Presbyter or higher, for general use in Sacraments, Mass and personal devotion; and

   (ii) *(Special) Holy Oil* is prepared from pure cannabis oil, consecrated by a Bishop or Patriarch, for use in special blessings, consecrations, unctions, last rites and Special Masses; and

   (iii) *(Extraordinary) Holy Oil* is prepared from the most ancient and sacred blending of oils to produce the true anointing oil of ancient prophets and kings being the blending of cannabis oil, olive oil, myrrh, cinnamon and frankincense, consecrated by a Patriarch for use in holy orders, major consecrations and extraordinary Masses.

Title VIII – Participants of Sacred Liturgy

VIII.I – PARTICIPANTS OF SACRED LITURGY

Participants of Sacred Liturgy

1. Participants are those who participate in a Liturgical Rite or Sacrament. All Celebrants, Assistants, Candidates, Sponsors, Congregants or Witnesses and Supplicants are by definition Participants, apart from any designated ecclesiastical or ceremonial title. There are five essential forms of Participants being *Celebrant, Assistant, Supplicant, Congregant* and *Witnesses*:

(i) A *Celebrant* is one ordained into Holy Orders and possessing the authority and powers to confer a particular Sacrament or celebrate Mass; and

(ii) An *Assistant* is a consecrated person, either clerical or laity, that assists the Celebrant in the conduct of Mass or the Sacraments; and

(iii) A *Supplicant* is a person having humbled themselves before Heaven and Earth under solemn oath and vow, comes before the Celebrant in the conduct of a certain Sacrament or Mass; and

(iv) A *Congregant* is an independent witness and arbitrator of the conferral of a certain Sacrament or conduct of Mass; and

(v) A *Witness* is a silent and independent witness, that through sacred silence testifies to the event, such as Ordinary Mass, where witnesses are forbidden to receive communion and only the Celebrant and participating clergy receive communion.

Obligation and Participation in Mass

2. True Faith is and has always been the free and intentional expression of fidelity to and observance of the authentic Magisterium of Christ, in trusting the proper teachings and sacred liturgy of the Universal Ecclesia of Christ, unhindered by threat or coercion or promise.

Neither fear nor coercion of obligation have ever been true signs of faith, even if superficially such traditional and customary habits may have inferred a deeper participation among the members of the People of God. No such untruth is sustainable forever and when people are finally given some space to breathe and express their free will and choice, a marked decline in participation is often a consequence.

Instead, true faith demands that each and every member of the Living Body of Christ find their voice, open their hearts and be willing to engage with the journey of New Evangelisation with the Universal Ecclesia, rather than being a passive observer.

All members of the united Living Body of Christ are called to honour and observe holy days of obligation by their own willingness to engage, to learn, to witness, to express, to participate and to acknowledge their own spirit and their own place in the cosmos of creation.

3. Clergy are expected to participate in Mass at least daily where possible. Obligation and Participation in Mass by Clergy

4. Members of the People of God are expected to observe and participate in the holy feast on every given Sunday as the completion of the seven Mysteries of Christ, as well as those holy days of observance that may fall within the week. Obligation and Participation in Mass by all Members

VIII.II – CELEBRANT

1. A *Celebrant*, or Officiant, is one empowered by Sacred Office to confer a sacred Sacrament, or Rite or celebrate Mass in accordance with the most sacred Covenants *Pactum De Singularis Caelum*, *Pactum De Singularis Christus* and the present sacred liturgical texts. Celebrant

2. A Celebrant is by definition a person authorised to hold a Sacred Office capable of ministering one or more of the Holy Sacraments and Rites as prescribed by the present sacred liturgical texts. Sacred Office of Celebrant

   Not every authorised Sacred Office demands the occupant take Holy Orders, yet no Sacred Office empowered to confer a sacred Sacrament or Rite is without clerical obligations or formality.

   Those entrusted with the gifts and powers of Heaven must necessarily be held to higher standards of fidelity, piety and honour. Such authorised occupants of Sacred Office are the gatekeepers of enlightened civilisation and the torchbearers of the promise of Christ.

   By accepting such obligation and burden, they may forgo the wealth and comforts of many of their peers, yet their reward for honouring their Sacred Office is a greater spiritual treasure.

   The health and future well being of Society depends upon all who hold Clerical Offices, to honour their oaths and execute their obligations and duties with the utmost care, diligence and respect.

3. No person may confer or dispense any Sacramental Power or Rite, unless duly installed into an appropriate Sacred Office conferring the necessary clerical powers. Sacramental Powers of Office of Celebrant

   Any action performed by a person without such authority in accord with the most sacred Covenants *Pactum De Singularis Caelum* and *Pactum De Singularis Christus* is therefore without legitimacy or validity. Thus, a Body Politic, or Judiciary, or Registry, or Court that defiles Divine Law has no legitimate power or authority, with all subsequent administrative acts, records, certificates and documents null and void from the beginning.

However, a Body Politic, or Judiciary, or Treasury, or Legislature or Registry that reforms and renews its commitment to Divine Law and the authority and powers of the Universal Ecclesia of One Christ, is capable of redemption and curing grievous errors and malfeasance.

In contrast, any Body Politic or entity, agency, claimed office or person thereof that remains obstinate in their refusal to redeem and reform for grievous error and injury against the very laws of sustaining civilised society and true Christian values, declares themselves a belligerent threat against all Heaven and Earth.

4. Some Sacraments are permitted to be conferred by competent juridic and sovereign authority, without the necessary religious profession of Holy Orders. Sacraments

However, the Sacraments of *Eucharist, Matrimony, Mercy, Convocation, Christening, Emancipation* and *Veneration* are reserved absolute to only those who have competently professed Holy Orders in accord with the most sacred Covenants *Pactum De Singularis Caelum, Pactum De Singularis Christus* and associated approved liturgy.

VIII.III – CONGREGANT

1. A *Congregant* is one who participates in a liturgical rite or Sacrament as a member of the congregation. There are two types of Participant within liturgical rites or Sacraments being a Communicant or Witness: Congregant

(i) *Communicant* is a member of the congregation who is allowed to receive communion and the Sacrament of the Holy Eucharist; and

(ii) *Witness* is a member of the congregation who is not permitted to participate in the proceeding of the liturgy other than to be a witness.

VIII.IV – ASSISTANT

1. An *Assistant* is a member of the laity or cleric holding a subordinate or auxiliary position during liturgy. Assistant

VIII.V – SUPPLICANT

1. A *Supplicant* is a participant of liturgy that gives a testimony, or petition or pleading. Supplicant

Title IX – Order of Mass

IX.I – ORDER OF MASS

1. **O**rder of Mass is the solemn and sacred order of service of Divine Liturgy associated with the four classes and formula for all forms of Mass including General, Special, Ordinary and Extraordinary.

Order of Mass

The term "Order of Mass" is so given, as it is an absolute and fundamental precept of Christian Faith that the proper Order of Divine Liturgy be followed in accord with the form and sequential order of the particular Mass.

Each and every word, gesture and function of the celebration has purpose and function. Thus a Celebrant is forbidden to extemporise or embellish the form of Divine Liturgy without severely impeding its function.

Similarly, all participants are expected to be familiar with the Order of Mass so that their engagement and involvement is one of authentic intention and knowledge.

Therefore, every effort must be made to ensure that each and every participant is given sufficient information and guidance and support in ensuring a level of competency exists.

2. Each and every element of the authentic form of Mass is so perfected and reasoned and divinely inspired as to its purpose and function that the entire Order of Mass represents the living embodiment and celebration of the thirty three most Holy Sacraments.

The Miracle and Mystery of the Elements of Mass and the Sacraments

Thus, when a Christian participates within a single ceremony of authentic Mass, they bear witness to the embodiment of the Mysteries of Christ, the Magisterium of Christ and the Divine Gifts of God, through his son the Risen Christ, assisted by the Holy Spirit.

IX.II – LITURGY OF THE PEOPLE OF GOD

1. First and foremost, Mass is the celebration of the Christian People in their witness and participation in their faith. Thus, the first part of Mass is called the *Liturgy of Christian People*.

Liturgy of the People of God

2. The *Entrance Antiphon* is a brief acclamation spoken by the congregation that expresses an immutable Christian logic and reason, as to a theme, or purpose or reason for their attendance. The Entrance Antiphon reflects the presence of the *Key Sacrament of Recognition* within the celebration of Mass.

Entrance Antiphon

The Entrance Antiphons for all sixty six Universal Feasts of the Seven

Mysteries of Christ of the Liturgical Year are all derived from the Book of Proverbs.

In the past the Entrance Antiphon was derived usually from a brief excerpt of an Old Testament Psalm. However, such phrases, despite their sacred antiquity, did not always reflect or resonate the intended theme or purpose of the sacred Liturgy of the day. Such tradition and custom of ancient Psalms is preserved within the Liturgy of Hours.

3. The *Greeting* is the formal conferral of the *Cardinal Sacrament of Convocation* within the celebration of Mass, through blessing and sacred invocation for divine presence and assistance at the commencement of the proceedings, for the duration of the proceedings. This sacred invocation and holy sacrament is further reinforced by the unique expression of the purpose and intention of the gathering by the celebrant, including a brief introduction to the sacred literature to be heard within the Liturgy of the Good News and the context of the celebration of the Holy Eucharist through the third phase of the Liturgy being the Liturgy of the Holy Eucharist. Greeting

4. The *Holy Blessing* is the formal conferral of the *Cardinal Sacrament of Sanctification (Consecration)* by Holy Water within the celebration of Mass to the whole congregation by the Celebrant. The Holy Blessing is to assist the participants to prepare themselves for hearing and witnessing the Liturgy of the Good News and receiving the Liturgy of the Holy Eucharist. The Holy Blessing is also a visible presence of the *Cardinal Sacrament of Sanctification* within the celebration of Mass. Holy Blessing

5. The *Penitential Rite* is the formal conferral of the 3rd form of the rite and *Cardinal Sacrament of Absolution* (the 1st rite being personal and the 2nd rite being communal), also known as the Rite of General Absolution, within the celebration of Mass. Penitential Rite

6. The *Gloria* is a moment of genuine Joy at just having received the sacrament of blessing and the sacrament of penance and forgiveness. The Gloria therefore reflects the manifest presence of the *Cardinal Sacrament of Mercy (Clemency)* within the celebration of Mass. Gloria

7. The *Will of the People* is a testament of the trust of the congregation in God and the Divine Creator as well as the Celebrant to represent their true intentions through the celebration of the Mass. The Will of the People reflects the presence of the *Key Sacraments of Obligation and Delegation* within the celebration of Mass. Will of the People

IX.III – LITURGY OF THE GOOD NEWS OF CHRIST

1. The ***Liturgy of the Good News of Christ*** celebrates the words of the Crucified and Risen Christ as the highest form of Revelation within the sixty six Universal Feasts of the Seven Mysteries of Christ of the Liturgical Year. Liturgy of the Good News of Christ

2. The *Magisterium* is a reading from revelation, or accounts of miracles or parables given by the Crucified and Risen Christ as a teaching example to the faithful. The arrangement of Magisterium readings is consistent with the liturgical season. Magisterium

3. The *Good News* is the revelation of the words of the Crucified and Risen Christ himself. Therefore to any Christian, they demand the highest respect and attention of all liturgy and scripture. The Book containing the Good News verse is raised for all to see; and the Celebrant introduces the Good News reading by making a small cross with his thumb, first on the words on the page, then a cross on his forehead, lips and heart as a mark of the highest respect. The Good News is the formal conferral of the *Cardinal Sacrament of Authorisation (Prescription)* within the celebration of Mass. Good News

4. The *Homily* is the explanation and teaching that comes from the Good News in the context of the First and Second Testimonies, in that order and priority. The word "homily"comes from the ancient Greek word meaning "conversation". Thus, the Homily of the Celebrant is ideally a conversation and inclusion. The Homily is the formal conferral of the *Cardinal Sacrament of Elucidation (Rescription)* within the celebration of Mass. Homily

5. The *Testament of Universal Faith* is a fundamental testament and promise of all members of the Congregation that upon hearing the Good News they shall act in the manner that marks a true Christian who follows the truth of the Crucified and Risen Christ. It is distinct from a creed or dogmatic expression of the tenets of a particular denomination, as the presence of the congregation and their participation within the Eucharist is rightly seen as living such creeds and dogmata. Testament of Universal Faith

   Furthermore, the Good News expressly compels all who seek to follow the Risen Christ, as it is in their manifest actions and not simply words that they will be measured. The Testament of Universal Faith reflects the presence of the *Key Sacraments of Invocation and Obligation* within the celebration of Mass.

6. The *Petition of the Faithful* are the humbling prayers of the faithful entrusted to the mercy, forgiveness and healing light of the Heavenly Petition of the Faithful

Father, through the intercession of his son and our saviour, the powers of the Holy Spirit and all the angels, saints and heroes of faith. The Petition of the Faithful is the formal conferral of the *Key Sacraments of Purification* within the celebration of Mass.

IX.IV – LITURGY OF THE EUCHARIST

1. The ***Liturgy of the Eucharist*** as celebration of the sacrament of the Eucharist as established in the context of Christian Life and mission, is the penultimate act of Mass, as a solemn and august ceremony that unites all Christians into one mission, one body and spirit of redemption, mercy and justice. Liturgy of the Eucharist

2. The *Offertory Antiphon* is a special invocation by all the participants in relation to the feast and intention of the Mass and their own individual intentions and offerings as a personal sacrifice before God and the Divine Creator. Offertory Antiphon

   The Offertory Antiphon reflects the presence of the *Key Sacrament of Invocation* within the celebration of Mass. The Offertory Antiphon is always taken from one of the Psalms.

3. The *Presentation of the Offering* follows the Offertory Antiphon whereby the symbol of the bread and wine becomes the symbol of the participants genuine offering of themselves, aided by the manifest presence of Christ. The Presentation of the Offering is the formal conferral of the *Key Sacrament of Obligation* within the celebration of Mass. Presentation of Offering

4. The *Prayer over the Offerings* follows the Presentation of the Offering and is the binding prayer and invocation between the participants, the celebrant and Christ himself as a petition of acceptance of Offering to God and the Divine Creator. Prayer over the Offerings

5. The *Preface* is the formal introduction to the Eucharistic Prayer and therefore reflects the context of the Holy Feast and context of the Mass as well as the true intentions of all participants. The Preface reflects the presence of the *Apostolic Life Sacrament of Incarnation* (Christening) within the celebration of Mass. Preface

6. The *Eucharistic Prayer*, also known as the Presidential Prayer, is the formal remembrance of the sacrifice of our Saviour Jesus Christ and binding the offerings of the faithful with the love, presence and forgiveness of Christ as one perfect offering to overcoming death and living a true Christian life. The Eucharistic Prayer reflects the presence of the *Apostolic Life Sacraments* within the celebration of Mass. Eucharistic Prayer

7. The *Acclamation* is the fundamental Acclamation of the Primary Acclamation

Mystery of Christianity that in bearing witness to the authentic Magisterium of Christ in unity, the people of God are themselves an essential fulfilment of Revelation. The Acclamation reflects the presence of the *Cardinal Sacrament of Testification* within the celebration of Mass.

8. The *Doxology* is an acclamation of the mystery of Divine Existence through the most Holy Trinity. The Doxology reflects the presence of the *Cardinal Sacrament of Conscription (Binding)* within the celebration of Mass. Doxology

9. *Christs' Prayer* is a formal invocation and sacred vow that testifies to the mission and calling of each and every Christian to live their lives according to the teachings and example of the Crucified and Risen Christ. Christs' Prayer is the formal conferral of the *Cardinal Sacrament of Vocation (Vow)* within the celebration of Mass. Christs' Prayer

10. The *Sign of Peace* is a visible sign of the fraternity and earnest amicability between Christians and all people. The Sign of Peace reflects the presence of the *Key Sacraments of Recognition and Satisfaction* within the celebration of Mass. Sign of Peace

11. The *Breaking of the Bread* is a reminder of the extraordinary fact that the Son of God, representing the singularity of all humanity, did make himself the lamb and did allow himself to be broken, so that all men and women be redeemed. The Breaking of the Bread reflects the presence of the *Cardinal Sacrament of Compassion (Mercy)* within the celebration of Mass. Breaking of the Bread

12. *Holy Communion* is the high point of the celebration of Mass. Christ revealed that he be the “bread of life”. Thus communion is literally and figuratively the meal where those accepted into communion partake in the meal of the bread of life. Holy Communion is the formal conferral of the *Cardinal Sacrament of Holy Eucharist* and reflects the presence of the *Cardinal Sacrament of Unification (Matrimony)* within the celebration of Mass. Holy Communion

13. The *Communion Antiphon* is a pronouncement by all the faithful as to their witness and participation. The Communion Antiphon reflects the presence of the *Key Sacrament of Satisfaction* within the celebration of Mass. Communion Antiphon

The Communion Antiphon is always taken from a brief account of prophecy and revelation in association with the Crucified and Risen Christ and the fulfilment of the promises of God the Divine Father to the People of God.

14. The *Prayer of Thanksgiving* is an essential prayer after Communion where the Celebrant speaks for all participants as to their thanks and gratitude as to the gifts provided through the celebration of Mass and the Liturgy of the People, the Liturgy of the Good News and the Liturgy of the Eucharist.

Prayer of Thanksgiving

The Prayer of Thanksgiving normally reflects in part the nature of the Feast Day. The Prayer of Thanksgiving reflects the presence of the *Key Sacrament of Recognition* within the celebration of Mass.

15. The *Promise of the People* is the final promise of the participants and the faithful that their authentic participation is a real engagement and renewal and that their sacred vows will translate into Christian action in mission. The Promise of the People is the formal conferral of the *Cardinal Sacrament of Volition (Oath)* within the celebration of Mass.

Promise of the People

16. The *Concluding Blessing* is the final blessing of the Celebrant as the Seal of Christ as protection and good will and care. The Concluding Blessing reflects the presence of the *Apostolic Life Sacraments* within the celebration of Mass.

Concluding Blessing

IX.V – LITURGY OF CHRISTIAN LIFE

1. The ***Liturgy of Christian Life*** celebrates the proper conferring of Cardinal and Apostolic Life Sacraments. The formula and order of actions are defined by the criteria and nature of the Sacraments and Rites themselves as enumerated within the Proper of Sacraments, Rites and Prayers.

Liturgy of Christian Life

The Liturgy of Christian Life replaces the Liturgy of the Good News as the second of the Tripartite Liturgy of a Special Mass.

2. The *Liturgy of Christian Life* is is able to replace and fulfil the Liturgy of the Good News of Christ within a Special Mass, as the imparting of Cardinal and Apostolic Life Sacraments and Rites to members of the faithful is one of the most visible signs of the loving and merciful Grace of the Divine Creator and Christ.

The Witness to the Imparting of the Sacraments as a Visible sign of Christ

Members of the congregation are able to witness first hand the manifest significance and joy that the imparting of the Sacred Gifts of Heaven may bring to a community to strengthen faith and communal fraternity.

IX.VI – LITURGY OF THE TESTIMONY OF SAINTS & HEROES

1. The ***Liturgy of the Testimony of Saints & Heroes*** celebrates and recognises the revelations and testimonies of heroes, saints and prophets, as exemplars of the Living Word of God. Liturgy of the Testimony of Saints & Heroes

In a Mass dedicated to one or more Saints and Heroes, it replaces the Liturgy of the Good News as the second of the Tripartite Liturgy of a Special Mass.

The details for particular dedications to Saints and Heroes in reference to the Liturgy of Saints & Heroes are to be found in the Proper of Saints and Heroes.

2. The *First Testimony* of *Revelation* is a reading of the words of an esteemed and venerated witness to the word of God. The First Testimony exists fundamentally as the first record and witness to the Truth of the Good News of Christ. First Testimony (or Revelation)

A reading of the First Testimony does not have to be restricted to only the Prophets or Apostles or earliest Church Fathers, but a witness whose testimony shines the brightest light to the revelations to be spoken during the ceremony of Mass within a particular Liturgical Season of Mystery of Christ. The First Testimony reflects the presence of the *Cardinal Sacrament of Testimony* within the celebration of Mass.

3. The *Second Testimony* is a reading of the words of an esteemed and venerated witness to the continuity and authenticity of the Universal Ecclesia. Therefore, the Second Testimony is permitted to be taken from the writings and teachings of a universally esteemed source among the Christian faithful over the past one thousand years to the present day. Second Testimony

The Second Testimony exists fundamentally as the second record and witness to the Truth of the Good News of Christ that unmistakably demonstrates continuity and unity in the faith in the Crucified and Risen Christ. The Second Testimony reflects the presence of the *Cardinal Sacrament of Testimony* within the celebration of Mass.

4. The *Homily* is the explanation and teaching that comes from First and Second Testimonies, in that order and priority. The word "homily"comes from the ancient Greek word meaning "conversation". Thus, the Homily of the Celebrant is ideally a conversation and inclusion. The Homily is the formal conferral of the *Cardinal Sacrament of Elucidation (Rescription)* within the celebration of Mass. Homily

5. The *Testament of Universal Faith* is a fundamental testament and promise of all members of the Congregation that upon hearing the Good News they shall act in the manner that marks a true Christian who follows the truth of the Crucified and Risen Christ. It is distinct from a creed or dogmatic expression of the tenets of a particular denomination, as the presence of the congregation and their participation within the Eucharist is rightly seen as living such creeds and dogmata. Furthermore, the Good News expressly compels all who seek to follow the Risen Christ, it is in their manifest actions and not simply words that they will be measured. The Testament of Universal Faith reflects the presence of the *Key Sacraments of Invocation and Obligation* within the celebration of Mass. Testament of Universal Faith

6. The *Petition of the Faithful* are the prayers of the faithful entrusted to the mercy, forgiveness and healing light of the Heavenly Father, through the intercession of his son and our saviour, the powers of the Holy Spirit and all the angels, saints and heroes of faith. The Petition of the Faithful is the formal conferral of the *Key Sacraments of Purification* within the celebration of Mass. Petition of the Faithful

IX.VII – LITURGY OF THE SERVANTS OF THE PEOPLE OF GOD

1. The ***Liturgy of the Servants of the People of God*** is the solemn opening Liturgy of Ordinary Mass as a celebration of Liturgy by Clergy that consciously and deliberately excludes the congregation from participation, other than as solemn and silent witnesses. It replaces the Liturgy of the People of God as the first of the Tripartite Liturgy of an Ordinary Mass. Liturgy of the Servants of the People of God

   In proper recognition of ancient custom and tradition, Ordinary Mass is the purest form of imitation of the immanent and transcendent nature of the Crucified and Risen Christ whereby the Celebrant or Co-Celebrants offer the Mass to God, *in persona Christi* being "in the physical and manifest person of Christ".

   However, the Liturgy of the Servants of the People of God should not be seen as "superior" to the Liturgy of the People of God, but complimentary as a vital channel between Heaven and Earth, for the health and well being of the Clergy of the Universal Ecclesia of Christ, especially in the relation to invoking the powers and systems of Heaven in answer to petitions and prayers of the community.

2. The *Incipit* is a brief invocation spoken by the Celebrant that expresses the deepest need and yearning, purpose and reason. The Incipit reflects the presence of the *Key Sacrament of Recognition* within the celebration of Mass. Incipit

3. The *Purification* is the formal conferral of the *Key Sacrament of Purification* by Holy Water within the celebration of Mass. The Holy Blessing is to assist the Celebrant to prepare for hearing and witnessing the Liturgy of the Good News and receiving the Liturgy of the Holy Eucharist. The Holy Blessing is also a visible presence of the *Cardinal Sacrament of Sanctification (Consecration)* within the celebration of Mass. Purification

4. The *Introit* is the formal conferral of the *Cardinal Sacrament of Convocation* within the celebration of Mass, through blessing and sacred invocation for divine presence and assistance at the commencement of the proceedings, for the duration of the proceedings. This sacred invocation and holy sacrament is further reinforced by the unique expression of the purpose and intention of the particular Mass and feast. Introit

5. The *Penitential Rite* is the formal conferral of the 3rd form of the rite and *Cardinal Sacrament of Absolution* (the 1st rite being personal and the 2nd rite being communal), also known as the Rite of General Absolution, within the celebration of Mass. Penitential Rite

6. The *Gloria* is a moment of genuine Joy at just having received the sacrament of blessing and the sacrament of penance and forgiveness. The Gloria therefore reflects the manifest presence of the *Cardinal Sacrament of Mercy (Clemency)* within the celebration of Mass. Gloria

7. The *Will of the Servant of the People of God* is a testament of the trust of the congregation in God and the Divine Creator as well as the Celebrant to represent their true intentions through the celebration of the Mass. The Will of the Servant of the People of God reflects the presence of the *Key Sacraments of Obligation and Delegation* within the celebration of Mass. Will of the Servant of the People of God

IX.VIII – LITURGY OF DIVINE REDEMPTION

1. The ***Liturgy of Divine Redemption*** is a special Liturgy reserved for Funerary Masses of the Tripartite form. It replaces the Liturgy of the Eucharist as the third of the Tripartite Liturgy of Mass. Liturgy of Divine Redemption

   The details of the licit forms of the Liturgy of Divine Redemption are to be found in the Proper of Sacraments, Rites and Prayers.

IX.IX – LITURGY OF DIVINE REVELATION

1. The ***Liturgy of Divine Revelation*** is an extraordinary Liturgy reserved for particular Extraordinary Masses of the Pentapartite form, associated with such Sacred Rites as Ordination, Coronation, Liturgy of Divine Revelation

Investiture and Inauguration.

The Liturgy of Divine Revelation is the context of consecration and conferral of certain Rights and Powers of Office. It is always accompanied with the Liturgy of Divine Mission.

In the Pentapartite form of an Extraordinary Mass, the Liturgy of Divine Revelation always comes as the third section before the Liturgy of the Eucharist (as the fourth key section).

The details of the different forms of the Liturgy of Divine Revelation are to be found with the appropriate Sacraments and Rites enumerated within the Proper of Sacraments, Rites and Prayers.

IX.X – LITURGY OF DIVINE MISSION

1. The ***Liturgy of Divine Mission*** is an extraordinary Liturgy reserved for particular Extraordinary Masses of the Pentapartite form, associated with such Sacred Rites as Ordination, Coronation, Investiture and Inauguration. Liturgy of Divine Mission

The Liturgy of Divine Mission is the context of sacred mission after the consecration and conferral of certain Rights and Powers of Office through the Liturgy of Divine Revelation.

In the Pentapartite form of an Extraordinary Mass, the Liturgy of Divine Mission always comes as the fifth and final section after the Liturgy of the Eucharist.

The details of the different forms of the Liturgy of Divine Mission are to be found with the appropriate Sacraments and Rites enumerated within the Proper of Sacraments, Rites and Prayers.

Title X – Preparation & Completion of Mass

X.I – PREPARATION & COMPLETION OF MASS

1. Divine Liturgy does not simply commence or conclude with the arrival or departure of the Celebrant from view of the Witnesses or Congregants, but by the deliberate and methodical *Preparations* and *Completions* of one entered into Consecrated Life who surrenders themselves fully to the sacred solemn obligation, honour and joy of *in persona Christi* being "in the physical and manifest person of Christ" throughout the proper celebration of Mass.

   Preparation & Completion of Mass

   These formal Preparations and Completions are as essential to the formula of Mass, as the prescribed forms specified for General, Special, Ordinary and Extraordinary forms.

2. The proper preparations and completions of Clergy before and after Mass has been recognised as an essential element of authentic celebration since the first formula of Divine Liturgy. Such ceremony, as evidence within the Holy Scripture demonstrates time and again the importance of the Celebrants of sacred ceremony in preparing the body, mind and spirit before commencing such ceremony and at its conclusion.

   Traditional and Customary Recognition of proper Preparation and Completion

   History has shown such preparation and completions before and after sacred ceremonies of different faiths as sometimes as intricate and elaborate and significant as the ceremony itself. Yet to authentic Christian devotion, such preparation and completion before and after Mass primarily exists to acknowledge right intention during the investiture of the Celebrant before Mass and heartfelt thanksgiving at its conclusion.

   Thus, it is not the volume of words or their form, or gestures or their order, or the presence of a brief window of silence or the sounds of multiple witnesses that validate and legitimise authentic Preparations and Completions, but the true heart and mind of the Celebrant that cannot be hidden from God or Heaven.

   Therefore, the Preparation Ceremony and Completion Ceremony prior to the commencement of Mass and after Mass are necessarily brief in nature, but abundantly clear in purpose and Christian intention.

X.II – PREPARATION BEFORE MASS

1. In matters of preparation of those things necessary to conduct the Mass properly, it is generally presumed that the Celebrant and Assistants are familiar with those things necessary for Mass and have made ready the place of worship, the altar and sacred objects. Thus, it

   Preparation before Mass

is the moments before the commencement of Mass when the Celebrant is mentally and physically preparing themselves that is properly called the Preparation before Mass.

In these moments, however brief, there are three essential Preparations for every Celebrant, being Right Intentions, Right Investiture and Right Discernment:

(i) *Right Intentions* are the first steps of preparation, formed to assist the Celebrant in clearing their mind and emotions to be able to focus on the clearest and purest of intentions in order to conduct Mass in the manner expected and prescribed by Christ, to be the embodiment of Christ in person; and

(ii) *Right Investiture* are the formal vesting prayers associated with the steps and sequence of the Celebrant being invested in the three primary Sacred Liturgical Vestments in preparation for Mass; and

(iii) *Right Discernment* is the final prayer made by the Celebrant prior to entering the sacred space of worship for Mass.

2. Right Intentions is a brief but powerful set of movements to assist the Celebrant in clearing their mind and emotions to be able to focus on the clearest and purest of intention:

Preparation of Right Intention

Upon entry to the Vestry or place where the Sacred Liturgical Vestments are prepared and laid out, the Celebrant makes the sign of the Cross

CELEBRANT

In the name of ✠ the Father, and of the Son, and of the Holy Spirit, I come forward to serve the People of God.

The Celebrant then bows down and kisses the vestments before him.

CELEBRANT

Lord Jesus, you know I am not worthy to stand as your person. Bless then these vestments so that they become a beacon for all to see your love, mercy and justice.

The Celebrant then reaches over and washes his hands in a bowl of pure water before drying his hands.

CELEBRANT

By cleansing my hands O Lord, may you help me cleanse my mind and heart of all distractions and negativities so that I may be a more perfect vessel.

3. Right Investiture are the formal vesting prayers associated with the steps and sequence of the Celebrant being invested in the three primary Sacred Liturgical Vestments in preparation for Mass:

Preparation of Right Investiture

The Celebrant puts on the Alb.

CELEBRANT

Here I am O Lord. Purify me, so that I may be your shining Light to all those struggling in a sea of uncertainty.

The Celebrant ties the Cincture around his waist.

CELEBRANT

Guard and Guide me O Lord, that I do not forget my sacred vows, nor suffer from hubris.

The Celebrant puts on the Chasuble.

CELEBRANT

I am ready Lord to serve your will.

4. Right Discernment is the final prayer made by the Celebrant prior to entering the sacred space of worship for Mass:

Preparation for Right Discernment

CELEBRANT

My God, My Divine Creator. I come to thee to honour you through your son, our Saviour Jesus Christ with the assistance of the Holy Spirit in the celebration of your most blessed Sacraments.

X.III – COMPLETION AFTER MASS

1. The formula of General, Special, Ordinary and Extraordinary Mass is such that the Mass is considered complete in all aspects upon the completion of the Concluding Rites.

Completion after Mass

However, a customary and traditional practice is permitted, whereby upon the Celebrant divesting, a short and brief prayer of thanksgiving is offered.

Such a brief prayer may be offered up in silence, whilst the Celebrant cleans up and puts away the sacred vestments. There is no need for the Celebrant to follow a formula for such a brief prayer. In fact, because such a prayer has its power by being a personal prayer of thanks from the Celebrant, no formula is permitted to be instructed or mandated;

as such an instruction contradicts the very nature of such a personal and intimate connection.

Title XI – General Mass

XI.I – GENERAL MASS

1. General Mass is a celebration of Liturgy in a form that is vital and essential to the life of a Christian Community. There are only three forms of General Mass being *Customary* (Traditional), *Community* (Family) and *Consecratory* (Sacramental): General Mass

(i) ***Customary*** (Traditional) Mass is a General Mass dedicated to the entire Christian Community. There must be at least one Customary (Traditional) Mass offered each day in each functioning church; and

(ii) ***Community*** (Family) Mass is a General Mass dedicated to the Christian Family; and so seeks to encourage and promote the participation of the Family in the Liturgy; and

(iii) ***Consecratory*** (Sacramental) Mass is a General Mass dedicated to the sacramental consecrations, healing and reconciliation of Christian members. There must be at least one Community or Consecratory Mass each day in each functioning church.

XI.II – CUSTOMARY (TRADITIONAL) MASS

1. Customary (Traditional) Mass is a General Mass dedicated to the entire Christian Community. Customary (Traditional) Mass

LITURGY OF THE PEOPLE OF GOD

Liturgy of the People of God

ENTRANCE ANTIPHON

Customary Entrance Antiphon

(NOTE: See the relevant feast within the Proper of Life & Mysteries of Christ for the correct ***Entrance Antiphon***.)

[Congregation stand.]

GREETING

Customary Greeting

CELEBRANT

In the name of ✠ the Father, and of the Son, and of the Holy Spirit.

ALL

Amen.

CELEBRANT

(C. joins his hands, then extends outward his hands:)

May the love of our Saviour Jesus Christ, the mercy of God and the strength of the Holy Spirit be with you all.

CONGREGATION

(Congregation all sit at conclusion of reply.)

And also with you.

[Congregation stand.]

CELEBRANT

(C. joins his hands:)

Dear Brothers and Sisters, we gather here today to celebrate [Name of feast] within the Liturgical Season of the Sacred Mystery of [Name of Mystery]; and to remember [Name of person or event]; and to bear true witness to the extraordinary mysteries of our faith. To renew our trust in the unconditional love, mercy and forgiveness of our Eternal Father and Creator of all Existence and all Heaven and Earth through his son, our Saviour Jesus Christ.

CELEBRANT (cont.)

(C. directs his hand toward the position of the Holy Bible, upon the lecturn:)

To help guide us in our celebration and remembrance as true witnesses to the Good News of Christ, we shall hear about a Teaching being [Name of Reading], before we reflect upon the deeper message of our Saviour Jesus Christ as recounted within the Sacred Gospel [Section of Gospel for Gospel Reading].

CELEBRANT (cont.)

(C. joins his hands:)

At the conclusion of the Gospel Reading, I shall then say a few words about the significance of our celebration and remembrance today; before I will invite all of you baptised and confirmed into the one Living Body of Christ, to testify and participate in the most holy of mysteries of the Risen Christ in the form of His Sacrament of the Eucharist; as a remembrance of his ultimate sacrifice for all of us, to wash away our sins; and to conquer death forever; and even now to continue to forgive each one of us our weaknesses and transgressions; as he calls us today to be a welcome guest at his Eucharistic Table.

CELEBRANT (cont.)

(C. extends outward his hands:)

Dear Brothers and Sisters, Let us prepare ourselves; by ridding ourselves of any negative distractions or regrets of our lives; and free ourselves from any burdens or impediment by humbly calling upon the Holy Spirit to open our hearts so that our earnest and meaningful participation today will be a true healing and renewal that not only sustains us for the days and week ahead, but brings healing, harmony and happiness to our family and friends and community.

ALL

Amen.

(Celebrant closes his hand and signals to one or two assistants to bring forth a bowl of water and a jar of sea salt from the middle of the church to him).

HOLY BLESSING

Customary
Holy Blessing

(The bowl of water and jar of sea salt are brought up by assistants to the Celebrant who accepts it and bows to the assistants, before returning to the altar and transfers the water into an aspersorium (sacramental bowl), then adding three pinches of salt, before using the aspergillum (holy water sprinkler) rotated once in a clockwise motion to mix the salt with the water, before completing the motion by making the sign of the cross).

CELEBRANT

Dear Brothers and Sisters, may this simple pure water and sea salt be a reminder to us all of our Baptism into the one, apostolic and united Universal Ecclesia of Christ. Let us ask God our Divine Creator of all things to bless this water mixed with the salt of the sea and to make it Holy.

CELEBRANT

(Celebrant opens his arms and looks up)

God our Father, your gift of pure water bring life and abundance to the Earth; it washes away our sins and brings us to eternal life. Help us rid and cleanse ourselves of all negativity and profanity that may cloak our mortal frames, and seek to prevent us from opening our hearts more fully to you.

CELEBRANT

(Celebrant brings his hands over the water in the aspersorium (sacramental bowl):)

We bless this water in the name ✠ of the Father, the Son and the Holy Spirit, that it become Holy and spiritually pure, without blemish nor the presence of any negative spirit; and that in the presence of such Holy Water any such negativity or spirit shall be compelled to withdraw so that we may renew the living spring of life within us and protect us in spirit and body.

We do this in the name of Jesus Christ, the Ruler of all Heaven and Earth and the Lord of Hosts whom no spirit can deny.

ALL

Amen.

(The Celebrant now moves through the church sprinkling all of the people while an antiphon or other song is sung. When the sprinkling and the song is finished, the priest concludes this rite as follows:)

CELEBRANT

By this blessing of Holy Water, may God the Divine Creator of all Existence and all Heaven and Earth free us of all such negativity and distractions, so we may be more conscious, willing and open to cleaning ourselves of our transgressions and therefore receiving more fully the love, mercy and forgiveness of our Father and Creator.

ALL

Amen.

PENITENTIAL RITE

Customary
Penitential Rite

CELEBRANT

As we prepare to celebrate the mystery of Christ's love, let us acknowledge our failures and ask the Lord for pardon and strength.

ALL

I confess before God and the Divine Creator of all Existence, that I have transgressed from your teachings and laws, by my thoughts and through my words and actions; and in what I have done and what I have failed to do.
Before all here present as witness, I admit that I am truly sorry and remorseful for my thoughts, my words and my actions and call out to our Mother Blessed Mary in Heaven, to all the angels and saints and our ancestors, to intercede for me.

[Congregation kneel.]

CELEBRANT

May God have mercy on us, forgive us our sins, and bring us to everlasting life.

ALL

Amen.

CELEBRANT

Jesus, we have earnestly confessed before all here present that we have transgressed against your teachings and rules. Jesus have mercy.

ALL

Jesus have mercy.

CELEBRANT

Christ sacrificed his own holy life, to forever end all forms of blood sacrifice; and to raise the dead to life; and to wash away our sins and the sins of every generation. Christ have mercy.

ALL

Christ have mercy.

CELEBRANT

Jesus you bring pardon and peace to the sinner. Accept our sincere contrition and help reconcile us to your love. Jesus have Mercy.

ALL

Jesus have mercy.

CELEBRANT

Christ, through your Divine Authority you gave us the Gift

of the Holy Sacrament of Penance, that through the demonstration of genuine remorse and contrition, your servants might administer the Rite of Absolution. Rise up then my Brother and Sisters!

[Congregation stand.]

CELEBRANT

In witness to the forgiveness and absolution of our Transgressions in the name of the Father and the Son and the Holy Spirit, in union our Blessed Mother Mary and all the angels, saints and ancestors, let us proclaim to the world the joy of such healing and peace and give glory to our Eternal Father.

GLORIA

Customary Gloria

ALL

Glory to God and all in Heaven,
And peace to all people on Earth.
Divine Creator of all Existence,
Our loving God and Father,
We worship you, we give you thanks,
We praise you for your mercy.
Glory be unto our Saviour Jesus Christ,
The Son of Man and the Lamb of God.
For you take away the sins of the world,
And set all us free from the bonds of slavery.
Have mercy upon all of us,
And receive our prayers.
For you alone are the Holy One,
You alone are the Absolute Sovereign Lord,
You alone are the most high Jesus Christ,
With the Holy Spirit in the glory of God our Father,
Amen.

WILL OF THE PEOPLE

Customary Will of the People

CELEBRANT

Let us pray.

Jesus, through your teachings and sacrifice we have come to no longer fear death, for you have given us eternal life so we can never die.

Heavenly Father, it is our Will and true intention in

gratitude for your gifts of healing and our reconciliation into your presence, that we seek to dedicate our lives more fully to enacting your teachings.

We pray you will accept our humble petition and promises as a sign of the truth of our intentions, through Jesus Christ your son.

ALL

Amen.

[Congregation sit.]

LITURGY OF THE GOOD NEWS OF CHRIST

Liturgy of Good News

MAGISTERIUM

Customary Magisterium

CELEBRANT

Let all those who have ears hear! Let all those who have eyes see! Behold! The Magisterium of Christ our Lord, according to [Magisterium Text]:

ALL

Glory be to you O Lord our Teacher.

(NOTE: See the relevant feast within the Proper of Life & Mysteries of Christ for the correct ***Magisterium***.)

GOOD NEWS

Customary Good News

CELEBRANT

The Lord be with you.

ALL

And also with you.

CELEBRANT

A Reading of the Good News of Christ according to ... [Matthew, Mark, Luke or John].

ALL

Praise to you, Jesus Christ!

(NOTE: See the relevant feast within the Proper of Life & Mysteries of Christ for the correct ***Good News passage***.)

CELEBRANT

This be then the Good News of Christ.

ALL

Glory be to our Saviour Jesus Christ!

[Congregation sit.]

HOMILY

Customary
Homily

[Homily taken from the significance of the Feast Day, the Liturgical Season, the Magisterium and especially the Gospel of the feast, including the relevance and context for the congregation.]

TESTAMENT OF UNIVERSAL FAITH

Customary
Testament of
Universal Faith

CELEBRANT

In honour of these teachings and examples given to us by Jesus Christ and in acknowledgement of the Love and Mercy of our Father in Heaven, let us stand as one and profess the true Testament of the Universal Christian Faith:

[Congregation stand.]

ALL

By the symbol of the Cross,
I pledge my mind and heart and spirit,
To the Golden Rule of Law,
That all are equal before the same laws,
And that no man or woman be enslaved,
Or be bound against their will.
With the sign of the Cross,
I promise that my word is my bond,
When given with my consent,
And that I shall live my life,
According to the seven Christian Virtues,
Of Respect, Honesty, Courage, Enthusiasm,
Compassion, Joy and Discernment,
And shall only give my word,
To those who do the same.
Through the symbol and sign of the Cross,
I vow to defend others against all evil,
So that no tyrant or false messenger,
Shall prevail against the Light of the Risen Christ.
Amen.

PETITION OF THE FAITHFUL

Customary
Petition of the Faithful

CELEBRANT

Let us pray.

[Petition sentence].
May our Saviour Jesus hear us!

ALL

Jesus hear our prayer.

[Congregation sit.]

LITURGY OF THE EUCHARIST

Liturgy of the Eucharist

OFFERTORY ANTIPHON

Customary
Offertory Antiphon

(NOTE: See the relevant feast within the Proper of Life & Mysteries of Christ for the correct ***Offertory Antiphon***.)

PRESENTATION OF OFFERING

Customary
Presentation of Offering

CELEBRANT

Blessed are you, God of all creation. Through your goodness we have this bread to offer, that the earth has given and human hands have made. It will become for us the bread of life.

ALL

Blessed be God for ever.

CELEBRANT

Blessed are you, God of all creation. Through your goodness we have this wine to offer, fruit of the vine and work of human hands. It will become for us a spiritual drink.

ALL

Blessed be God for ever.

CELEBRANT

Pray, my brothers and sisters, that our offerings may be acceptable to God, our heavenly Father.

[Congregation stand.]

ALL

May God our Father accept these offerings through your hands, for the praise and glory of his name, for our good, and the good of the one true apostolic Universal Church.

PRAYER OVER THE OFFERINGS

Customary Prayer over the Offerings

(NOTE: See the relevant feast within the Proper of Life & Mysteries of Christ for the correct ***Prayer over the Offerings***.)

ALL

Amen.

PREFACE

Customary Preface

CELEBRANT

Christ be with us!

ALL

And Christ be with you.

CELEBRANT

Open then our hearts!

ALL

We open them to the truth!

CELEBRANT

Let us remember and give thanks to our Saviour Jesus Christ.

ALL

It is right we give him our thanks and praise!

CELEBRANT

It is right and proper that we give thanks and praise to our Saviour Jesus Christ as we contemplate this Holy Feast of [Name of Feast] during this Liturgical Season as the Sacred Mystery of [Name of Mystery].

Through the Crucified and Risen Christ, God our Father makes all things new again, re-affirming our forgiveness and redemption; and breathing the rejuvenating strength and life of the Holy Spirit into the Holy Vine that is your Ecclesia.

And so with the Angels and all the Saints, we praise you and acclaim:

ALL

Holy, Holy, Holy Christ,
God of all Powers and Majesty,
Heaven and Earth are full of your Glory,
Hosanna in the highest.
Blessed are they who come
In the name of the Risen Christ.
Hosanna in the Highest.

[Congregation kneel.]

EUCHARISTIC PRAYER

Customary Eucharistic Prayer

CELEBRANT

We come before you, Father, with humility and thanksgiving, through Jesus Christ your Son.

CELEBRANT (cont.)

(C. joins his hands, making the sign of the cross over both bread and chalice:)

Through him, we ask you to accept and bless ✠ these gifts we offer you as a manifest symbol of our own personal sacrifice.

CELEBRANT (cont.)

(C. Extends outward his hands:)

We offer them for your one true and holy Apostolic Universal Ecclesia. Watch over us; and guide us; grant us the grace and unity of being one living body of your son Jesus Christ, through our good works in this world. We offer them for N. our Holy Father, for N, our Bishop; and for all who hold true and teach the authentic Christian faith that comes to us from your apostles.

Customary *Remembrance*

CELEBRANT (cont.)

(C. joins hands briefly, before bowing head in moment of silence after the reciting of names:)

Remember your faithful servants, especially those for whom we now pray, N. et N.

CELEBRANT (cont.)

(C. lifts his head and extends his arms and hands outward in gesture toward the whole congregation:)

Heavenly Father, remember all of us gathered here before you. You know how firmly we trust in you and dedicate ourselves to you. We offer you our personal sacrifice and praise for our well-being and redemption and for all those who are dear to us.

CELEBRANT (cont.)

(C. lifts his head and eyes upward whilst also tilting upward his already extended hands:)

In union with all members of the Universal Ecclesia of Christ, we honour Mary, the blessed mother of Jesus and our universal mother. We honour Joseph, her husband, the apostles and martyrs Peter and Paul and all the apostles and saints. May their merits and prayers grant us your constant help and protection. Father, please accept our authentic offering. Bestow upon us your peace and good graces in this life; as we ask to be granted nothing more than the same mercy and forgiveness in death as we have shown to others in our lifetime.

CELEBRANT (cont.)

(C. lowers his head and eyes to the congregation and rotates his palms and hand to them whilst arms remain outstretched:)

We ask all this in the name of Christ, our Saviour.

ALL

Amen.

Customary
Consecration

CELEBRANT (cont.)

(C. takes the bread and, raising it a little above the altar, continues:)

The day before he suffered, Jesus took some bread in his own hands,

CELEBRANT (cont.)

(C. looks upward:)

And looking up to Heaven, to you, our Divine Father, he gave you thanks and praise. He then broke the bread, gave it to each of his disciples, saying,

CELEBRANT (cont.)

(C. shows the consecrated host to the people.)

Take this, all of you, and eat it: this is my flesh that will be given up for you.

(C. places the consecrated host on the paten, and genuflects in adoration.)

CELEBRANT (cont.)

(C. takes the chalice, and raising it a little above the altar, continues.)

Jesus then took a cup of wine. Again he gave you thanks and praise, before giving the cup to his disciples, saying.

CELEBRANT (cont.)

(C. shows the consecrated chalice to the people.)

Take this all of you and drink from it. This is the cup of my blood, the blood of the new and everlasting covenant. It will be shed for you and for all mankind so that every sin may be forgiven.

(C. places it on the corporal, and genuflects in adoration.)

ACCLAMATION

Customary Acclamation

(C. extends his arms:)

In honour of the memory of the sacrifice of our Saviour and our own humble offerings, let us rise up and proclaim the mystery of our faith:

[Congregation stand.]

ALL

Christ suffered and died for us; Christ is risen for us; Christ has returned through us as his united living body.

CELEBRANT (cont.)

(C. with hands extended, the priest says:)

Divine Father, we celebrate the memory of Christ, your Son. We, your people and your ministers, recall his passion, his resurrection from the dead, and his ascension into Heaven; and from the many gifts you have given us we offer to you, this, our humble and heartfelt personal sacrifice: symbolised by these, the bread of life and the cup of merciful salvation. We trust you look favourably upon our reverent and faithful offerings and accept them.

CELEBRANT (cont.)

(C. bows, with hands joined:)

In your name Heavenly Father, in honour of the will of your son, and through the power and authority of the Holy Spirit, we pray these perfect symbols of your New Covenant are transformed into the Bread and Fruits of Eternal Spiritual Life as the spiritual manifestation of the most sacred body of the Risen Christ,

CELEBRANT (cont.)

(C. stands up straight and makes the sign of the cross, saying:)

✠ That as disciples of Christ, and in partaking in the blessed Eucharist, we too may be filled with the strength and grace of the Holy Spirit,

CELEBRANT (cont.)

(C. joins his hands:)

As the one true living Body of Christ.

ALL

Amen.

DOXOLOGY

Customary
Doxology

CELEBRANT (cont.)

(C. joins his hands:)

Through him, with him, and in him. In unity with the Holy Spirit, all glory and honour is yours our Heavenly Father, for ever and ever.

ALL

Amen.

CHRISTS' PRAYER

Customary
Christs' Prayer

[Congregation stand.]

CELEBRANT

It is Christ that taught us to call the Divine Creator of all Existence our Father. Let us pray with confidence to our Father in the manner and Spirit our Saviour taught us.

ALL

Our Father of All Creation,
We beseech thee and honour your name,
For your Rule be united as One,
And your Laws be equal to All,

On Earth as it is in Heaven,
Grant us the means to sustenance,
As we shall give alms to those in need.
Save us from trickery and false oaths,
As our vows and our oaths shall be true.
Forgive us our debits and transgressions,
As we shall forgive the debits and transgressions of others.
Release us from any curse and ills,
As we shall not curse nor wish ill upon another.
We ask most humbly and with deep gratitude,
For let then your will be done.
Amen.

CELEBRANT

Deliver us, Jesus, from every evil, and grant us peace in our day. In your mercy help us to free ourselves from transgressions and protect us from all fear as we defend and proclaim the authentic mysteries of our Christian Faith.

ALL

For the kingdom, the power, and the glory are yours, now and forever.

SIGN OF PEACE

Customary Sign of Peace

CELEBRANT

Jesus, you said to your apostles: I leave you peace, my peace I give you. Look not on our transgressions, but on the courage and faith of your Church, and grant us the peace and unity of your kingdom where you live for ever and ever.

ALL

Amen.

CELEBRANT

The Peace of Jesus Christ be with you always.

ALL

And also with you.

CELEBRANT

As true Christians, let us express to one another, the signs of peace and goodwill.

[The ministers and all the people exchange an embrace, handshake, or other appropriate gesture of peace with those near them, according to local custom.]

BREAKING OF BREAD

Customary Breaking of Bread

ALL

Lamb of God, you take away the transgressions of the world: have mercy on us.
Lamb of God, you take away the transgressions of the world: have mercy on us.
Lamb of God, you take away the transgressions of the world: grant us peace.

[Congregation kneel.]

COMMUNION

Customary Communion

CELEBRANT

This is the Lamb of God who takes away all the sins of the world. Happy are those who are called to his supper.

ALL

Though I am not worthy to receive you, I Trust in your Divine Promise that none be turned away and I shall be healed.

COMMUNION MINISTER

The Bread of Eternal Life

COMMUNICANT

Amen.

COMMUNION MINISTER

The Fruits of Spiritual Renewal

COMMUNICANT

Amen.

COMMUNION ANTIPHON

Customary Communion Antiphon

[Congregation sit.]

(NOTE: See the relevant feast within the Proper

of Life & Mysteries of Christ for the correct ***Communion Antiphon***.)

PRAYER AFTER COMMUNION

Customary
Prayer after
Communion

CELEBRANT

[Announcements, etc.]

[If there are any announcements, acknowledgements, reflections, eulogies, or similar actions, these are best included here, after the Prayer after Communion and before the Concluding Rite. The people may remain standing, or may be invited to sit, depending on the length of the announcements or activity.]

CELEBRANT

Let us pray.

[Congregation stand.]

(A prayer chosen by the Celebrant, or members of the Congregation relevant to the life of the community and the feast.)

CELEBRANT

We humbly petition and ask for your help, through your son, Jesus Christ.

ALL

Amen.

CONCLUDING RITE

Customary
Concluding Rite

CELEBRANT

May Jesus always be with you.

ALL

And also with you.

CELEBRANT

Just as God our Father has forgiven us of our transgressions and his son Jesus Christ has healed us with his love and mercy and the Holy Spirit has filled us with renewed strength and courage to do better, let us make a firm promise now, before we depart, to live and act in each moment of our lives as true and authentic Christians.

ALL

We do honestly and sincerely promise.

CELEBRANT

May our God and Divine Creator bless you, ✠the Father, and the Son and the Holy Spirit.

ALL

Amen

CELEBRANT

Go forth with the peace and love of Christ.

ALL

Thanks be to God!

XI.III – COMMUNITY (FAMILY) MASS

1. Community (Family) Mass is a General Mass dedicated to the Christian Family.

Community (Family) Mass

LITURGY OF THE PEOPLE OF GOD

Liturgy of the People of God

ENTRANCE ANTIPHON

(NOTE: See the relevant feast within the Proper of Life & Mysteries of Christ for the correct ***Entrance Antiphon***.)

Community Entrance Antiphon

[Congregation stand.]

GREETING

Community Greeting

CELEBRANT

In the name of ✠the Father, and of the Son, and of the Holy Spirit.

ALL

Amen.

CELEBRANT

(C. joins his hands, then extends outward his hands:)

May the joyous love of our Saviour Jesus Christ, the merciful protection of God and the unifying strength of the Holy Spirit be with you all.

CONGREGATION

(Congregation all sit at conclusion of reply.)

And also with you.

[Congregation stand.]

CELEBRANT

(C. joins his hands:)

Dear Brothers and Sisters, we gather here today as one united family to celebrate [Name of feast] within the Liturgical Season of the Sacred Mystery of [Name of Mystery]; and to remember [Name of person or event]; and to bear true witness to the extraordinary mysteries of our faith. To renew our trust in the unconditional love, mercy and forgiveness of our Eternal Father and Creator of all Existence and all Heaven and Earth through his son, our Saviour Jesus Christ; and to call upon the blessed intercession of the Saints and Angels and our Ancestors to help guard, support and nurture our individual and collective families; and comfort us in our times of economic or relationship troubles; to calm our woes and frustrations and help heal our spirits, minds and bodies.

CELEBRANT (cont.)

(C. directs his hand toward the position of the Holy Bible, upon the lecturn:)

To help guide us in our celebration and remembrance as true witnesses to the Good News of Christ, we shall hear about a Teaching being [Name of Reading], before we reflect upon the deeper message of our Saviour Jesus Christ as recounted within the Sacred Gospel [Section of Gospel for Gospel Reading].

CELEBRANT (cont.)

(C. joins his hands:)

At the conclusion of the Gospel Reading, I shall then say a few words about the significance of our celebration and remembrance today [some very brief points as to theme of homily]; before I will invite all of you baptised and confirmed into the one Living Body of Christ, to testify and participate in the most holy of mysteries of the Risen Christ in the form of His Sacrament of the Eucharist; as a remembrance of his ultimate sacrifice for all of us, to wash away our sins; and to conquer death forever; and even now to continue to forgive each one of us our weaknesses and transgressions; as he calls us today to be a welcome guest at his Eucharistic Table.

CELEBRANT (cont.)

(C. extends outward his hands:)

Dear Brothers and Sisters, Let us prepare ourselves; by ridding ourselves of any negative distractions or regrets of our lives; and free ourselves from any burdens or impediment by humbly calling upon the Holy Spirit to open our hearts so that our earnest and meaningful participation today will be a true healing and renewal that not only sustains us for the days and week ahead, but brings healing, harmony and happiness to our family and friends and community.

ALL

Amen.

(Celebrant closes his hand and signals to one or two assistants to bring forth a bowl of water and a jar of sea salt from the middle of the church to him).

HOLY BLESSING

Community
Holy Blessing

(The bowl of water and jar of sea salt are brought up by assistants to the Celebrant who accepts it and bows to the assistants, before returning to the altar and transfers the water into an aspersorium (sacramental bowl), then adding three pinches of salt, before using the aspergillum (holy water sprinkler) rotated once in a clockwise motion to mix the salt with the water, before completing the motion by making the sign of the cross).

CELEBRANT

Dear Brothers and Sisters, may this simple pure water and sea salt be a reminder to us all of our Baptism into the family of one, apostolic and united Universal Ecclesia of Christ. Let us ask God our Divine Creator of all things to bless this water mixed with the salt of the sea and to make it Holy.

CELEBRANT

(Celebrant opens his arms and looks up)

God our Father, your gift of pure water bring life and abundance to the Earth; it washes away our sins and brings us to eternal life. Help us rid and cleanse ourselves of all negativity and profanity that may cloak our mortal frames, and seek to prevent us from opening our hearts more fully to you.

CELEBRANT

(Celebrant brings his hands over the water in the aspersorium (sacramental bowl):)

We bless this water in the name ✠ of the Father, the Son and the Holy Spirit, that it become Holy and spiritually pure, without blemish nor the presence of any negative spirit; and that in the presence of such Holy Water any such negativity or spirit shall be compelled to withdraw so that we may renew the living spring of life within us and protect us in spirit and body.

We do this in the name of Jesus Christ, the Ruler of all Heaven and Earth and the Lord of Hosts whom no spirit can deny.

ALL

Amen.

(The Celebrant now moves through the church sprinkling all of the people while an antiphon or other song is sung. When the sprinkling and the song is finished, the priest concludes this rite as follows:)

CELEBRANT

By this blessing of Holy Water, may God the Divine Creator of all Existence and all Heaven and Earth, protect our families and especially our children. Keep them healthy and safe from all forms of harm; and free them and all of us from any negativities and pain from social gossip or bullying; and help us overcome any feelings of depression or isolation or helplessness, so that we may be more conscious, willing and open to receiving the abundant love, mercy and healing of our Father and Creator.

ALL

Amen.

PENITENTIAL RITE

CELEBRANT

As we prepare to celebrate the mystery of Christ's love, let us acknowledge our own failures and ask the Lord for pardon and strength.

ALL

I confess before God and the Divine Creator of all Existence, that I have transgressed from your teachings and laws, by my thoughts and through my words and actions; and in what I have done and what I have failed to do.
Before all here present as witness, I admit that I am truly sorry and remorseful for my thoughts, my words and my actions and call out to our Mother Blessed Mary in Heaven, to all the angels and saints and our ancestors, to intercede for me.

[Congregation kneel.]

CELEBRANT

May God have mercy on us, just as we shall show mercy to others. Jesus have mercy.

ALL

Jesus have mercy.

CELEBRANT

May God forgive us our transgressions, as we honestly forgive those that transgress against us; and in doing so, free ourselves from any burden of hate or anger or regret. Christ have mercy.

ALL

Christ have mercy.

CELEBRANT

May God free us from any pain, or anxiety, or frustration, or negativity or feelings of isolation or helplessness, so that we feel our hearts once more and know with certainty that in the eyes of God we are absolutely loved and that our existence truly matters. Christ have mercy.

ALL

Christ have mercy.

CELEBRANT

Christ, through your Divine Authority you gave us the Gift of the Holy Sacrament of Penance, that through the demonstration of genuine remorse and contrition, your servants might administer the Rite of Absolution. Rise up then my Brother and Sisters!

[Congregation stand.]

CELEBRANT

In witness to the forgiveness and absolution of our Transgressions in the name of the Father and the Son and the Holy Spirit, in union our Blessed Mother Mary and all the angels, saints and ancestors, let us proclaim to the world the joy of our healing and peace and give glory to our Eternal Father.

GLORIA

Community Gloria

ALL

Glory to God and all in Heaven,
And peace to all people on Earth.
Divine Creator of all Existence,
Our loving God and Father,
We worship you, we give you thanks,
We praise you for your mercy.
Glory be unto our Saviour Jesus Christ,
The Son of Man and the Lamb of God.
For you take away the sins of the world,
And set all us free from the bonds of slavery.
Have mercy upon all of us,
And receive our prayers.
For you alone are the Holy One,
You alone are the Absolute Sovereign Lord,
You alone are the most high Jesus Christ,
With the Holy Spirit in the glory of God our Father,
Amen.

WILL OF THE PEOPLE

Community Will of the People

CELEBRANT

Let us pray.

Jesus, thanks to your teachings and your love we can overcome even the most impossible of negative circumstances, when we might have felt there was no way forward or reason to keep going.

Heavenly Father, it is our Will and true intention, in gratitude for your healing and forgiveness and our reconciliation into your presence, that we seek to dedicate our lives and the unity of our family more fully to enacting your teachings.

We pray you will accept our humble petitions and gifts as a sign of the truth of our intentions, through Jesus Christ your son.

ALL

Amen.

CELEBRANT

Let us be seated then to witness the Testimonies and Good News of the Liturgy of Christ.

[Congregation sit.]

LITURGY OF THE GOOD NEWS

Liturgy of the Good News

MAGISTERIUM

Customary Magisterium

CELEBRANT

Let all those who have ears hear! Let all those who have eyes see! Behold! The Magisterium of Christ our Lord, according to [Text]:

ALL

Glory be to you O Lord our Teacher.

(NOTE: See the relevant feast within the Proper of Life & Mysteries of Christ for the correct ***Magisterium***.)

GOOD NEWS

Customary Good News

CELEBRANT

The Lord be with you.

ALL

And also with you.

CELEBRANT

A Reading of the Good News of Christ according to ... [Matthew, Mark, Luke or John].

ALL

Praise to you, Jesus Christ!

(NOTE: See the relevant feast within the Proper of Life & Mysteries of Christ for the correct ***Good News passage***.)

CELEBRANT

This be then the Good News of Christ.

ALL

Glory be to our Saviour Jesus Christ!

[Congregation sit.]

HOMILY

Community
Homily

[Homily taken from the significance of the Feast Day, the Liturgical Season, the Magisterium and especially the Gospel of the feast, including the relevance and context for the congregation.]

TESTAMENT OF UNIVERSAL FAITH

Community
Testament of Universal Faith

CELEBRANT

In honour of these teachings and examples given to us by Jesus Christ and in acknowledgement of the Love and Mercy of our Father in Heaven, let us stand as one and profess the true Testament of the Universal Christian Faith:

[Congregation stand.]

ALL

By the symbol of the Cross,
I pledge my mind and heart and spirit,
To the Golden Rule of Law,
That all are equal before the same laws,
And that no man or woman be enslaved,
Or be bound against their will.
With the sign of the Cross,
I promise that my word is my bond,
When given with my consent,
And that I shall live my life,
According to the seven Christian Virtues,
Of Respect, Honesty, Courage, Enthusiasm,
Compassion, Joy and Discernment,
And shall only give my word,

To those who do the same.
Through the symbol and sign of the Cross,
I vow to defend others against all evil,
So that no tyrant or false messenger,
Shall prevail against the Light of the Risen Christ.
Amen.

PETITION OF THE FAITHFUL

Community
Petition of the Faithful

(The attendants now bring a petition box and set it in front of the Altar as the Celebrant moves around (and arrange a microphone) to the side of the box.

CELEBRANT

I now invite those of you, who have prepared an intention and any personal gift and sealed it in one of the envelopes to step forward and express the brief sentence you've written as summary of your petition, followed by the words Jesus hear us, so that the congregation may endorse and support your petition with the words Christ hear our prayer. As a special blessing, I shall then bless each Supplicant, as a further sign of the true intention our Saviour Jesus Christ that this be a moment of charity and unity of our family and community.

(Supplicants come forward and stand at the front of the church.)

CELEBRANT

Let us pray.

SUPPLICANT (1, 2, 3, etc)

[Petition sentence]. Jesus hear us.

ALL

Christ hear our prayer.

(At the response of the congregation, the Supplicant places their petition into the box. The Supplicant then kneels in front of the Celebrant.

CELEBRANT

Your faith has redeemed you. I bless you in the name of ✠ the Father and the Son and the Holy Spirit.

SUPPLICANT

Amen.

(This process is repeated until all Supplicants have made their petitions and have been individually blessed. The box is then removed to the side by the Attendants and taken safely to the sacristy at the conclusion of the Mass.)

[Congregation sit.]

LITURGY OF THE EUCHARIST

Liturgy of the Eucharist

OFFERTORY ANTIPHON

Community
Offertory Antiphon

(NOTE: See the relevant feast within the Proper of Life & Mysteries of Christ for the correct ***Offertory Antiphon***.)

PRESENTATION OF OFFERING

Community
Presentation of Offering

CELEBRANT

Blessed are you, God of all creation. Through your goodness we have this bread to offer, that the earth has given and human hands have made. It will become for us the bread of life.

ALL

Blessed be God for ever.

CELEBRANT

Blessed are you, God of all creation. Through your goodness we have this wine to offer, fruit of the vine and work of human hands. It will become for us a spiritual drink.

ALL

Blessed be God for ever.

CELEBRANT

Pray, my brothers and sisters, that our offerings may be acceptable to God, our heavenly Father.

[Congregation stand.]

ALL

May God our Father accept these offerings

through your hands, for the praise and glory of his name, for our good, and the good of the one true apostolic Universal Church.

PRAYER OVER THE OFFERINGS

Community
Prayer over the Offerings

(NOTE: See the relevant feast within the Proper of Life & Mysteries of Christ for the correct ***Prayer over the Offerings***.)

ALL

Amen.

PREFACE

Community
Preface

CELEBRANT

Christ be with us!

ALL

And Christ be with you.

CELEBRANT

Open then our hearts!

ALL

We open them to the truth!

CELEBRANT

Let us remember and give thanks to our Saviour Jesus Christ.

ALL

It is right we give him our thanks and praise!

CELEBRANT

It is right and proper that we give thanks and praise to our Saviour Jesus Christ as we contemplate this Holy Feast of [Name of Feast] during this Liturgical Season as the Sacred Mystery of [Name of Mystery].

Through the Crucified and Risen Christ, God our Father makes all things new again, re-affirming our forgiveness and redemption; and breathing the rejuvenating strength and life of the Holy Spirit into the Holy Vine that is your Ecclesia.

And so with the Angels and all the Saints, we praise you and acclaim:

ALL

Holy, Holy, Holy Christ,
God of all Powers and Majesty,
Heaven and Earth are full of your Glory,
Hosanna in the highest.
Blessed are they who come
In the name of the Risen Christ.
Hosanna in the Highest.

[Congregation kneel.]

EUCHARISTIC PRAYER

Community
Eucharistic Prayer

CELEBRANT

We come before you, Father, with humility and thanksgiving, through Jesus Christ your Son.

CELEBRANT (cont.)

(C. joins his hands, making the sign of the cross over both bread and chalice:)

Through him, we ask you to accept and bless ✠ these gifts we offer you as a manifest symbol of our own personal sacrifice.

CELEBRANT (cont.)

(C. Extends outward his hands:)

We offer them for your one true and holy Apostolic Universal Ecclesia. Watch over us; and guide us; grant us the grace and unity of being one living body of your son Jesus Christ, through our good works in this world. We offer them for N. our Holy Father, for N, our Bishop; and for all who hold true and teach the authentic Christian faith that comes to us from your apostles.

Community
Remembrance

CELEBRANT (cont.)

(C. joins hands briefly, before bowing head in moment of silence after the reciting of names:)

Remember your faithful servants, especially those for whom we now pray, N. et N.

CELEBRANT (cont.)

(C. lifts his head and extends his arms and hands outward in gesture toward the whole congregation:)

Heavenly Father, remember all of us gathered here before you. You know how firmly we trust in you and dedicate ourselves to you. We offer you our personal sacrifice and praise for our well-being and redemption and for all those who are dear to us.

CELEBRANT (cont.)

(C. lifts his head and eyes upward whilst also tilting upward his already extended hands:)

In union with all members of the Universal Ecclesia of Christ, we honour Mary, the blessed mother of Jesus and our universal mother. We honour Joseph, her husband, the apostles and martyrs Peter and Paul and all the apostles and saints. May their merits and prayers grant us your constant help and protection. Father, please accept our authentic offering. Bestow upon us your peace and good graces in this life; as we ask to be granted nothing more than the same mercy and forgiveness in death as we have shown to others in our lifetime.

CELEBRANT (cont.)

(C. lowers his head and eyes to the congregation and rotates his palms and hand to them whilst arms remain outstretched:)

We ask all this in the name of Christ, our Saviour.

ALL

Amen.

Community
Consecration

CELEBRANT (cont.)

(C. takes the bread and, raising it a little above the altar, continues:)

The day before he suffered, Jesus took some bread in his own hands,

CELEBRANT (cont.)

(C. looks upward:)

And looking up to Heaven, to you, our Divine Father, he gave you thanks and praise. He then broke the bread, gave it to each of his disciples, saying,

CELEBRANT (cont.)

(C. shows the consecrated host to the people.)

Take this, all of you, and eat it: this is my flesh that will be given up for you.

(C. places the consecrated host on the paten,

and genuflects in adoration.)

CELEBRANT (cont.)

(C. takes the chalice, and raising it a little above the altar, continues.)

Jesus then took a cup of wine. Again he gave you thanks and praise, before giving the cup to his disciples, saying.

CELEBRANT (cont.)

(C. shows the consecrated chalice to the people.)

Take this all of you and drink from it. This is the cup of my blood, the blood of the new and everlasting covenant. It will be shed for you and for all mankind so that every sin may be forgiven.

(C. places it on the corporal, and genuflects in adoration.)

ACCLAMATION

Community Acclamation

(C. extends his arms:)

In honour of the memory of the sacrifice of our Saviour and our own humble offerings, let us rise up and proclaim the mystery of our faith:

[Congregation stand.]

ALL

Christ suffered and died for us; Christ is risen for us; Christ has returned through us as his united living body.

CELEBRANT (cont.)

(C. with hands extended, the priest says:)

Divine Father, we celebrate the memory of Christ, your Son. We, your people and your ministers, recall his passion, his resurrection from the dead, and his ascension into Heaven; and from the many gifts you have given us we offer to you, this, our humble and heartfelt personal sacrifice: symbolised by these, the bread of life and the cup of merciful salvation. We trust you look favourably upon our reverent and faithful offerings and accept them.

CELEBRANT (cont.)

(C. bows, with hands joined:)

In your name Heavenly Father, in honour of the will of your son, and through the power and authority of the Holy Spirit, we pray these perfect symbols of your New Covenant are transformed into the Bread and Fruits of Eternal Spiritual Life as the spiritual manifestation of the most sacred body of the Risen Christ,

CELEBRANT (cont.)

(C. stands up straight and makes the sign of the cross, saying:)

✠That as disciples of Christ, and in partaking in the blessed Eucharist, we too may be filled with the strength and grace of the Holy Spirit,

CELEBRANT (cont.)

(C. joins his hands:)

As the one true living Body of Christ.

ALL

Amen.

DOXOLOGY

Community
Doxology

CELEBRANT (cont.)

(C. joins his hands:)

Through him, with him, and in him. In unity with the Holy Spirit, all glory and honour is yours our Heavenly Father, for ever and ever.

ALL

Amen.

CHRISTS' PRAYER

Community
Christs' Prayer

[Congregation stand.]

CELEBRANT

It is Christ that taught us to call the Divine Creator of all Existence our Father. Let us pray with confidence to our Father in the manner and Spirit our Saviour taught us.

ALL

Our Father of All Creation,
We beseech thee and honour your name,
For your Rule be united as One,
And your Laws be equal to All,
On Earth as it is in Heaven,

Grant us the means to sustenance,
As we shall give alms to those in need.
Save us from trickery and false oaths,
As our vows and our oaths shall be true.
Forgive us our debits and transgressions,
As we shall forgive the debits and transgressions of others.
Release us from any curse and ills,
As we shall not curse nor wish ill upon another.
We ask most humbly and with deep gratitude,
For let then your will be done.
Amen.

CELEBRANT

Deliver us, Jesus, from every evil, and grant us peace in our day. In your mercy help us to free ourselves from transgressions and protect us from all fear as we defend and proclaim the authentic mysteries of our Christian Faith.

ALL

For the kingdom, the power, and the glory are yours, now and forever.

SIGN OF PEACE

Community
Sign of Peace

CELEBRANT

Jesus, you said to your apostles: I leave you peace, my peace I give you. Look not on our transgressions, but on the courage and faith of your Church, and grant us the peace and unity of your kingdom where you live for ever and ever.

ALL

Amen.

CELEBRANT

The Peace of Jesus Christ be with you always.

ALL

And also with you.

CELEBRANT

As true Christians, let us express to one another, the signs of peace and goodwill.

[The ministers and all the people exchange an embrace, handshake, or other appropriate gesture of peace with those near them, according to local custom.]

BREAKING OF BREAD

Community
Breaking of Bread

ALL

Lamb of God, you take away the transgressions of the world: have mercy on us.
Lamb of God, you take away the transgressions of the world: have mercy on us.
Lamb of God, you take away the transgressions of the world: grant us peace.

[Congregation kneel.]

COMMUNION

Community
Communion

CELEBRANT

This is the Lamb of God who takes away the transgressions of the world. Happy are those who are called to his supper.

ALL

Jesus, though I am not worthy to receive you, I trust in your promise that none be turned away and all shall be healed.

COMMUNION MINISTER

The Bread of Eternal Life

COMMUNICANT

Amen.

COMMUNION MINISTER

The Fruits of Spiritual Renewal

COMMUNICANT

Amen.

COMMUNION ANTIPHON

Community
Communion Antiphon

[Congregation sit.]

(NOTE: See the relevant feast within the Proper of Life & Mysteries of Christ for the correct

Communion Antiphon.)

PRAYER AFTER COMMUNION

Community
Prayer after
Communion

CELEBRANT
[Announcements, etc.]

[If there are any announcements, acknowledgements, reflections, eulogies, or similar actions, these are best included here, after the Prayer after Communion and before the Concluding Rite. The people may remain standing, or may be invited to sit, depending on the length of the announcements or activity.]

CELEBRANT
Let us pray.

[Congregation stand.]

(A prayer chosen by the Celebrant, or members of the Congregation relevant to the life of the community and the feast.)

CELEBRANT
We humbly petition and ask for your help, through your son, Jesus Christ.

ALL
Amen.

CONCLUDING RITE

Community
Concluding Rite

CELEBRANT
May Jesus always be with you.

ALL
And also with you.

CELEBRANT
Just as God our Father has forgiven us of our transgressions and his son Jesus Christ has healed us with his love and mercy and the Holy Spirit has filled us with renewed strength and courage to do better, let us make a firm promise now, before we depart, to live and act in each moment of our lives as true and authentic Christians.

ALL

We do honestly and sincerely promise.

CELEBRANT

May our God and Divine Creator bless you, ✠the Father, and the Son and the Holy Spirit.

ALL

Amen

CELEBRANT

Go forth with the peace and love of Christ.

ALL

Thanks be to God!

XI.IV – CONSECRATORY (SACRAMENTAL) MASS

Consecratory (Sacramental) Mass

1. Consecratory (Sacramental) Mass is a General Mass dedicated to sacramental consecrations, healing and reconciliation of Christian members.

Liturgy of the People of God

LITURGY OF THE PEOPLE OF GOD

Consecratory Entrance Antiphon

ENTRANCE ANTIPHON

(NOTE: See the relevant feast within the Proper of Life & Mysteries of Christ for the correct ***Entrance Antiphon***.)

[Congregation stand.]

Consecratory Greeting

GREETING

CELEBRANT

In the name of ✠the Father, and of the Son, and of the Holy Spirit.

ALL

Amen.

CELEBRANT

(C. joins his hands, then extends outward his hands:)

May the abundant love of our Saviour Jesus Christ, the merciful forgiveness of God and the healing strength of the Holy Spirit be with you all.

CONGREGATION

(Congregation all sit at conclusion of reply.)

And also with you.

[Congregation stand.]

CELEBRANT

(C. joins his hands:)

Dear Brothers and Sisters, we gather here today to celebrate [Name of feast] within the Liturgical Season of the Sacred Mystery of [Name of Mystery]; and to remember [Name of person or event]; and to bear true witness to the extraordinary mysteries and powers of our faith. To renew our trust in the unconditional love, mercy and forgiveness of our Eternal Father and Creator of all Existence and all Heaven and Earth through his son, our Saviour Jesus Christ; and to call upon the blessed intercession of the Saints and Angels and our Ancestors to help comfort us in our times of troubles; to calm our woes and pain and help heal our wounded spirits, minds and bodies.

CELEBRANT (cont.)

(C. directs his hand toward the position of the Holy Bible, upon the lecturn:)

To help guide us in our petitions and remembrance as true witnesses to the Good News of Christ, we shall hear about a Teaching being [Name of Reading], before we reflect upon the deeper message of our Saviour Jesus Christ as recounted within the Sacred Gospel [Section of Gospel for Gospel Reading].

CELEBRANT (cont.)

(C. joins his hands:)

At the conclusion of the Gospel Reading, I shall then share a few words about the significance of our remembrance and call for healing today [some very brief points as to theme of homily]; before I will invite all of you baptised and confirmed into the one Living Body of Christ, who wish, to come forward with your special and individual prayers and petitions and any offering you choose to make, sealed up in the envelopes you should find at the end of each [pew/aisle] and testify and participate in the most holy of mysteries of the Risen Christ in the form of His Sacrament of the Eucharist; as a remembrance of his ultimate sacrifice for all of us, to wash away our sins; and to conquer death forever; and even now to continue to support and help each one of us in our times of pain and grief; as he welcomes each and every one us today to be a welcome guest at his Eucharistic Table, despite our previous transgressions.

CELEBRANT (cont.)

(C. extends outward his hands:)

Dear Brothers and Sisters, Jesus calls all of us to his real and manifest healing presence here today. Even if our return is after a lapse of many months or even years, our Saviour does not condemn us, but welcomes you as his Prodigal Children, seeking to robe you in new spiritual garments of love and to heal your broken heart and spirit. Even if we have strayed from our sacred promises and vows of faithfulness in holy matrimony, Jesus is here now, waiting patiently with open arms to forgive us and help us. Even if we have felt angry or hurt with God and with Jesus that we turned our backs on his unfailing love, God has not turned his back on you, as demonstrated by our calling today. Let this moment in time and space be its most sacred and profound, so that it become a foundation stone of healing and forgiveness. Let us first prepare ourselves for this sacred encounter; by receiving the blessing of Special Holy Water of Healing and Sanctity as a manifest grace upon each of us to assist us in our healing, in ridding ourselves of the burdens of unresolved regret, negativity, hate, anger or jealousy; and to free ourselves by humbly calling upon the Holy Spirit to open our hearts so that our earnest and meaningful participation today will be a true and lasting healing and renewal that not only sustains us for the days and week ahead, but brings healing, harmony and happiness to our family and friends and community.

ALL

Amen.

(Celebrant closes his hand and signals to one or two assistants to bring forth a jar of Special Holy Water from the middle of the church to him).

HOLY BLESSING

(The jar of Special Holy Water is brought up by assistants to the Celebrant who accepts it and bows to the assistants, before returning to the altar and transfers the Special Holy Water into an aspersorium (sacramental bowl).

CELEBRANT

Dear Brothers and Sisters, may this Special Holy Water of Healing and Sanctity, that was consecrated and dedicated in the presence of the Holy Spirit and a Company of Guardian Angels of Heaven, for the express purpose that when dispensed it should be for such intentions and needs of healing, consecration and reconciliation as we have already pronounced. Let this Special Blessing also be a reminder to us all of our Baptism into the one, apostolic and united Universal Ecclesia of Christ.

CELEBRANT

(Celebrant opens his arms and looks up)

God our Father, your gift of pure water bring life and abundance to the Earth; it washes away our sins and brings us to eternal life. With this Special Holy Water of Healing and Sanctity, help us rid and cleanse ourselves of all negativity and profanity that may cloak our mortal frames, and seek to prevent us from opening our hearts more fully to your forgiveness and healing.

CELEBRANT

(Celebrant brings his hands over the water in the aspersorium (sacramental bowl):)

We now bind our healing intentions and dedications to this Special Holy Water in the name ✠ of the Father, the Son and the Holy Spirit; and that upon receiving this blessing that any negative foreign form of physical invader or parasite be expelled from the cells and organs of our bodies; and that with the assistance of the Guardian Angels any such negativity or negative spirits shall be expelled from our bodies, so that we may renew the living spring of life within us and protect us in spirit and body.

We do this in the name of Jesus Christ, the Ruler of all Heaven and Earth and the Lord of Hosts whom no spirit can deny.

ALL

Amen.

(The Celebrant now moves through the church sprinkling all of the people while an antiphon or other song is sung. When the sprinkling and the song is finished, the priest concludes this rite as follows:)

CELEBRANT

By this blessing of Special Holy Water, may God the Divine Creator of all Existence and all Heaven and Earth help heal us and free us of all such negativity and distractions, so we may be more conscious, willing and open to cleansing ourselves of our transgressions and therefore receiving more fully the love, mercy and forgiveness of our Father and Creator.

ALL

Amen.

PENITENTIAL RITE

CELEBRANT

As we prepare to celebrate the mystery of Christ's love, let us acknowledge our failures and ask the Lord for pardon and strength.

ALL

I confess before God and the Divine Creator of all Existence, that I have transgressed from your teachings and laws, by my thoughts and through my words and actions; and in what I have done and what I have failed to do.
Before all here present as witness, I admit that I am truly sorry and remorseful for my thoughts, my words and my actions and call out to our Mother Blessed Mary in Heaven, to all the angels and saints and our ancestors, to intercede for me.

[Congregation kneel.]

CELEBRANT

May God have mercy on us, forgive us our sins, and bring us to everlasting life.

ALL

Amen.

CELEBRANT
Jesus, we have earnestly confessed before all here present that we have transgressed against your teachings and rules. Jesus have mercy.

ALL
Jesus have mercy.

CELEBRANT
Christ sacrificed his own holy life, to forever end all forms of blood sacrifice; and to raise the dead to life; and to wash away our sins and the sins of every generation. Christ have mercy.

ALL
Christ have mercy.

CELEBRANT
Jesus you bring pardon and peace to the sinner. Accept our sincere contrition and help reconcile us to your love. Jesus have Mercy.

ALL
Jesus have mercy.

CELEBRANT
Christ, through your Divine Authority you gave us the Gift of the Holy Sacrament of Penance, that through the demonstration of genuine remorse and contrition, your servants might administer the Rite of Absolution. Rise up then my Brother and Sisters!

[Congregation stand.]

CELEBRANT
In witness to the forgiveness and absolution of our Transgressions in the name of the Father and the Son and the Holy Spirit, in union our Blessed Mother Mary and all the angels, saints and ancestors, let us proclaim to the world the joy of such healing and peace and give glory to our Eternal Father.

GLORIA

Consecratory
Gloria

ALL
Glory to God and all in Heaven,
And peace to all people on Earth.

**Divine Creator of all Existence,
Our loving God and Father,
We worship you, we give you thanks,
We praise you for your mercy.
Glory be unto our Saviour Jesus Christ,
The Son of Man and the Lamb of God.
For you take away the sins of the world,
And set all us free from the bonds of slavery.
Have mercy upon all of us,
And receive our prayers.
For you alone are the Holy One,
You alone are the Absolute Sovereign Lord,
You alone are the most high Jesus Christ,
With the Holy Spirit in the glory of God our Father,
Amen.**

WILL OF THE PEOPLE

Consecratory
Will of the People

CELEBRANT

Let us pray.

Jesus, through your teachings and sacrifice we have come to no longer fear death, for you have given us eternal life so we can never die.

Heavenly Father, it is our Will and true intention in thanks to our reconciliation into your presence as well as your gifts of healing, that we seek to dedicate our lives more fully to enacting your teachings.

We pray you will accept our humble petitions and personal gifts as a sign of the truth of our intentions, through Jesus Christ your son.

ALL

Amen.

CELEBRANT

Let us be seated then to witness the Testimonies and Good News of the Liturgy of Christ.

[Congregation sit.]

LITURGY OF THE GOOD NEWS

Liturgy of the Good News

MAGISTERIUM

Consecratory
Magisterium

CELEBRANT

Let all those who have ears hear! Let all those who have eyes see! Behold! The Magisterium of Christ our Lord, according to [Text]:

ALL

Glory be to you O Lord our Teacher.

(NOTE: See the relevant feast within the Proper of Life & Mysteries of Christ for the correct ***Magisterium***.)

GOOD NEWS

Consecratory
Good News

CELEBRANT

The Lord be with you.

ALL

And also with you.

CELEBRANT

A Reading of the Good News of Christ according to ... [Matthew, Mark, Luke or John].

ALL

Praise to you, Jesus Christ!

(NOTE: See the relevant feast within the Proper of Life & Mysteries of Christ for the correct ***Good News passage***.)

CELEBRANT

This be then the Good News of Christ.

ALL

Glory be to our Saviour Jesus Christ!

[Congregation sit.]

HOMILY

Consecratory
Homily

[Homily taken from the significance of the Feast Day, the Liturgical Season, the Magisterium and especially the Gospel of the feast, including the relevance and context for the congregation.]

TESTAMENT OF UNIVERSAL FAITH

Consecratory
Testament of Universal Faith

CELEBRANT

In honour of these teachings and examples given to us by Jesus Christ and in acknowledgement of the Love and

Mercy of our Father in Heaven, let us stand as one and profess the true Testament of the Universal Christian Faith:

[Congregation stand.]

ALL

By the symbol of the Cross,
I pledge my mind and heart and spirit,
To the Golden Rule of Law,
That all are equal before the same laws,
And that no man or woman be enslaved,
Or be bound against their will.
With the sign of the Cross,
I promise that my word is my bond,
When given with my consent,
And that I shall live my life,
According to the seven Christian Virtues,
Of Respect, Honesty, Courage, Enthusiasm,
Compassion, Joy and Discernment,
And shall only give my word,
To those who do the same.
Through the symbol and sign of the Cross,
I vow to defend others against all evil,
So that no tyrant or false messenger,
Shall prevail against the Light of the Risen Christ.
Amen.

PETITION OF THE FAITHFUL

Consecratory
Petition of the Faithful

(The attendants now bring a petition box and set it in front of the Altar as the Celebrant moves around (and arrange a microphone) to the side of the box.

CELEBRANT

I now invite those of you, who have prepared an intention and any personal gift and sealed it in one of the envelopes to step forward and express the brief sentence you've written as summary of your petition, followed by the words Jesus hear us, so that the congregation may endorse and support your petition with the words Christ hear our prayer. As a special blessing, I shall then bless each Supplicant with Holy Oil, as a further sign of the true intention our Saviour Jesus Christ that this be a moment of healing and forgiveness.

(Supplicants come forward and stand at the front of the church.)

CELEBRANT

Let us pray.

SUPPLICANT (1, 2, 3, etc)

[Petition sentence]. Jesus hear us.

ALL

Christ hear our prayer.

(At the response of the congregation, the Supplicant places their petition into the box. The Supplicant then kneels in front of the Celebrant (or the Supplicant bends down if disabled) and marks the forehead of the Supplicant with a cross in Special Holy Oil.)

CELEBRANT

Your faith has saved you. I consecrate you with Holy Oil of Healing in the name of ✠ the Father and the Son and the Holy Spirit.

SUPPLICANT

Amen.

(This process is repeated until all Supplicants have made their petitions and have been consecrated with Special Holy Oil. The box is then removed to the side by the Attendants and taken safely to the sacristy at the conclusion of the Mass.)

[Congregation sit.]

LITURGY OF THE EUCHARIST

Liturgy of the Eucharist

OFFERTORY ANTIPHON

Consecratory Offertory Antiphon

(NOTE: See the relevant feast within the Proper of Life & Mysteries of Christ for the correct ***Offertory Antiphon***.)

PRESENTATION OF OFFERING

Consecratory Presentation of Offering

CELEBRANT

Blessed are you, God of all creation. Through your

goodness we have this bread to offer, that the earth has given and human hands have made. It will become for us the bread of life.

ALL

Blessed be God for ever.

CELEBRANT

Blessed are you, God of all creation. Through your goodness we have this wine to offer, fruit of the vine and work of human hands. It will become for us a spiritual drink.

ALL

Blessed be God for ever.

CELEBRANT

Pray, my brothers and sisters, that our offerings may be acceptable to God, our heavenly Father.

[Congregation stand.]

ALL

May God our Father accept these offerings through your hands, for the praise and glory of his name, for our good, and the good of the one true apostolic Universal Church.

PRAYER OVER THE OFFERINGS

Consecratory
Prayer over the Offerings

(NOTE: See the relevant feast within the Proper of Life & Mysteries of Christ for the correct ***Prayer over the Offerings***.)

ALL

Amen.

PREFACE

Consecratory
Preface

CELEBRANT

Christ be with us!

ALL

And Christ be with you.

CELEBRANT

Open then our hearts!

ALL

We open them to the truth!

CELEBRANT

Let us remember and give thanks to our Saviour Jesus Christ.

ALL

It is right we give him our thanks and praise!

CELEBRANT

It is right and proper that we give thanks and praise to our Saviour Jesus Christ as we contemplate this Holy Feast of [Name of Feast] during this Liturgical Season as the Sacred Mystery of [Name of Mystery].

Through the Crucified and Risen Christ, God our Father makes all things new again, re-affirming our forgiveness and redemption; and breathing the rejuvenating strength and life of the Holy Spirit into the Holy Vine that is your Ecclesia.

And so with the Angels and all the Saints, we praise you and acclaim:

ALL

Holy, Holy, Holy Christ,
God of all Powers and Majesty,
Heaven and Earth are full of your Glory,
Hosanna in the highest.
Blessed are they who come
In the name of the Risen Christ.
Hosanna in the Highest.

[Congregation kneel.]

EUCHARISTIC PRAYER

Consecratory Eucharistic Prayer

CELEBRANT

We come before you, Father, with humility and thanksgiving, through Jesus Christ your Son.

CELEBRANT (cont.)

(C. joins his hands, making the sign of the cross over both bread and chalice:)

Through him, we ask you to accept and bless ✠ these gifts we offer you as a manifest symbol of our own personal sacrifice.

CELEBRANT (cont.)

(C. Extends outward his hands:)
We offer them for your one true and holy Apostolic Universal Ecclesia. Watch over us; and guide us; grant us the grace and unity of being one living body of your son Jesus Christ, through our good works in this world. We offer them for N. our Holy Father, for N, our Bishop; and for all who hold true and teach the authentic Christian faith that comes to us from your apostles.

Consecratory
Remembrance

CELEBRANT (cont.)
(C. joins hands briefly, before bowing head in moment of silence after the reciting of names:)
Remember your faithful servants, especially those for whom we now pray, N. et N.

CELEBRANT (cont.)
(C. lifts his head and extends his arms and hands outward in gesture toward the whole congregation:)
Heavenly Father, remember all of us gathered here before you. You know how firmly we trust in you and dedicate ourselves to you. We offer you our personal sacrifice and praise for our well-being and redemption and for all those who are dear to us.

CELEBRANT (cont.)
(C. lifts his head and eyes upward whilst also tilting upward his already extended hands:)
In union with all members of the Universal Ecclesia of Christ, we honour Mary, the blessed mother of Jesus and our universal mother. We honour Joseph, her husband, the apostles and martyrs Peter and Paul and all the apostles and saints. May their merits and prayers grant us your constant help and protection. Father, please accept our authentic offering. Bestow upon us your peace and good graces in this life; as we ask to be granted nothing more than the same mercy and forgiveness in death as we have shown to others in our lifetime.

CELEBRANT (cont.)
(C. lowers his head and eyes to the congregation and rotates his palms and hand to them whilst arms remain outstretched:)

We ask all this in the name of Christ, our Saviour.

ALL

Amen.

CELEBRANT (cont.)

Consecration

(C. takes the bread and, raising it a little above the altar, continues:)

The day before he suffered, Jesus took some bread in his own hands,

CELEBRANT (cont.)

(C. looks upward:)

And looking up to Heaven, to you, our Divine Father, he gave you thanks and praise. He then broke the bread, gave it to each of his disciples, saying,

CELEBRANT (cont.)

(C. shows the consecrated host to the people.)

Take this, all of you, and eat it: this is my flesh that will be given up for you.

(C. places the consecrated host on the paten, and genuflects in adoration.)

CELEBRANT (cont.)

(C. takes the chalice, and raising it a little above the altar, continues.)

Jesus then took a cup of wine. Again he gave you thanks and praise, before giving the cup to his disciples, saying.

CELEBRANT (cont.)

(C. shows the consecrated chalice to the people.)

Take this all of you and drink from it. This is the cup of my blood, the blood of the new and everlasting covenant. It will be shed for you and for all mankind so that every sin may be forgiven.

(C. places it on the corporal, and genuflects in adoration.)

ACCLAMATION

Consecratory
Acclamation

(C. extends his arms:)

In honour of the memory of the sacrifice of our Saviour and our own humble offerings, let us rise up and proclaim the mystery of our faith:

[Congregation stand.]

ALL

Christ suffered and died for us; Christ is risen for us; Christ has returned through us as his united living body.

CELEBRANT (cont.)

(C. with hands extended, the priest says:)

Divine Father, we celebrate the memory of Christ, your Son. We, your people and your ministers, recall his passion, his resurrection from the dead, and his ascension into Heaven; and from the many gifts you have given us we offer to you, this, our humble and heartfelt personal sacrifice: symbolised by these, the bread of life and the cup of merciful salvation. We trust you look favourably upon our reverent and faithful offerings and accept them.

CELEBRANT (cont.)

(C. bows, with hands joined:)

In your name Heavenly Father, in honour of the will of your son, and through the power and authority of the Holy Spirit, we pray these perfect symbols of your New Covenant are transformed into the Bread and Fruits of Eternal Spiritual Life as the spiritual manifestation of the most sacred body of the Risen Christ,

CELEBRANT (cont.)

(C. stands up straight and makes the sign of the cross, saying:)

✠ That as disciples of Christ, and in partaking in the blessed Eucharist, we too may be filled with the strength and grace of the Holy Spirit,

CELEBRANT (cont.)

(C. joins his hands:)

As the one true living Body of Christ.

ALL

Amen.

DOXOLOGY

Consecratory
Doxology

CELEBRANT (cont.)

(C. joins his hands:)

Through him, with him, and in him. In unity with the Holy Spirit, all glory and honour is yours our Heavenly Father, for ever and ever.

ALL

Amen.

CHRISTS' PRAYER

Consecratory
Christs' Prayer

[Congregation stand.]

CELEBRANT

It is Christ that taught us to call the Divine Creator of all Existence our Father. Let us pray with confidence to our Father in the manner and Spirit our Saviour taught us.

ALL

Our Father of All Creation,
We beseech thee and honour your name,
For your Rule be united as One,
And your Laws be equal to All,
On Earth as it is in Heaven,
Grant us the means to sustenance,
As we shall give alms to those in need.
Save us from trickery and false oaths,
As our vows and our oaths shall be true.
Forgive us our debits and transgressions,
As we shall forgive the debits and transgressions of others.
Release us from any curse and ills,
As we shall not curse nor wish ill upon another.
We ask most humbly and with deep gratitude,
For let then your will be done.
Amen.

CELEBRANT

Deliver us, Jesus, from every evil, and grant us peace in our day. In your mercy help us to free ourselves from transgressions and protect us from all fear as we defend and proclaim the authentic mysteries of our Christian Faith.

ALL

For the kingdom, the power, and the glory are

yours, now and forever.

SIGN OF PEACE

Consecratory
Sign of Peace

CELEBRANT

Jesus, you said to your apostles: I leave you peace, my peace I give you. Look not on our transgressions, but on the courage and faith of your Church, and grant us the peace and unity of your kingdom where you live for ever and ever.

ALL

Amen.

CELEBRANT

The Peace of Jesus Christ be with you always.

ALL

And also with you.

CELEBRANT

As true Christians, let us express to one another, the signs of peace and goodwill.

[The ministers and all the people exchange an embrace, handshake, or other appropriate gesture of peace with those near them, according to local custom.]

BREAKING OF BREAD

Consecratory
Breaking of Bread

ALL

Lamb of God, you take away the transgressions of the world: have mercy on us.
Lamb of God, you take away the transgressions of the world: have mercy on us.
Lamb of God, you take away the transgressions of the world: grant us peace.

[Congregation kneel.]

COMMUNION

Consecratory
Communion

CELEBRANT

This is the Lamb of God who takes away the transgressions of the world. Happy are those who are called to his supper.

ALL

Jesus, though I am not worthy to receive you, I trust in your promise that none be turned away and I shall be healed.

COMMUNION MINISTER

The Bread of Eternal Life

COMMUNICANT

Amen.

COMMUNION MINISTER

The Fruits of Spiritual Renewal

COMMUNICANT

Amen.

COMMUNION ANTIPHON

Consecratory
Communion
Antiphon

[Congregation sit.]

(NOTE: See the relevant feast within the Proper of Life & Mysteries of Christ for the correct ***Communion Antiphon***.)

PRAYER AFTER COMMUNION

Consecratory
Prayer after
Communion

CELEBRANT

[Announcements, etc.]

[If there are any announcements, acknowledgements, reflections, eulogies, or similar actions, these are best included here, after the Prayer after Communion and before the Concluding Rite. The people may remain standing, or may be invited to sit, depending on the length of the announcements or activity.]

CELEBRANT

Let us pray.

[Congregation stand.]

(A prayer chosen by the Celebrant, or members of the Congregation relevant to the life of the community and the feast.)

CELEBRANT

We humbly petition and ask for your help, through your son, Jesus Christ.

ALL

Amen.

CONCLUDING RITE

CELEBRANT

May Jesus always be with you.

ALL

And also with you.

CELEBRANT

Just as God our Father has forgiven us of our transgressions and his son Jesus Christ has healed us with his love and mercy and the Holy Spirit has filled us with renewed strength and courage to do better, let us make a firm promise now, before we depart, to live and act in each moment of our lives as true and authentic Christians.

ALL

We do honestly and sincerely promise.

CELEBRANT

May our God and Divine Creator bless you, ✠ the Father, and the Son and the Holy Spirit.

ALL

Amen

CELEBRANT

Go forth with the peace and love of Christ.

ALL

Thanks be to God!

Title XII – Special Mass

XII.I – SPECIAL MASS

1. Special Mass is a celebration of Liturgy dedicated for specific persons and members of a Christian Community. As the participation in the Eucharist is limited to such persons, such a Mass is called "Special" rather than "General" for the whole community. There are nine (9) main forms of Special Mass being Memorial, Matrimonial, Apostolic, Funerary, Dedicatory, Consecratory, Investiture, Coronation and Pilgrim: Special Mass

(i) *Memorial Mass* is a Special Mass dedicated to the memory and honour of one or more deceased persons, whereby filial or fraternal members of the deceased are invited to participate in the holy sacrament of the Eucharist, with remaining members of the congregation as witnesses to the event; and

(ii) *Matrimonial Mass* is a Special Mass dedicated to the consecration, honouring and celebration of the solemn vows of a man and woman entering into Holy Matrimony and participating exclusively in the holy sacrament of the Eucharist, with remaining members of the congregation as witnesses to the event; and

(iii) *Apostolic Mass* is a Special Mass dedicated to the initiation, consecration and blessing of members of the Community having qualified to participate in one of the Apostolic Life Rites such as *Annunciation, Baptism, Christening, First Communion, Majority, Maturity, Seniority or Elderity* whereby such members participate exclusively in the holy sacrament of the Eucharist, with remaining members of the congregation as witnesses to the event; and

(iv) *Funerary Mass* is a Special Mass dedicated to the consecration, blessing, emancipation and honouring of a departed member of the community, whereby family and friends participate exclusively in the holy sacrament of the Eucharist, with remaining members of the congregation as witnesses to the event; and

(v) *Dedicatory Mass* is a Special Mass dedicated to the consecration of sacred places and spaces, particularly new places of worship; and

(vi) *Consecratory Mass* is a Special Mass dedicated to consecration of sacred objects, Holy Orders and the consecration of higher vows of office; and

(vii) *Investiture Mass* is a Special Mass dedicated to blessing, protecting and honouring one or more living members of the Christian community, particularly in association with the rite of Investiture, or the renewal of Oaths or Vows; and

(viii) *Coronation Mass* is a Special Mass dedicated to the consecration and investiture of Christian Sovereigns having a legitimate and valid Divine Mandate; and

(ix) *Pilgrim Mass* is a Special Mass dedicated to the healing, reconciliation and blessing of Christian Pilgrims whilst they remain on their solemn Pilgrimage, whereby such persons participate exclusively in the holy sacrament of the Eucharist, with remaining members of the congregation as witnesses to the event.

2. By definition, a Special Mass is a celebration of Liturgy dedicated to specific persons and members of a Christian Community. Therefore, the purpose of a Special Mass is to set apart one or more members of the community, in order for such events and celebrations to signify an important milestone in the journey of life and spirit; and as a manifest symbol of encouragement and support for the entire Community.

Special Mass and Participants

As sentient as well as sapient beings, all human beings by their innate nature, place greater emphasis upon those places, times and events of such spiritual, mental and physical significance. Therefore, the restoration and presence of such milestones greatly assist each and every member of the Christian Community from more fully immersing and embracing their journey in life and the promise of a heavenly afterlife.

3. The full mystery and meaning of the Eucharist is revealed when seen not only from the celebration of General Mass, but Special Mass. The Christian Mission to live and act according to the Magisterium of Christ is most visually demonstrated in Liturgy when members of the community willingly and faithfully choose to participate in the Sacrament of the Holy Eucharist for special causes.

Special Mass and Congregation

The Sacrament of Holy Matrimony as a Special Mass becomes an opportunity to witness the mystery of the Eucharist as a wedding feast when the bride and groom choose through their sacred vows to sacrifice their individual selfish desires to choose to be united as one spirit recognised in Heaven and upon the Earth.

The celebration and consecration of Pilgrims as a Special Mass becomes an opportunity to see the Holy Eucharist as the greater events of the Mysteries and Life of Christ, when people of faith, chose to sacrifice their fears and constraints and take up their staff to follow

Jesus.

The recognition and honouring of men and women of office and service, who keep and renew their oaths and vows to protect and serve the community is a further opportunity to witness the Holy Eucharist from the vocation and calling of Disciples not to abandon the world, but to live and work within communities, by harnessing their talents and sacrificing their worship of money as an end in itself, and any form of hardness of heart and lack of empathy, to devote their lives to making their communities a better place and that none are left behind.

XII.II – LITURGY OF SPECIAL MASS

1. The ***Liturgy of Special Mass*** is Tripartite in form in the same way that the three (3) forms of General Mass or Ordinary Mass are Tripartite. Liturgy of Special Mass

2. The first section of Liturgy for a Special Mass may follow the Liturgy of the People of God according to the same formula of a General Mass, or if celebrated alone by an ordained minister according to the Liturgy of the Servants of the People of God. First Section of Liturgy

3. The second section of Liturgy for a Special Mass depends upon its purpose; and shall generally fall into one of two forms being the Liturgy of Saints & Heroes or the Liturgy of Christian Life. Second Section of Liturgy

   The form for the Liturgy of Saints and Heroes can be found in the Proper of Saints & Heroes. The form for the Liturgy of Christian Life may be found in the Proper of Sacraments, Rites & Prayers.

4. Except for a Special Funerary Mass, the third section of a Special Mass is always the Liturgy of the Eucharist. In the case of Funerary Rites it is one of the licit forms of the Liturgy of Christian Redemption. Third Section of Liturgy

Title XIII – Ordinary Mass

XIII.I – ORDINARY MASS

1. **O**rdinary Mass is a celebration of Liturgy by Clergy that consciously and deliberately excludes the congregation from participation, other than as solemn and silent witnesses. Only Ordinary Masses or High Masses of the extraordinary form may be recited in Latin. However, only Ordinary Masses may be said *Ad Orientem* and such custom is strictly forbidden in all other forms of Mass. There are only two forms of Ordinary Mass being Solitary and Fraternal:

Ordinary Mass

(i) *Solitary Mass* is an Ordinary Mass dedicated whereby a single Celebrant vocalises and performs the Mass as if they are completely alone; and to the total exclusion of interaction with any members of the congregation or laity that may be present; and

(ii) *Fraternal Mass* is an Ordinary Mass of two or more Clergy, whereby the co-celebrants and clergy vocalise and perform Mass as if they are the sole community; and to the total exclusion of interaction with any members of the congregation or laity that may be present.

2. The formal and traditional nature of Ordinary Mass whereby the Celebrant or Co-Celebrants offer the Mass to God, *in persona Christi* being "in the physical and manifest person of Christ" is a profound devotion that absolutely precludes the congregation and laity from participation other than as faithful witness to such sacred mystery.

The absolute exclusion of congregation and laity from Ordinary Mass

In proper recognition of ancient custom and tradition, Ordinary Mass is the purest form of imitation of the immanent and transcendent nature of the Crucified and Risen Christ. It serves as a vital channel between Heaven and Earth, for the health and well being of the Universal Ecclesia of Christ, especially in the relation to invoking the powers and systems of Heaven in answer to petitions and prayers of the community.

Therefore, the Ordinary form of Mass cannot usurp the General Form, just as the General form of Mass cannot usurp the Special form of Mass, as each form has specific function, purpose and place in the authentic living liturgy of Christ.

3. In strict honour to the purpose and function of the Ordinary form of Mass, the congregation and laity that may be present are absolutely excluded and forbidden to receive Holy Communion, nor participate in any vocalisation of the Liturgy of the Eucharist. Any clergy, or diocese, or traditional or customary rite that permits the congregation

The exclusion of congregation and laity from Communion in Ordinary Form or laity present at an Ordinary Mass to receive Holy Communion is culpable of a grave delict against the sacraments of the Universal Ecclesia. However, the congregation and laity should always be welcome to observe in silent reverence at such sacred mystery.

4. Ordinary Mass is the only form of Liturgy permitted to be performed *Ad Orientem*, meaning "to the east" in honour of the light and revelation of the Risen Christ and the unity of the one, true apostolic Universal Ecclesia as the fulfilment of prophecy as the authentic Living Body of Christ. Any claim or assertion of its use, as a rejection of authentic liturgy, or as a challenge to the true Magisterium of Christ is a gross error and falsity.

Ad Orientem

Ad Orientem is reserved exclusively for Ordinary Mass, precisely because of the profound and sacred purpose of the Ordinary form of Mass and not to diminish the significance of custom and tradition, nor such formality.

XIII.II – SOLITARY MASS

1. *Solitary Mass* is an Ordinary Mass dedicated whereby a single Celebrant vocalises and performs the Mass as if they are completely alone; and to the total exclusion of interaction with any members of the congregation or laity that may be present.

Solitary Mass

LITURGY OF THE SERVANTS OF THE PEOPLE OF GOD

Liturgy of the Servants of the People of God

INCIPIT

Solitary
Incipit

CELEBRANT

(The Celebrant comes to the front of the Altar and kneels, facing the tabernacle. He stretches out his arms and in a strong and firm voice directing his attention toward the shrine of the tabernacle he cries out.)

My God! My Lord! My Spirit!
Hear me! Help me! Guide me!
Let me honour and purify this sacred circumscribed space,
This sacred sanctuary and holy temple in your name,
So that nothing impure nor malevolent may impede,
My humble petitions and offerings,
In the name of your son, our Saviour Jesus Christ.
For you are the one true Divine Creator of all Existence,
And all Heaven and Earth and all life and human life.
You alone are the highest Lord and Master of all Reason.

Hear then the cries of your humble servant,
And grant me the aid of your strongest angels,
That they may make their presence manifest,
Together with Mary, our Blessed Mother and protector,
And all the heroic martyrs, saints and ancestors,
So that in offering this simple sacrifice of myself,
As a renewal of my solemn vows and vocation,
By dedicating myself to serving you this day,
You will accept my humble offering,
And help strengthen my limbs to continue to stand and walk in your name,
And fill my heart with your abundant love to care and support all others in your name,
And in the name of your one true apostolic Universal Ecclesia.

PURIFICATION

Solitary
Purification

(The celebrant arises and collects the incense burner and then performs the incensing of the Altar and around the Altar in silence, before returning the incense burner to its place.)

INTROIT

Solitary
Introit

CELEBRANT

(Whisper quietly.)

In the name of ✠ the Father, and of the Son, and of the Holy Spirit. Amen.

(C. joins his hands, then extends outward his hands:)

May the love of our Saviour Jesus Christ, the mercy of God and the strength of the Holy Spirit be present.

(C. joins his hands:)

Our Father in Heaven, you called me to witness and testify to the extraordinary mysteries of our faith, by following in the footsteps and true teachings of your son Jesus.

To cast off the false securities and material desires of this world. To reject the temptations of comfortable indifference. To guard against the falsity of pride and spiritual hubris.

Look kindly upon us; May you forgive your servant for all our transgressions and our weaknesses and inadequacies in failing to more completely devote ourselves to fulfilling your Divine Mission.

Verily, we acknowledge the test of our calling, is that even the smallest moments of doubt; even the tiniest seed of pride or self-righteousness may impair our moral duties; especially in seeking to celebrate [Name of feast] within the Liturgical Season of the Sacred Mystery of [Name of Mystery]; and to remember [Name of person or event]; and to bear true witness to the extraordinary mysteries of our faith; and to renew our trust in the unconditional love, mercy and forgiveness of our Eternal Father and Creator of all Existence and all Heaven and Earth through his son, our Saviour Jesus Christ.

Therefore, I prepare myself by ridding myself of any negative distractions or regrets of my life; and free myself from any burdens or impediment by humbly calling upon the Holy Spirit to open my heart so that this ceremony shall be be a true healing and renewal that sustains and strengthens me for the days ahead for the healing, harmony and happiness to our family and friends and community.

PENITENTIAL RITE

Solitary Penitential Rite

CELEBRANT

I confess before God and the Divine Creator of all Existence, that I have transgressed from your teachings and laws, by my thoughts and through my words and actions; and in what I have done and what I have failed to do.

Before all here present as witness, I admit that I am truly sorry and remorseful for my thoughts, my words and my actions and call out to our Mother Blessed Mary in Heaven, to all the angels and saints and our ancestors, to intercede for me.

CELEBRANT

May God have mercy on me, forgive me my sins, and bring

me to his everlasting life. Amen.

GLORIA

Solitary
Gloria

CELEBRANT

Glory to God and all in Heaven,
And peace to all people on Earth.
Divine Creator of all Existence,
Our loving God and Father,
We worship you, we give you thanks,
We praise you for your mercy.
Glory be unto our Saviour Jesus Christ,
The Son of Man and the Lamb of God.
For you take away the sins of the world,
And set all us free from the bonds of slavery.
Have mercy upon all of us,
And receive our prayers.
For you alone are the Holy One,
You alone are the Absolute Sovereign Lord,
You alone are the most high Jesus Christ,
With the Holy Spirit in the glory of God our Father,
Amen.

WILL OF THE SERVANT OF THE PEOPLE

Solitary
Will of the Servant of the People

CELEBRANT

Loving Eternal Father, It is our Will and intention, to serve you with all our heart and minds and spirit. To be your instruments of peace, mercy and justice. To clothe and feed the hungry. To shelter the abandoned. To bring life to your promise of redemption for all life and humanity.

LITURGY OF CHRIST

Liturgy of Christ

GOOD NEWS

Solitary
Good News

CELEBRANT

May my head, my lips and my heart be blessed, that I may speak the Good News of our Saviour Jesus Christ.

A Reading from the Holy Testament according to ... [Matthew, Mark, Luke or John].

(NOTE: See the relevant Proper of Heroes & Saints, or Mystery or Rite for the correct ***Good***

News passage.)

CELEBRANT
This be then the Good News of Christ.

TESTAMENT OF UNIVERSAL FAITH

Solitary
Testament of Universal Faith

CELEBRANT
In honour of these teachings and examples given by Jesus Christ and in acknowledgement of the the Love and Mercy of our Father in Heaven, I stand and profess the true Testament of the Universal Christian Faith:

By the symbol of the Cross,
I pledge my mind and heart and spirit,
To the Golden Rule of Law,
That all are equal before the same laws,
And that no man or woman be enslaved,
Or be bound against their will.
With the sign of the Cross,
I promise that my word is my bond,
When given with my consent,
And that I shall live my life,
According to the seven Christian Virtues,
Of Respect, Honesty, Courage, Enthusiasm,
Compassion, Joy and Discernment,
And shall only give my word,
To those who do the same.
Through the symbol and sign of the Cross,
I vow to defend others against all evil,
So that no tyrant or false messenger,
Shall prevail against the Light of the Risen Christ.
Amen.

PETITION OF THE FAITHFUL

Solitary
Petition of the Faithful

CELEBRANT
Today, I pray for N,

I pray to you our Lord Jesus, that you hear our prayers.

LITURGY OF THE EUCHARIST

Liturgy of the Eucharist

OFFERTORY ANTIPHON

Solitary
Offertory

(NOTE: See the relevant Proper of Heroes & Saints, or Mystery or Rite for the correct ***Offertory Antiphon***.)

Antiphon

PRESENTATION OF OFFERING

Solitary
Presentation of Offering

CELEBRANT

Blessed are you, God of all creation. Through your goodness we have this bread to offer, that the earth has given and human hands have made. It will become for us the bread of life.

Blessed are you, God of all creation. Through your goodness we have this wine to offer, fruit of the vine and work of human hands. It will become for us a spiritual drink.

May God our Father accept these offerings through these hands, for the praise and glory of his name, for our good, and the good of his one true apostolic Universal Church.

PRAYER OVER THE OFFERINGS

Solitary
Prayer over the Offerings

(NOTE: See the relevant feast within the Proper of Life & Mysteries of Christ for the correct ***Prayer over the Offerings***.)

CELEBRANT

Amen.

PREFACE

Solitary
Preface

CELEBRANT

Holy, Holy, Holy Christ,
God of all Powers and Majesty,
Heaven and Earth are full of your Glory,
Hosanna in the highest.
Blessed are they who come
In the name of the Risen Christ.
Hosanna in the Highest.

EUCHARISTIC PRAYER

Solitary
Eucharistic Prayer

CELEBRANT (cont.)

I come before you, Father, with humility and thanksgiving,

through Jesus Christ your Son.

(C. joins his hands, making the sign of the cross over both bread and chalice:)

Through him, I ask you to accept and bless ✠ these gifts we offer you as a manifest symbol of our own sacrifice.

(C. Extends outward his hands:)

I offer them for your one true and holy Apostolic Universal Ecclesia. Watch over your family; and guide us; grant us the grace and unity of being one living body of your son Jesus Christ, through our good works in this world. I offer them for N. our Holy Father, for N, our Bishop; and for all who hold true and teach the authentic Christian faith that comes to us from your apostles.

Solitary *Remembrance*

CELEBRANT (cont.)

(C. joins hands briefly, before bowing head in moment of silence after the reciting of names:)

Remember your faithful servants, especially those for whom I now pray, N. et N.

(C. lifts his head and extends his arms and hands outward in gesture toward the whole congregation:)

Heavenly Father, remember your humble servant here before you. You know how firmly I trust in you and dedicate ourselves to you. I offer you my sacrifice and praise for our well-being and redemption and for all those who are dear me.

(C. lifts his head and eyes upward whilst also tilting upward his already extended hands:)

In union with all members of the Universal Ecclesia of Christ, I honour Mary, the blessed mother of Jesus and our universal mother. I honour Joseph, her husband, the apostles and martyrs Peter and Paul and all the apostles and saints. May their merits and prayers grant us your constant help and protection. Father, please accept our authentic offering. Bestow upon us your peace and good graces in this life; as I ask to be granted nothing more than the same mercy and forgiveness in death as we have shown to others in our lifetime.

(C. lowers his head and eyes to the congregation and rotates his palms and hand to them whilst arms remain outstretched:)

I ask all this most humbly in the name of Christ, our Saviour. Amen.

CELEBRANT (cont.)

Solitary
Consecration

(C. takes the bread and, raising it a little above the altar, continues:)

The day before he suffered, Jesus took some bread in his own hands,

(C. looks upward:)

And looking up to Heaven, to you, our Divine Father, he gave you thanks and praise. He then broke the bread, gave it to each of his disciples, saying,

(C. shows the consecrated host to the people.)

Take this, all of you, and eat it: this is my flesh that will be given up for you.

(C. places the consecrated host on the paten, and genuflects in adoration.)

(C. takes the chalice, and raising it a little above the altar, continues.)

Jesus then took a cup of wine. Again he gave you thanks and praise, before giving the cup to his disciples, saying.

(C. shows the consecrated chalice to the people.)

Take this all of you and drink from it. This is the cup of my blood, the blood of the new and everlasting covenant. It will be shed for you and for all mankind so that every sin may be forgiven.

(C. places it on the corporal, and genuflects in adoration.)

ACCLAMATION

Solitary
Acclamation

(C. extends his arms:)

In honour of the memory of the sacrifice of our Saviour

and our own humble offerings, I proclaim the mystery of our faith:

Christ suffered and died for us; Christ is risen for us; Christ has returned through us as his united living body.

(C. with hands extended, the priest says:)

Divine Father, I celebrate the memory of Christ, your Son. As your minister, I recall his passion, his resurrection from the dead, and his ascension into Heaven; and from the many gifts you have given us all I offer to you, this, our humble and heartfelt sacrifice: symbolised by these, the bread of life and the cup of merciful salvation. I trust you look favourably upon our reverent and faithful offerings and accept them.

(C. bows, with hands joined:)

In your name Heavenly Father, in honour of the will of your son, and through the power and authority of the Holy Spirit, I pray these perfect symbols of your New Covenant are transformed into the Bread and Fruits of Eternal Spiritual Life as the spiritual manifestation of the most sacred body of the Risen Christ,

(C. stands up straight and makes the sign of the cross, saying:)

✠That as a disciple of Christ, and in partaking in the blessed Eucharist, we too may be filled with the strength and grace of the Holy Spirit,

(C. joins his hands:)

As the one true living Body of Christ. Amen.

DOXOLOGY

Solitary
Doxology

CELEBRANT (cont.)

(C. joins his hands:)

Through him, with him, and in him. In unity with the Holy Spirit, all glory and honour is yours our Heavenly Father, for ever and ever. Amen.

CHRISTS' PRAYER

Solitary
Christs' Prayer

CELEBRANT

Our Father of All Creation,

We beseech thee and honour your name,
For your Rule be united as One,
And your Laws be equal to All,
On Earth as it is in Heaven,
Grant us the means to sustenance,
As we shall give alms to those in need.
Save us from trickery and false oaths,
As our vows and our oaths shall be true.
Forgive us our debits and transgressions,
As we shall forgive the debits and transgressions of others.
Release us from any curse and ills,
As we shall not curse nor wish ill upon another.
We ask most humbly and with deep gratitude,
For let then your will be done.
Amen.

Deliver us all, Jesus, from every evil, and grant us peace in our day. In your mercy help us to free ourselves from transgressions and protect us from all fear as we defend and proclaim the authentic mysteries of our Christian Faith.

For the kingdom, the power, and the glory are yours, now and forever.

SIGN OF PEACE

Solitary
Sign of Peace

CELEBRANT

May the peace and love of the Crucified and Risen Christ be upon and throughout the lands of this Earth.

BREAKING OF BREAD

Solitary
Breaking of Bread

CELEBRANT

Lamb of God, you take away the transgressions of the world: have mercy on us.
Lamb of God, you take away the transgressions of the world: have mercy on us.
Lamb of God, you take away the transgressions of the world: grant us peace.

COMMUNION

Solitary
Communion

CELEBRANT

This is the Lamb of God who takes away the transgressions of the world. Happy are those who are called to his supper.

Jesus, though I am not worthy to receive you, I trust in your promise that none be turned away and I shall be healed.

The Bread of Eternal Life. Amen

The Fruits of Spiritual Renewal. Amen.

COMMUNION ANTIPHON

Solitary Communion Antiphon

(NOTE: See the relevant Proper of Heroes & Saints, or Mystery or Rite for the correct ***Communion Antiphon***.)

CONCLUDING RITE

Solitary Concluding Rite

CELEBRANT

Just as God our Father has forgiven us of our transgressions and his son Jesus Christ has healed us with his love and mercy and the Holy Spirit has filled us with renewed strength and courage to do better, I make a firm promise now, before we depart, to live and act in each moment of my life as true and authentic Christian.
I do honestly and sincerely promise in the name of ✠ the Father, and the Son and the Holy Spirit. Amen.

Title XIV – Proper of Mystery of Immanent Christ

XIV.I – MYSTERY OF IMMANENT CHRIST

1. The most *Sacred Immanent Mystery of Christ*, also known as *Advent* and *Christmastide*, is a variable liturgical season of approximately 41 to 47 days and a maximum of 11 holy feast days, beginning on the *Feast of the Divine Light of the World* (1st Sunday after *Mission Sunday*), then rising to the solemnity of *Holy Nativity Day*, also known as *Christmas Day* (25th December); and concluding on the solemnity of *New Years Day* (1st January). Immanent Mystery of Christ

   The liturgical season of the *Immanent Mystery of Christ* exists as a time of preparation and anticipation for the coming of Christ and the necessary and constant need for person and community renewal, rebirth and rejuvenation.

   The term "Immanent" encompasses both Advent and Christmastide as elements of the liturgical season and is chosen as the core theme of the mystery of the Singularity of Christ choosing to become flesh and to experience the pains and trials of human life.

2. The Sacred Colour for the liturgical season of the *Immanent Mystery of Christ* is **purple**, representing the Divine Imperial Authority of Christ as the Singularity of all Humanity. All Vestments used in relation to all feast days of the liturgical season and all dressings and fabrics used throughout the church during this period, should adhere to the colour of purple. Sacred Colour of Season and Vestments

---

XIV.II – FEAST OF THE DIVINE LIGHT OF THE WORLD

(First Sunday after Mission Sunday)

Solemnity

1. The Universal Feast of the Divine Light of the World (1st Sunday after Mission Sunday), is the opening Feast of the liturgical season. Feast of the Divine Light of the World

Entrance Antiphon: Prov. 11: 30

> The fruit of the righteous is the tree of life, and those whose lives are saved.

Magisterium: Daniel Daniel 9:24-27

> Seventy weeks are determined upon thy people and upon thy holy city, to finish all transgression, and to make an end of sins, and to make reconciliation for iniquity, and to bring in everlasting righteousness, and to seal up the vision and prophecy, and to anoint the most Holy. Know therefore and understand, that from the going forth of the commandment to restore and to build a new Jerusalem unto the Messiah the Prince shall be seven weeks, and

threescore and two weeks: the street shall be built again, and the wall, even in troubled times. And after threescore and two weeks shall the Messiah be cut off, but not for himself: and the people of the prince that shall come shall destroy the city and the sanctuary; and the end thereof shall be with a flood, and unto the end of the war desolations are determined. And he shall confirm a new covenant of Heaven with many for one week: and in the midst of the week he shall cause blood sacrifice and oblation to cease, and for the overspreading of such abominations he shall make it desolate in the temple, until the consummation of the new covenant, and all that shall be determined shall be poured upon the new temple.

Good News: John

John: 1-14

In the beginning was the Word, and the Word was with Him, and the Word was God. The same was in the beginning with God. All things were made by him; and all men and women were made in his image. In him is everlasting life; and his life is the light for all mankind. And such light shines through the darkness; as the darkness comprehends it not. For there were men sent from God, whose names are known, to bear witness as Sons of the Light, so that all men through them might have true faith. They are not the Light, but witnesses of the Light. The true Light that knows the soul of every man and woman that comes into the world. He through whom the world was made, was in the world, and the world treated him as a stranger. He came to what was his own, and they who were his own gave him no welcome. But all those who did welcome him, he empowered to become the Brothers and Sisters of the Light over all who claimed to serve and rule in his name: authority that was born not by blood right, or birthright, nor the will of the flesh, nor the will of man, but of God the Divine Creator. And the Word was made flesh and came to dwell among us, full of grace and truth.

Offertory Antiphon

O God and Divine Creator of all Life and Light, grant us the light of your wisdom and the promise of eternal life. Through our Lord Jesus Christ, your Son, who lives and reigns with you in the unity of the Holy Spirit, one God, for ever and ever.

Prayer over the Offerings

May God and the Divine Creator accept and sanctify these humble gifts as symbols of the genuine personal offerings we make in respect and honour of your *Holy Feast of the Divine Light of the World*. Through Christ our Light and Saviour.

Communion Antiphon — Psalm 43: 3

Send out thy light and thy truth: let them lead me. Let them bring me unto thy holy mountain, and to thy tabernacle.

Prayer after Communion

Heavenly Father and God of all Creation, we give thanks for the nourishment of your heavenly gifts of the Bread and Fruits of Eternal Spiritual Life. May our earnest participation in your *Holy Feast of the Divine Light of the World* bring forth favourable blessings upon our lives, our community and your Holy Apostolic Universal Ecclesia. Through your Son our Lord Jesus Christ.

XIV.III – FEAST OF THE ANNUNCIATION OF BLESSED MARY

Feast of the Annunciation of Blessed Mary

1. The Universal Feast of the Annunciation of Blessed Mary, also known as Annunciation Sunday, is the 1st Sunday after the Feast of the Divine Light of the World.

Entrance Antiphon: — Prov. 15: 30

The Light of the Messenger brings joy to the heart, and such good news heals the soul.

Magisterium: Isaiah — Isaiah 7:10-15

Moreover, God did speak again to Ahaz, saying, You may ask thee a sign of the Lord thy God either of the Earth or of the Heavens above. But Ahaz was fearful and said, I dare not ask such a thing; neither will I tempt my God. And God said to him: Hear me now, O House of Messengers, it is one thing for you to weary men with your doubts, but will ye also weary your God? Therefore, I myself shall give you a sign: Behold! a virgin shall conceive and bear a son and shall call his name Emmanuel. Butter and honey shall he eat in his youth, so that he may know of his own to refuse the evil and may choose good.

Good News: Luke — Luke 1:26-35

When the sixth month had passed, God sent his angel

Gabriel to a town in the lands of Galilee called Nazareth, where a young virgin named Mary did dwell, betrothed to a man named Joseph of the royal line of David. Into her presence the angel came, and said, Hail, Mary, full of Grace, God is with thee. Blessed are you among all women. When Mary saw the vision of the angel and his words, she was deeply frightened and confused, before the angel Gabriel did say to her, Mary, do not be afraid. For you have found great favour in the sight of God. Behold! Thou shall conceive in thy womb, and shall bear a son, and shall call him Jesus. He shall be great, and men will know him for the Son of the most High; and the Lord God shall give unto him the throne of his father David, and he shall reign over the house of Jacob eternally; and his kingdom shall have no end. Then Mary said unto the angel, How can that be, seeing I know not yet of a man? And the angel Gabriel answered her, The Holy Spirit will come upon thee, and the power of the most High will overshadow thee. Therefore, your holy offspring shall be called the Son of God.

Offertory Antiphon

O God and Divine Creator of all Wisdom, who willed that your Word be made manifest in this reality as human flesh, upon the humble acceptance and unblemished holiness of the Virgin Mary, grant that we may serve you in a meaningful way as part of your Divine Plan. Through our Lord Jesus Christ, your Son, who lives and reigns with you in the unity of the Holy Spirit, one God, for ever and ever.

Prayer over the Offerings

May God and the Divine Creator accept and sanctify these humble gifts as symbols of the genuine personal offerings we make in respect and honour of your *Holy Feast of the Annunciation of our Blessed Mother Mary*. Through Christ our Light and Saviour.

Communion Antiphon — Psalm 139 :13-14

Holy Spirit and guide of my inmost being, you did help form me in my mother's womb I praise thee for my wondrous fashioning, for all the wonders of thy creation.

Prayer after Communion

Heavenly Father and God of all Wisdom, we give thanks for the nourishment of your heavenly gifts of the Bread and Fruits of Eternal Spiritual Life. May our earnest participation in your *Holy Feast of the Annunciation of our Blessed Mother Mary* bring forth favourable blessings upon our lives, our community and your Holy Apostolic Universal Ecclesia. Through your Son our Lord Jesus Christ.

XIV.IV – FEAST OF ST. JOSEPH

1. The Universal Feast of St Joseph, also known as St Joseph Sunday, is the 2nd Sunday after the Feast of the Divine Light of the World. Feast of St. Joseph

Entrance Antiphon: Prov. 3: 5-6

Trust in the Divine Creator with all your heart and mind; and rest not on your own presumptions. In every way commit to God, and he will make your path straight.

Magisterium: Deuteronomy Deut. 18:14-15

And God said unto Moses, Do not let those that follow suffer such addictions as to constantly seek the counsel of astrologers and soothsayers to divine the plans of God; for in time, the Lord your God shall raise up unto the people a Prophet, like you, from your kin and your brethren and unto him all shall listen.

Good News: Matthew Matt. 1:18-25

Now the birth of Christ was in the following manner. His mother Mary was betrothed to Joseph according to the law, yet they had not yet come together in Holy Matrimony, when she was found to be with child, by the power of the Holy Spirit. Whereupon Joseph, being a just and honourable man, and not desiring to make a public scandal against her, did contemplate banishing Mary away in secret. Yet while he was still dwelling on these things, an angel of God did appear unto him in a vivid dream, and said, Joseph, son of the line of David, do not be afraid to take thy wife Mary to thyself, for it is by the power of the Holy Spirit that she is conceived with child; and she will bear a son, whom thou shall call Jesus as the Emmanuel, for he shall save all people from their transgressions. For all this is so done, to fulfil the promise of God to all his people through his prophets when he said: Behold!, a virgin shall be with child, and shall bear a son, and they shall call him Emmanuel. Upon awaking from sleep, Joseph obeyed as the angel commanded and did bind himself in Holy Matrimony unto Mary as his wife; and did refrain from entering the marital chamber with her until after she had brought forth her first born son, they named Jesus.

Offertory Antiphon

O God and Divine Creator of all Existence, who endowed the human species with extraordinary talents, grant that we may follow the example of Saint Joseph in willingly accepting our duty and that we complete the works you set us to do with humility and courage, even if none but God may fully appreciate our achievements in your service. Through our Lord Jesus Christ, your Son, who lives and reigns with you in the unity of the Holy Spirit, one God, for ever and ever.

Prayer over the Offerings

May God and the Divine Creator accept and sanctify these humble gifts as symbols of the genuine personal offerings we make in respect and honour of your *Holy Feast of St Joseph*. Through Christ our Light and Saviour.

Communion Antiphon — Psalm 61: 7

In God is my salvation and my glory: the rock of my strength, and my refuge.

Prayer after Communion

Heavenly Father and God of all Existence, we give thanks for the nourishment of your heavenly gifts of the Bread and Fruits of Eternal Spiritual Life. May our earnest participation in your *Holy Feast of St Joseph* bring forth favourable blessings upon our lives, our community and your Holy Apostolic Universal Ecclesia. Through your Son our Lord Jesus Christ.

XIV.V – FEAST OF THE MAGNIFICAT

1. The Universal Feast of the Magnificat of Mary Mother of Mankind, also known as Magnificat Sunday Mother of all,is the 3rd Sunday after the Feast of the Divine Light of the World. — Feast of the Magnificat

Entrance Antiphon: — Prov. 4: 7

The beginning of wisdom is to get wisdom. Though it may cost all you have, seek true knowledge of the Divine.

Magisterium: Isaiah — Isaiah 9:5-7

Isaiah did reveal, For every battle of the warrior is fraught with confused noise and garments rolled in blood; but this one shall be with a sacrifice of a different fuel and fire. For unto us a child shall be born; unto us a son shall be given: and the authority and knowledge of law and government shall be upon his shoulders: and his name shall be called Wonderful, Counsellor, The mighty God, The everlasting Father, The Prince of Peace. Of the increase of his government and peace there shall be no end, upon the throne of messiah kings, and unto his kingdom, to order it, and to establish it with judgement and with justice from henceforth even for ever. The enthusiasm and eagerness of God will make this manifest.

Good News: Luke Luke 1:39-53

In the days soon after the visitation of the angel Gabriel, Mary did hastily prepare to travel to the settlement of Zachariah to visit her older cousin Elizabeth. Yet no sooner had Mary arrived and begun to greet her cousin, when the child leapt within the womb of Elizabeth and she was immediately filled with the Holy Spirit; and did proclaim with a loud voice saying, Blessed are you among all women, and blessed is the fruit of thy womb. How then have I come to deserve such a visit from the mother of my Lord? For, as soon as the voice of your greeting sounded in my ears, the child in my womb leapt for joy. Blessed are thou for your faith in the message that was brought to thee from God, for it shall be fulfilled. Mary did then embrace her cousin and say, My soul does praise and give glory to God; and my spirit rejoices before our Lord and Saviour. For He looks ever graciously upon even the lowliest of handmaidens. Behold!, from this day forward all generations will count me as blessed; because of He who is mighty and whose name is most holy. Verily, His mercy is everlasting to all those who respect him, from generation to generation. He has revealed his strength and reach. He scatters the arrogant so filled with contempt in their hearts; and He casts down the mightiest from their proud thrones and instead exalts those most humble. He fills the hungry with the greatest of treasures; yet the rich he dismisses from his sight, empty handed. He comes to the aid of the faithful People of God, in remembrance of his holy promises, as he did speak to our fathers and to his holy messengers for all future generations forever. And Mary did stay with Elizabeth for about three months, before returning to her own house.

Offertory Antiphon

O God and Divine Creator of all Life, who through the Holy Spirit inspired Elizabeth to bear witness to your Divine Mission, grant that we receive the inspiration and strength of the Holy Spirit to proclaim your Divine Mission of New Evangelisation and the Renewal of your Universal Ecclesia. Through our Lord Jesus Christ, your Son, who lives and reigns with you in the unity of the Holy Spirit, one God, for ever and ever.

Prayer over the Offerings

May God and the Divine Creator accept and sanctify these humble gifts as symbols of the genuine personal offerings we make in respect and honour of your *Holy Feast of the Magnificat of Mary Mother of Mankind*. Through Christ our Light and Saviour.

Communion Antiphon — Psalm 86: 15 -16

O God you are full of compassion, and gracious, long suffering, and plenteous in mercy and truth. Hear me and have mercy upon me. Give thy strength unto thy servant.

Prayer after Communion

Heavenly Father and God of all Life, we give thanks for the nourishment of your heavenly gifts of the Bread and Fruits of Eternal Spiritual Life. May our earnest participation in your *Holy Feast of the Magnificat of Mary Mother of Mankind* bring forth favourable blessings upon our lives, our community and your Holy Apostolic Universal Ecclesia. Through your Son our Lord Jesus Christ.

XIV.VI – FEAST OF THE NATIVITY OF JOHN THE BAPTIST

1. The Universal Feast of the Nativity of John the Baptist, also known as St. John the Baptist Sunday is the 4th Sunday after the Feast of the Divine Light of the World. — Feast of the Nativity of John the Baptist

Entrance Antiphon: — Prov. 3: 9-10

Honour the Divine Creator with your wealth, with the first fruits of your own making; so that your barns will be filled to overflowing, and your vats will brim over with new wine.

Magisterium: Isaiah — Isaiah 40:3-5

Isaiah did say, Behold! a voice shall cry out in the wilderness to prepare the way of the Lord; make straight in the desert a highway for our God. Every valley shall be lifted up, and every mountain and hill be made low; the uneven ground shall become level, and the rough places a plain.

Good News: Luke

Luke 1:5-25

In the days when Herod was king, there was a priest who served the High Priest of Obiah, whose name was Zachariah, who had married a woman named Elizabeth of the Line of Aaron. Both Zachariah and Elizabeth were heroic in their virtue before God, following in all commandments and observances of the law, without fault. Yet, they had no children as Elizabeth could not conceive; and they both were now well advanced in years. One time, Zachariah was tending to his duties within the inner sanctuary of the holy temple, burning sacred incense at the altar during an hour of obligation, while the multitude prayed in the outer area of the temple, when an Angel of God did appear, standing to the right side of the altar. Zachariah was immediately bewildered at the sight and overcome with fear, before the angel said to him, do not be afraid Zachariah; thy prayers have been received, and thy wife is to bear thee a son, to whom thou shall give the name of John. Joy and gladness shall be thine, and many hearts shall rejoice over his birth, for he is to be high in the favour of God. He is to drink neither wine nor strong drink; and from the time when he is yet a child in his mother's womb he shall be filled with the Holy Spirit. He shall lead many of the sons and daughters to return to their faith in God, ushering in his advent in the spirit and power of Elijah. He shall unite the hearts of all, the fathers with the children, and teach the disobedient the wisdom that makes men just, preparing for the Lord a people fit to receive him. And Zachariah said to the angel, By what sign am I to be assured of this? I am an old man now, and my wife is far advanced in age. The angel answered, my name is Gabriel, and my place is within the direct presence of God; I have been sent to speak with thee, and to bring thee this good news. Behold, thou shall therefore be dumb, and have no power of speech, until the day when all this is accomplished; and that, because thou hast not believed my promise, which shall in due time be fulfilled. At the end of the time of Obligation, all the people outside the inner sanctuary were waiting for Zachariah, and wondered what had delayed him in the temple so long; but when Zachariah did come out, he could speak no word to them; whereupon the people as witnesses were sure among themselves that he had seen some vision in the inner sanctuary. Zachariah could but stand there making signs to them, yet he remained dumb. And so, when the days of his ministry were at an end, Zachariah returned to his house. It was after those days that his wife Elizabeth conceived, and for five months she dwelt retired; she said, It is the Lord who has done this for me, visiting me at his own time, to take away my reproach among men.

Offertory Antiphon

O God and Divine Creator of all Miracles, who ordained that your faithful priest Zachariah and Elizabeth be blessed with a son, grant that we have the courage to never doubt our faith and your ability to transform any situation. Through our Lord Jesus Christ, your Son, who lives and reigns with you in the unity of the Holy Spirit, one God, for ever and ever.

Prayer over the Offerings

May God and the Divine Creator accept and sanctify these humble gifts as symbols of the genuine personal offerings we make in respect and honour of your *Holy Feast of the Nativity of John the Baptist*. Through Christ our Light and Saviour.

Communion Antiphon Psalm 28: 6-7

Blessed be God, because he has heard the voice of my supplications. Christ is my strength and my shield; and my heart trusts in him, because I am helped by him.

Prayer after Communion

Heavenly Father and God of all Miracles, we give thanks for the nourishment of your heavenly gifts of the Bread and Fruits of Eternal Spiritual Life. May our earnest participation in your *Holy Feast of the Nativity of John the Baptist* bring forth favourable blessings upon our lives, our community and your Holy Apostolic Universal Ecclesia. Through your Son our Lord Jesus Christ.

XIV.VII – FEAST OF EMMANUEL

1. The Universal Feast of Emmanuel, also known as Immanuel Sunday is the Sunday before Christmas Day as the 5th Sunday of the liturgical season when Christmas Day falls on a Wednesday, Thursday, Monday or Tuesday. Feast of Emmanuel

Entrance Antiphon: Prov. 9: 9

Instruct the wise and they will be wiser still; teach the righteous and they will add to their learning.

Magisterium: Isaiah Isaiah 42:1-4

And God said unto Isaiah, Behold! my servant, whom I uphold; mine elect, in whom my soul delights; I have put my spirit upon him: he shall bring forth judgement to all people. He shall not cry, nor lift up, nor cause his voice to be heard in the street. A bruised reed shall he not break, and the smoking flax shall he not quench: he shall bring forth judgement unto truth. He shall not fail nor be discouraged, till he have set judgement upon the earth: and the nations shall wait for his law.

Good News: Luke Luke 1:57-79

Meanwhile, the time had come for Elizabeth to bear her child, and she bore a son. Her neighbours and her kinsfolk, hearing how wonderfully God had shown his mercy to her, came to rejoice with her; and now, when they assembled on the eighth day for the circumcision of the child, they were for calling him Zachary, because of the name of his father; but his mother answered, No, he is to be called John. And they said, There is none of thy kindred that is called by this name, and began asking his father by signs, what name he would have him called by. So he asked for a tablet, and wrote on it the words, His name is John; and they were all astonished. At that moment, his lips and his tongue were unloosed, and he broke into speech, giving praise to God; so that fear and wonder came upon all the people in the settlement and throughout the lands on news of these happenings. All that witnessed Zachariah and the bearing of his new born son took such signs into their hearts, saying, What manner of child shall this be! For truly the hand of God is with him. And his father Zachariah was willed with the Holy Spirit and did speak in revelation, saying: Blessed be the People of God, for God has truly visited us and granted all people Redemption;

and has raised up a herald of salvation for us from the house of his servant David, as he promised through the mouths of his holy messengers since the beginning of time: That we shall be saved from our enemies, and from the hands of all those who hate us, so the mercy promised to our fathers shall be performed in remembrance of his most Holy Covenant to all people, the Divine Oath given even to the first of the prophets, that God would grant unto each of us, that we be delivered out of darkness, so that we might serve his will without fear, in holiness and righteousness, all the days of our lives. Verily, though this child shall be called a prophet of the Highest; for he shall go before the face of our Lord to prepare a way for him, to make known to the People of God the salvation and remission of all their transgressions. Such is the merciful kindness of the Divine Creator of all, who has come to visit us, like a dawning from on high, to give light to all those who live in darkness and in the shadow of death; and to guide our feet into the way of peace.

Offertory Antiphon

O God and Divine Creator of all Authentic Revelation, who inspired the prophets and messengers to foretell the signs of your Divine Mission through authenticProphecy, grant us patience in your message and Divine Plan. Through our Lord Jesus Christ, your Son, who lives and reigns with you in the unity of the Holy Spirit, one God, for ever and ever.

Prayer over the Offerings

May God and the Divine Creator accept and sanctify these humble gifts as symbols of the genuine personal offerings we make in respect and honour of your *Holy Feast of Emmanuel*. Through Christ our Light and Saviour.

Communion Antiphon

Psalm 7: 8

All the nations shall gather about thee, when thou comes to thy throne to rule over them.

Prayer after Communion

Heavenly Father and God of all Authentic Revelation, we give thanks for the nourishment of your heavenly gifts of the Bread and Fruits of Eternal Spiritual Life. May our earnest participation in your *Holy Feast of Emmanuel* bring forth favourable blessings upon our lives, our community and your Holy Apostolic Universal Ecclesia. Through your Son our Lord Jesus Christ.

XIV.VIII – VIGIL OF CHRISTMAS
December 24

1. Christmas Vigil (December 24th) is the night before Christmas. Vigil of Christmas

Entrance Antiphon: Prov. 27: 18

The one who guards a fig tree will eat of its fruit, and whoever protects the name of the Lord shall be honoured.

Magisterium: Micah Micah 5:2

And the prophet Micah said, But you, O fruit of Bethlehem, though you be small among the thousands of sacred dwelling places of the Spirit of the Lord, yet out of thee shall he come forth for all: one that is to be ruler of all the People of God: one whose coming has been foretold since ancient days.

Good News: Luke Luke 2: 1-7

It happened that a decree went out at this time from the emperor Augustus, enjoining that the whole world should be registered for taxes at the place they were born; and this tax register was the first one made during the time when Cyrinus was governor of Syria. And fearing the emperor and his legions, all went to their towns and cities where they were born. And Joseph also went up from Galilee, out of the town of Nazareth, to the town of Bethlehem where he was born, to be registered and taxed with Mary his lawful wife, despite she being advanced in pregnancy. And so it was that, while they were there, the time came for her delivery. Mary brought forth a son, her first-born, whom she wrapped in his swaddling-clothes, and laid in a manger, because there was no room for them in the inn. In the field near the town, there were some shepherds still awake in the fields, keeping night-watches over their flock, whereupon all at once a troop of angels of God came and stood by them, and the glory of Heaven shone about them, so that the shepherds were overcome with fear and the others awoke. But the lead angel said to them, Do not be afraid; Behold!, We bring you Good News and a great rejoicing for all people. Upon this day, in the town of Bethlehem, the Lord Saviour has been born for you and for all the world. Verily, the sign whereby you arc to know him shall be as an infant in swaddling-clothes, lying in a manger. Then, a multitude of the heavenly army did appear around the angels, giving praise to God, and saying, Glory to God in the highest and peace and goodwill to all people.

Offertory Antiphon

O God and Divine Creator of Divine Love and Mercy, who so loves us, that he brought forth a "singularity" of all human beings that have lived or will ever live, in the form of his flesh and blood, grant us the serenity to remember the Divine Message of your son that your true nature be one of Divine Love, Mercy and Redemption and not wrath and harsh judgement. Through our Lord Jesus Christ, your Son, who lives and reigns with you in the unity of the Holy Spirit, one God, for ever and ever.

Prayer over the Offerings

May God and the Divine Creator accept and sanctify these humble gifts as symbols of the genuine personal offerings we make in respect and honour of your *Holy Feast of the Vigil of the Nativity of our Lord*. Through Christ our Light and Saviour.

Communion Antiphon — Psalm 66: 4

All the earth shall worship thee, and shall sing unto thee; they shall sing praises to thy name.

Prayer after Communion

Heavenly Father and God of Divine Love and Mercy, we give thanks for the nourishment of your heavenly gifts of the Bread and Fruits of Eternal Spiritual Life. May our earnest participation in your *Holy Feast of the Vigil of the Nativity of our Lord* bring forth favourable blessings upon our lives, our community and your Holy Apostolic Universal Ecclesia. Through your Son our Lord Jesus Christ.

XIV.IX– HOLY NATIVITY – MIDNIGHT *CHRISTMAS*

(December 25)

Solemnity

1. Christmas Midnight is the December 25th. — Christmas Midnight

Entrance Antiphon: — Prov. 29: 25

The fears of men are a proven snare, but he who trusts in

the Lord shall be kept safe.

Magisterium: Samuel 2 Sam. 7: 12-16

And God said to Samuel, When thy days be fulfilled, and thou shall sleep with thy fathers, I will set up thy seed after thee, which shall proceed out of thy bowels, and I will establish his kingdom. He shall build a house for my name, and I will establish the throne of his kingdom for ever. I will be his father, and he shall be my son. If he commit iniquity, I will chasten him with the rod of men, and with the stripes of the children of men: But my mercy shall not depart away from him, as I took it from Saul, whom I put away before thee. And thine house and thy kingdom shall be established for ever before thee: thy throne shall be established for ever.

Good News: Luke Luke 2: 1-7

It happened that a decree went out at this time from the emperor Augustus, enjoining that the whole world should be registered for taxes at the place they were born; and this tax register was the first one made during the time when Cyrinus was governor of Syria. And fearing the emperor and his legions, all went to their to their towns and cities where they were born. And Joseph also went up from Galilee, out of the town of Nazareth, to the town of Bethlehem where he was born, to be registered and taxed with Mary his lawful wife, despite she being advanced in pregnancy. And so it was that, while they were there, the time came for her delivery. Mary brought forth a son, her first-born, whom she wrapped in his swaddling-clothes, and laid in a manger, because there was no room for them in the inn. In the field near the town, there were some shepherds still awake in the fields, keeping night-watches over their flock, whereupon all at once a troop of angels of God came and stood by them, and the glory of Heaven shone about them, so that the shepherds were overcome with fear and the others awoke. But the lead angel said to them, Do not be afraid; Behold!, We bring you Good News and a great rejoicing for all people. Upon this day, in the town of Bethlehem, the Lord Saviour has been born for you and for all the world. Verily, the sign whereby you are to know him shall be as an infant in swaddling-clothes, lying in a manger. Then, a multitude of the heavenly army did appear around the angels, giving praise to God, and saying, Glory to God in the highest and peace and goodwill to all people.

Offertory Antiphon

O God and Divine Creator of all Life, who so loves us, that he brought forth a "singularity" of all human beings that have lived or will ever live, in the form of his flesh and blood, grant us the serenity to remember the Divine Message of your son that your true nature be one of Divine Love, Mercy and Redemption and not wrath and harsh judgement. Through our Lord Jesus Christ, your Son, who lives and reigns with you in the unity of the Holy Spirit, one God, for ever and ever.

Prayer over the Offerings

May God and the Divine Creator accept and sanctify these humble gifts as symbols of the genuine personal offerings we make in respect and honour of your Holy Feast in celebration of the hour Our Lord was born as flesh. Through Christ our Light and Saviour.

Communion Antiphon — Psalm 2: 10-11

Princes and leaders, take warning; and learn your lesson, those of you that claim to rule the world. Tremble, and serve Christ, rejoicing in his presence, but with awe in your hearts.

Prayer after Communion

Heavenly Father and God of all Life, we give thanks for the nourishment of your heavenly gifts of the Bread and Fruits of Eternal Spiritual Life. May our earnest participation in your Holy Feast in celebration of the hour Our Lord was born as flesh bring forth favourable blessings upon our lives, our community and your Holy Apostolic Universal Ecclesia. Through your Son our Lord Jesus Christ.

XIV.X– HOLY NATIVITY – DAY
CHRISTMAS

(December 25)

Solemnity

1. Holy Nativity Day, also known as Christmas Day is the December 25th. Christmas Day

Entrance Antiphon: — Prov. 3: 19-20

By wisdom the Divine Creator laid the foundations of the Earth and by understanding he set the heavens in place. By his knowledge the watery depths were divided, and the clouds let their drops bring forth abundance.

Magisterium: Isaiah — Isaiah 11:1-4

And there shall come forth a rod out of the stem of line of Holly Messenger Kings, and a Branch shall grow out of his roots: And the spirit of God shall rest upon him, the spirit of wisdom and understanding, the spirit of counsel and might, the spirit of knowledge and of the mind of the Divine. And God shall make him of quick of understanding in the mind of the Divine: and he shall not judge after the sight of his eyes, neither reprove after the hearing of his ears: But with righteousness shall he judge the poor, and reprove with justice for the meek of the earth: and he shall smite the earth with the rod of his mouth, and with the breath of his lips shall he slay the wicked.

Good News: Matthew — Matt. 2:1-12

Jesus was born at Bethlehem, in the days of king Herod. And thereupon certain wise men came out of the east to Jerusalem, who asked, Where is he that has been born, the Messiah King? We have seen his star out in the east, and we have come to worship him. King Herod was troubled when he heard it, and all Jerusalem with him; so that he assembled all the chief priests and learned men among the people, and enquired of them where it was that Christ would be born. And they told him, At Bethlehem; so it has been written by the prophet: And thou, Bethlehem, art far from the least among the princes, for out of thee will arise a leader who is to be the shepherd of my people. Then, summoning the wise men in secret, Herod questioned them closely upon the time of the star's appearing. And he sent them on their way to Bethlehem, saying to them, Go and enquire carefully for the child, and when you have found him, bring me back word, so that I too may come and worship him. They obeyed the king, and went on their journey; and all at once the star which they had seen in the east was there going before them, till at last it stood still over the place where the child was. Then, when they saw the star, were glad beyond measure; and so, going into the dwelling, they found the child there, with his mother Mary, and fell down to worship him; and, opening their store of treasures, they offered him the rarest of anointing gifts, of cinnamon and frankincense and myrrh. Afterwards, because they had received a warning in a dream forbidding them to go back to Herod, they returned to their own country by a different way.

Offertory Antiphon

O God and Divine Creator of all Existence, who so loves us, that he brought forth a "singularity" of all human beings that have lived or will ever live, in the form of his flesh and blood, grant us the serenity to remember the Divine Message of your son that your true nature be one of Divine Love, Mercy and Redemption and not wrath and harsh judgement. Through our Lord Jesus Christ, your Son, who lives and reigns with you in the unity of the Holy Spirit, one God, for ever and ever.

Prayer over the Offerings

May God and the Divine Creator accept and sanctify these humble gifts as symbols of the genuine personal offerings we make in respect and honour of your Holy Feast in celebration of the birth of Our Lord. Through Christ our Light and Saviour.

Communion Antiphon — Psalm 113: 4-7

God is high above all nations, and his glory above the heavens. Who is like unto the Lord our God, who dwells on high, who humbled himself to behold the things that are in heaven, and upon the earth! He raises up the poor out of the dust, and lifts the needy out of their oppression.

Prayer after Communion

Heavenly Father and God of all Existence, we give thanks for the nourishment of your heavenly gifts of the Bread and Fruits of Eternal Spiritual Life. May our earnest participation in your Holy Feast in celebration of the birth of Our Lord bring forth favourable blessings upon our lives, our community and your Holy Apostolic Universal Ecclesia. Through your Son our Lord Jesus Christ.

XIV.XI – FEAST OF HOLY TESTAMENT

1. The Universal Feast of Holy Testament, also known as Testament Sunday as the Sunday before New Years Day, when Christmas Day falls on a Wednesday, Thursday, Friday, Monday or Tuesday. Feast of Holy Testament

Entrance Antiphon: — Prov. 14: 5

An honest witness does not deceive, but a false witness pours out falsities.

Magisterium: Malachi

Malachi 3:1

And God said to Malachi. Behold, I shall send my messenger, and he will prepare the way before me. And the Lord whom you seek will suddenly come to his temple; and the messenger of the covenant in whom you delight, behold, he is coming.

Good News: Luke

Luke 2:15-20

When the angels had left them, and gone back into heaven, the shepherds said to one another, Come, let us make our way to Bethlehem, and see for ourselves this happening which God has made known to us. And so they went with all haste, and found Mary and Joseph there, with the child lying in the manger. On seeing him, they discovered the truth of what had been told them about this child. All those who witnessed it were full of amazement at the story that the shepherds told them; but Mary treasured up all these sayings, and reflected on them in her heart. And the shepherds went home giving praise and glory to God, at seeing and hearing that all was as it had been told them.

Offertory Antiphon

O God and Divine Creator of all Truth, grant us the fortitude and grace to speak the truth to all people of your salvation and forgiveness of all transgressions and that the presence of your son Jesus Christ is living proof you neither condemn the world nor wish to see its destruction. Through our Lord Jesus Christ, your Son, who lives and reigns with you in the unity of the Holy Spirit, one God, for ever and ever.

Prayer over the Offerings

May God and the Divine Creator accept and sanctify these humble gifts as symbols of the genuine personal offerings we make in respect and honour of your *Feast of Holy Testament*. Through Christ our Light and Saviour.

Communion Antiphon

Psalm 27: 4

May I dwell in the house of God all the days of my life, to behold the beauty of our Divine Creator and to honour the earth as his temple.

Prayer after Communion

Heavenly Father and God of all Truth, we give thanks for the nourishment of your heavenly gifts of the Bread and Fruits of Eternal Spiritual Life. May our earnest participation in your *Feast of Holy Testament* bring forth favourable blessings upon our lives, our community and your Holy Apostolic Universal Ecclesia. Through your Son our Lord Jesus Christ.

XIV.XII – NEW YEARS DAY

1. New Years Day is the 1st January. New Years Day

Entrance Antiphon: Prov. 16: 3

Commit to God whatever you do, and he will help establish your plans.

Magisterium: Jeremiah Jeremiah 31:31

Behold, the days are coming, declares the Lord, when I will make a new covenant with the People of God and make a new sacred dwelling place.

Good News: Luke Luke 2:25-35

At this time there was a virtuous and devout old priest named Simeon living in Jerusalem, who prayed and waited patiently for his own passing; and for the miracle of comfort to be brought to the People of God. One day, the Holy Spirit came upon him; and revealed in answer to his prayers, that he was not to meet death, until he had seen the living Christ with his own eyes. The Spirit then directed Simeon to get up and go to the temple on the same occasion that Joseph and Mary did bring forth and present the infant Jesus in honour of the laws and customs of the time. On seeing Mary and the infant Jesus, Simeon requested he hold him and in taking the infant Jesus into his arms, did proclaim, saying: Blessed be God forever! Let now thy humble servant depart in peace, according to thy word: Verily, my own eyes have seen thy Redemption that thou has prepared before the face of all nations. The light that shall give true revelation to all faiths and to the glory of the People of God. Upon hearing the words of Simeon, Joseph and Mary were amazed, before the old priest blessed them as a family and then said to Mary, Behold! this child is destined to bring about the fall of empires and the rise of a new kingdom of conscience; and to reveal many signs of God, that some will speak against such truth; so that the thoughts and hearts of all men and women shall be revealed.

Offertory Antiphon

O God and Divine Creator of all Time and Seasons, grant us a fresh start, with clear intentions and commitment to live every day and year as a blessing to serve your Divine Mission; and to learn and experience greater self knowledge. Through our Lord Jesus Christ, your Son, who lives and reigns with you in the unity of the Holy Spirit, one God, for ever and ever.

Prayer over the Offerings

May God and the Divine Creator accept and sanctify these humble gifts as symbols of the genuine personal offerings we make in respect and honour of your *Holy Feast of New Years Day*. Through Christ our Light and Saviour.

Communion Antiphon Psalm 118: 1

This is the day that God has made. Let us rejoice and give thanks for all to come.

Prayer after Communion

Heavenly Father and God of all Time and Seasons, we give thanks for the nourishment of your heavenly gifts of the Bread and Fruits of Eternal Spiritual Life. May our earnest participation in your *Holy Feast of New Years Day* bring forth favourable blessings upon our lives, our community and your Holy Apostolic Universal Ecclesia. Through your Son our Lord Jesus Christ.

Title XV – Proper of Mystery of Filial Christ

XV.I – MYSTERY OF FILIAL CHRIST

1. The most *Sacred Filial Mystery of Christ*, is a variable liturgical season of approximately 36 to 44 days and a maximum of 7 holy feast days, beginning on the *Feast of the Holy Exodus* (the first Sunday of January after New Years Day), then rising to the solemnity of Holy Baptism Day (1st Sunday after feast of Epiphany of Christ); and concluding on the solemnity of *Confirmation Sunday* (mid-February and Sunday before Ash Wednesday). Filial Mystery of Christ

   The liturgical season of the *Filial Mystery of Christ* exists as a time of family, learning, initiation, tolerance, communication and commitment as necessary qualities of family life and the transition from infant to child, from child to youth and from youth to adulthood.

2. The Sacred Colour for the liturgical season of the *Filial Mystery of Christ* is **blue**, representing the eternal trust and covenant between the Divine Creator and all Humanity. All Vestments used in relation to all feast days of the liturgical season and all dressings and fabrics used throughout the church during this period, should adhere to the colour of blue. Sacred Colour of Season and Vestments

---

XV.II – FEAST OF THE HOLY EXODUS

1. The Universal Feast of the Holy Exodus, also known as Exodus Sunday and Refugee Sunday is the first Sunday after New Years Day. Feast of the Holy Exodus

Entrance Antiphon: Prov. 3: 24-26

> When you find shelter, you will not be afraid; when you rest, your sleep will be sweet. Have no fear of sudden disaster or of the ruin that overtakes the wicked, for the Lord will be at your side and will keep your feet from being snared.

Magisterium: Hosea Hosea 11:1

> When he was a child, I loved him and out of Egypt I called my son.

Good News: Matthew Matt. 2:13-15

> As soon as the wise men had departed, an Angel of God appeared to Joseph in a vivid dream, and said to him, Rise up, take with thee the child and his mother, and flee to Egypt; there remain, until I give thee word. For Herod will soon be making search for the child, to destroy him. Joseph awoke while it was still night, and obeying the warning of the Angel, took the child and his mother with

him from Bethlehem, and withdrew into Egypt, where they remained until the death of Herod, in fulfilment of the Revelation of God spoken to his prophet, when he said, I called my son out of Egypt.

Offertory Antiphon

O God and Divine Creator of all Families and Communities, grant us peace and security during this time that all our families and community be safe. Through our Lord Jesus Christ, your Son, who lives and reigns with you in the unity of the Holy Spirit, one God, for ever and ever.

Prayer over the Offerings

May God and the Divine Creator accept and sanctify these humble gifts as symbols of the genuine personal offerings we make in respect and honour of your *Holy Feast of the Holy Exodus*. Through Christ our Light and Saviour.

Communion Antiphon — Psalm 91: 2-3

My God is my refuge and my fortress. In him will I trust. Surely he shall deliver me from the those that seek to entrap me, and from the noisome pestilence of this world.

Prayer after Communion

Heavenly Father and God of all Families and Communities, we give thanks for the nourishment of your heavenly gifts of the Bread and Fruits of Eternal Spiritual Life. May our earnest participation in your *Holy Feast of the Holy Exodus* bring forth favourable blessings upon our lives, our community and your Holy Apostolic Universal Ecclesia. Through your Son our Lord Jesus Christ.

XV.III – FEAST OF THE HOLY INNOCENTS

1. The Universal Feast of the Holy Innocents, also known as Children Sunday is the 1st Sunday after feast of the Holy Exodus. — Feast of the Holy Innocents

Entrance Antiphon: — Prov. 30: 8-9

Speak up for those who cannot speak for themselves, for the rights of all who are destitute. Speak up and judge fairly; defend the rights of the poor and needy.

Magisterium: Jeremiah — Jeremiah 31:15

Thus says the Lord: A voice is heard in Ramah, lamentation and bitter weeping. Rachel is weeping for her children; she refuses to be comforted for her children, because they are no more.

Good News: Matthew

Matt. 2:16-18

When King Herod discovered that the wise men had not trusted in him, he was enraged; and ordered his forces to murder all the male children of the age of two or younger in Bethlehem and surrounding lands, according to the time reckoned by the visitation of the wise men. It was then that the words spoken by the prophet Jeremiah were fulfilled: A great cry was heard, of lamentation and weeping and great mourning, of Rachel weeping for her children. For she could not be comforted, because none were spared. But as soon as Herod was dead, an angel of the Lord appeared to Joseph in Egypt in a dream, and said: Rise up, take with thee the child and his mother, and return to the land of your forefathers; for those who sought the child's life are dead. So he arose, and took the child and his mother with him, and came into the lands of his ancestors. But, when he heard that Archelaus was king in the place of his father Herod, he was afraid to return there; and so, receiving a warning in a dream, he withdrew into the region of Galilee; where he came to live in a town called Nazareth, in fulfilment of what was said by the prophets, They shall be called seekers of truth (Nazarenes).

Offertory Antiphon

O God and Divine Creator of all Life, watch over and protect the innocence of new born children and keep them safe from harm; and grant us the courage and vigilance to do everything in our power to protect the innocence and safety of your children. Through our Lord Jesus Christ, your Son, who lives and reigns with you in the unity of the Holy Spirit, one God, for ever and ever.

Prayer over the Offerings

May God and the Divine Creator accept and sanctify these humble gifts as symbols of the genuine personal offerings we make in respect and honour of your *Feast of the Holy Innocents*. Through Christ our Light and Saviour.

Communion Antiphon

Psalm 36: 7

How excellent is thy loving kindness, O God! For we entrust the protection and care of our children under the shadow of thy wings.

Prayer after Communion

Heavenly Father and God of all Life, we give thanks for the nourishment of your heavenly gifts of the Bread and Fruits of Eternal Spiritual Life. May our earnest participation in your *Feast of the Holy Innocents* bring forth favourable blessings upon our lives, our community and your Holy Apostolic Universal Ecclesia. Through your Son our Lord Jesus Christ.

XV.IV – FEAST OF THE EPIPHANY OF CHRIST

1. The Universal Feast of the Epiphany of Christ, also known as Epiphany Sunday 2nd Sunday after feast of the Holy Exodus. Feast of the Epiphany of Christ

Entrance Antiphon: Prov. 1: 8-9

Hear the instruction of thy father, and forsake not the law of thy mother: For they shall be an ornament of grace unto thy head, and chains about thy neck.

Magisterium: Isaiah Isaiah 35: 3-7

And the Spirit of God said to Isaiah, Strengthen the weak of hands, and confirm courage upon those of feeble knees. Say to them that are of a true heart, Be strong, fear not: behold, your God will come not with vengeance, but with redemption and forgiveness and save you. Then the eyes of the blind shall be opened, and the ears of the deaf shall be made clear. Then shall the lame man leap as an dancer, and the tongue of the dumb sing: for in the wilderness shall waters break out, and streams in the desert. And the parched ground shall become a pool, and the thirsty land springs of water: even midst the habitation of monsters, where each man lay, shall be grass with reeds and rushes.

Good News: Luke Luke 2: 40-52

So it was that the child Jesus grew and came to his strength, full of wisdom; and the grace of God rested upon him. Every year, his parents used to go up to Jerusalem at the paschal feast. And when he was twelve years old, after going up to Jerusalem, as the custom was at the time of the feast, and completing the days of its observance, they set about their return home. But the boy Jesus, unknown to his parents, continued his stay in Jerusalem. And they, thinking that he was among their travelling companions, had gone a whole day's journey before they made enquiry for him among their kinsfolk and acquaintances. When they could not find him, they made their way back to Jerusalem in search of him, and it was only after three days that they found him. He was sitting in the temple, in the midst of those who taught there, listening to them and asking them questions; and all those who heard him were in amazement at his quick understanding and at the answers he gave. Seeing him there, they were full of wonder, and his mother said to him, My Son, why hast thou treated us so? Think, what anguish your father and I have endured, searching for thee. But the young boy asked them, *What reason had you to search for me? Do you not see that I must be about the business of my true Father?* These words that he spoke to them they did not understand, nor did he resist them. Instead, Jesus returned with them to Nazareth and did live obediently under their rules, while his mother kept in her heart the memory of all these events. And so Jesus advanced in wisdom with the years, and in favour both with God and with men.

Offertory Antiphon

O God and Divine Creator of all Inspiration, grant us through the Holy Spirit your inspiration and dedication to learn and develop the talents you have given us. Through our Lord Jesus Christ, your Son, who lives and reigns with you in the unity of the Holy Spirit, one God, for ever and ever.

Prayer over the Offerings

May God and the Divine Creator accept and sanctify these humble gifts as symbols of the genuine personal offerings we make in respect and honour of your *Holy Feast of the Epiphany of Christ*. Through Christ our Light and Saviour.

Communion Antiphon

Psalm 64: 9

Let all men and women respect and declare the good works of God. For it is the wise that acknowledge the mercy and kindness of his actions.

Prayer after Communion

Heavenly Father and God of all Inspiration, we give thanks for the nourishment of your heavenly gifts of the Bread and Fruits of Eternal Spiritual Life. May our earnest participation in your *Holy Feast of the Epiphany of Christ* bring forth favourable blessings upon our lives, our community and your Holy Apostolic Universal Ecclesia.

Through your Son our Lord Jesus Christ.

XV.V – FEAST OF THE HOLY BAPTISM OF CHRIST

1. The Universal Feast of the Holy Baptism of Christ, also known as Holy Baptism Sunday is the 3rd Sunday after feast of the Holy Exodus. Feast of the Holy Baptism of Christ

Entrance Antiphon: Prov. 3: 21-22

Let not wisdom nor understanding out of your sight, and preserve all sound judgement and discretion; for they too will bring new life for you, and be an ornament to grace your neck.

Magisterium: Malachi Malachi 3:1

Behold, I send my messenger, and he will prepare the way before me. And the Lord whom you seek will suddenly come to his temple; and the messenger of the covenant in whom you delight, behold, he is coming, says the Spirit of the Lord.

Good News: Matthew Matt. 3:1-17

In those days John the Baptist did appear, preaching in the wilderness and saying: Repent ye all: for the kingdom of heaven is at hand. For it was John that the prophet Isaiah spoke of, when he said, The voice of the one crying in the wilderness, shall prepare the way of the Lord and straighten his paths. And in great austerity, John, wore rough garments of camel's hair, and a leather girdle about his loins, and mere locusts and wild honey were his food. Thereupon Jerusalem and all those who dwelt around Jordan and all of Palestine, went out to see him, and John did baptise them in the River Jordan, while they confessed their transgressions. But when he saw many of the Pharisees and Sadducees come down to his baptisms, he said unto them, O generation of vipers, who said to you that you could flee from the justice that soon draws near? Come, then now, yield the acceptable fruit of genuine repentance; and think not to say within ourselves we know the doctrines of our fathers as our protection: for I say unto you, that God is able to make these stones speak as witnesses than all your laws and doctrines. Verily, the axe is laid before the root of each tree: and every tree that does not bring forth good fruit shall be cut down and cast into the fire. As for me, I am baptising you with water, for your repentance; but one is to come after me who is mightier than I, and whose shoes I am not worthy to bear, behold! He shall baptise you with the fire of the Holy Spirit. For He holds his winnowing-fan ready, to sweep the threshing-floor clean; He will gather the wheat into his barn, but the chaff he will consume with fire that can never be quenched. So it was then that Jesus came from Galilee and stood before John at the River Jordan, to be baptised by him. But upon seeing Jesus and recognising him, John protested saying, It is I that am in need of being baptised by thee. Why then does thou come to me? Jesus answered saying, *It be my time now to accept my obligation: for thus it is necessary that all fulfil such observance*. John then baptised him, and as he came straight up out of the water, the sky and heavens did open unto him, and the Spirit of God did descend like a dove and rest upon him. And with that, a voice came from heaven, which said, This is my beloved Son, in whom I am well pleased.

Offertory Antiphon

O God and Divine Creator of all Redemption and Rebirth, grant us the clarity and understanding of the significance and importance of all your Holy Sacraments; and the remembrance of your gift of Redemption and Rebirth into new life. Through our Lord Jesus Christ, your Son, who lives and reigns with you in the unity of the Holy Spirit, one God, for ever and ever.

Prayer over the Offerings

May God and the Divine Creator accept and sanctify these humble gifts as symbols of the genuine personal offerings we make in respect and honour of your *Feast of the Holy Baptism of Christ*. Through Christ our Light and Saviour.

Communion Antiphon Psalm 67: 1

God be merciful unto us, and bless us; and cause your face to shine upon us.

Prayer after Communion

Heavenly Father and God of all Redemption and Rebirth, we give thanks for the nourishment of your heavenly gifts of the Bread and Fruits of Eternal Spiritual Life. May our earnest participation in your *Feast of the Holy Baptism of Christ* bring forth favourable blessings upon our lives, our community and your Holy Apostolic Universal Ecclesia. Through your Son our Lord Jesus Christ.

XV.VI – FEAST OF THE APPRENTICES

1. The Universal Feast of the Apprentices, also known as Apprentice Sunday is the 4th Sunday after feast of the Holy Exodus. Feast of the Apprentices

Entrance Antiphon: Prov. 13: 24

Whoever spares the rod spoils their children, but the one who loves their children is careful to keep discipline.

Magisterium: Isaiah Isaiah 52: 13-15

Behold, my servant shall deal prudently, he shall be exalted and extolled, and be very high. As many were astonished at thee; for his vision of the Divine be more than any man, and his form more than the sons of men: So shall he sprinkle many nations; the kings shall shut their mouths at him: for they shall see the knowledge never before told to them; and such wisdom they have not heard before they shall acknowledge.

Good News: Mark Mark 1:14-28

After John the Baptist had been put in prison, Jesus began coming to the shores of Galilee, speaking to strangers about the kingdom of God saying: *The time is soon fulfilled and the Kingdom of God is at hand. Repent and trust in the Good News!* And as he passed along the sea of Galilee, he saw Simon and Simon's brother Andrew casting a net into the sea. Jesus said to them, *Come and follow me; and I will make you into fishers of men.* And straight away they dropped their nets and followed him. Then he went a little further, and saw James, the son of Zebedee, and his brother John; these too were in their boat, repairing their nets; all at once he called them, and they, leaving their father Zebedee in the boat with the hired men, turned aside after him. So Jesus and his first followers made their way to the city of Capharnaum; here, as soon as the Sabbath came, he went into the synagogue and taught; and those that were witnesses were amazed by his teaching, for he sat there teaching them like one who had authority, not like the scribes. And there, in the synagogue, was a man possessed by an unclean spirit, who cried aloud: Leave us alone! What have we to do with thee, thou Jesus of Nazareth? Has thou come to destroy us? For I know who thou are, the Holy One of God. And Jesus was deeply troubled and rebuked him strongly saying: *Silence! Begone from here!* And the unclean spirit at first threw the man into convulsions and loud growls and moaning, before finally coming out of the man and leaving him. All who witnessed were full of astonishment and said to themselves, what can this be? What be the source of this new teaching? they said to one another. See how he has authority to command even the unclean spirits and they obey him. And soon after his fame quickly spread throughout the region of Galilee.

Offertory Antiphon

O God and Divine Creator of all Skills and Talents, bless all those in our families and our community that are seeking to find new work and starting out at their first jobs, that may be encouraged to respect the gifts and talents given to them and to honour the responsibilities and duties bestowed upon them to perform the best they can. Through our Lord Jesus Christ, your Son, who lives and reigns with you in the unity of the Holy Spirit, one God, for ever and ever.

Prayer over the Offerings

May God and the Divine Creator accept and sanctify these humble gifts as symbols of the genuine personal offerings we make in respect and honour of your *Holy Feast of the Apprentices*. Through Christ our Light and Saviour.

Communion Antiphon — Psalm 62: 12

God is mercy. For he renders in return to every man and woman according to their works.

Prayer after Communion

Heavenly Father and God of all Skills and Talents, we give thanks for the nourishment of your heavenly gifts of the Bread and Fruits of Eternal Spiritual Life. May our earnest participation in your *Holy Feast of the Apprentices* bring forth favourable blessings upon our lives, our community and your Holy Apostolic Universal Ecclesia. Through your Son our Lord Jesus Christ.

XV.VII – FEAST OF THE TEACHERS

Feast of the Teachers

1. Feast of the Teachers, also known as Teachers Sunday, is the Sunday before Confirmation Day as the 5th Sunday of the liturgical season after the feast of the Holy Exodus when New Years Day falls on a

Friday or Wednesday or Saturday.

Entrance Antiphon: Prov. 1: 20-21

All the while Wisdom is publishing her message, crying it aloud in the open streets; never a meeting of roads, never a gateway, but her voice is raised, echoing above the din of it.

Magisterium: Malachi Malachi 4:5-6

Behold, I will send you one like the prophet Elijah before the great and awesome day of the Lord comes. And he will turn the hearts of fathers to their children and the hearts of children to their fathers, lest I come and strike the land with a decree of utter destruction.

Good News: Luke Luke 12: 49 -59

Jesus said, It is fire of illumination, not water, that I have come to spread all over the Earth; and it be my deepest Will that it should be kindled! There is another baptism after water that is the Light by the Holy Spirit that I must also be baptised; and how impatient am I for its accomplishment! Did you think that I have simply come to fulfil the corrupted prophecies of the wicked priests and doctors of law? Verily, I have come to first bring dissension to all their houses, before there be peace. Henceforward for a time, five in the same house will be found at variance, three against two and two against three; the father will be at variance with his son, and the son with his father, the mother against her daughter, and the daughter against her mother, the mother-in-law against her daughter-in-law, and the daughter-in-law against her mother-in-law. And Jesus then said to the multitudes, When you find a cloud rising out of the west, you say at once, There is rain coming, and so it does; when you find the south wind blowing, you say, It will be hot, and so it is. Alas, how wilfully ignorant and arrogant you have become! Verily, you know well enough how to interpret the face of land and sky; yet you refuse to acknowledge and interpret the signs of the times that you live in! Does not your own experience teach you to make the right decision? If one has a claim against thee, and thou are going with him to the magistrate, then do thy utmost, while you are still on the road, to be quit of his claim; or it may be he will drag thee into the presence of the judge, and the judge will hand thee over to his officer, and the officer will cast thee into prison.

Be sure of this, thou wilt find no discharge from it until thou hast paid the last coin.

Offertory Antiphon

O God and Divine Creator of all Knowledge and Guidance, bless all the teachers and educators in our community that are helping to forge the next generation of minds and imagination. May they be afforded the highest respect and dignity that rightly signifies such positions of absolute trust and integrity and that they are inspired by the Holy Spirit to be the best mentors our children and young adults need and deserve Through our Lord Jesus Christ, your Son, who lives and reigns with you in the unity of the Holy Spirit, one God, for ever and ever.

Prayer over the Offerings

May God and the Divine Creator accept and sanctify these humble gifts as symbols of the genuine personal offerings we make in respect and honour of your *Holy Feast of the Teachers*. Through Christ our Light and Saviour.

Communion Antiphon — Psalm 25: 4-5

Show us thy ways, O God and teach us your paths. Guide us in your truth and teach us. For thou are the God of our salvation.

Prayer after Communion

Heavenly Father and God of all Knowledge and Guidance, we give thanks for the nourishment of your heavenly gifts of the Bread and Fruits of Eternal Spiritual Life. May our earnest participation in your *Holy Feast of the Teachers* bring forth favourable blessings upon our lives, our community and your Holy Apostolic Universal Ecclesia. Through your Son our Lord Jesus Christ.

XV.VIII – FEAST OF HOLY CONFIRMATION

1. The Universal Feast of Holy Confirmation, also known as Confirmation Day is the mid-February and Sunday before Ash Wednesday. — Feast of Holy Confirmation

Entrance Antiphon: — Prov. 27: 10

Forsake not your friend or a friend of your family, and do not go to the house of a relative when disaster strikes you— better a good neighbour nearby than a relative far away.

Magisterium: Wisdom

Wisdom 2:12-20

Let us lie in wait for the righteous man, because he is inconvenient to us and opposes our actions; he reproaches us for sins against the law, and accuses us of sins against our training. He professes to have knowledge of God, and calls himself a child of the Lord. He became to us a reproof of our thoughts; the very sight of him is a burden to us, because his manner of life is unlike that of others, and his ways are strange. We are considered by him as something base, and he avoids our ways as unclean; he calls the last end of the righteous happy, and boasts that God is his father. Let us see if his words are true, and let us test what will happen at the end of his life; for if the righteous man is God's son, he will help him, and will deliver him from the hand of his adversaries. Let us test him with insult and torture, that we may find out how gentle he is, and make trial of his forbearance. Let us condemn him to a shameful death, for, according to what he says, he will be protected.

Good News: John

John 2:1-11

There was a wedding-feast in Galilee where the parents of Jesus were present. And Jesus himself, was called to be in the official party, with his disciples as guests. So when the supply of wine for all the guests did run dry, Mary said unto to him, there is no wine. Jesus answered her saying, *Woman what have I to do with thee? My time has not yet come*. His mother then said unto the servants, Whatever he says unto you, do it. And the house for the feast possessed six ceremonial water pots for purification rites of some thirty to thirty six gallons apiece, whereupon Jesus said unto the head servant, *fill the water pots* with water, and they filled them to the brim. And Jesus then said to them, *draw out now and bring it unto the master of the feast*, and they did bring an urn, and the master of the feast tasted the water, now turned into wine. Yet he did not know from whence it came as only the servants that had witnessed the instruction knew first the truth. The master of the feast then called to bridegroom and said to him, It is ever the good wine that men set out first, and the worse kind only when all have drunk deep. Yet thou hast kept the good wine till now. Thus in Galilee, Jesus began his miracles, and made known the glory that was his, so that his disciples learned to believe in him.

Offertory Antiphon

O God and Divine Creator of all Ages, grant us the awareness of respect and maturity to acknowledge the important stages in and milestones of age in our lives; and to gladly accept our responsibilities to our family and to our community. Through our Lord Jesus Christ, your Son, who lives and reigns with you in the unity of the Holy Spirit, one God, for ever and ever.

Prayer over the Offerings

May God and the Divine Creator accept and sanctify these humble gifts as symbols of the genuine personal offerings we make in respect and honour of your *Feast of Holy Confirmation*. Through Christ our Light and Saviour.

Communion Antiphon

Psalm 121:7-8

Verily, God shall guard thee from all evil, for the Lord protects the faithful from danger. He protects our spirits upon our journeying and thy home-coming, henceforth and for ever.

Prayer after Communion

Heavenly Father and God of all Ages, we give thanks for the nourishment of your heavenly gifts of the Bread and Fruits of Eternal Spiritual Life. May our earnest participation in your *Feast of Holy Confirmation* bring forth favourable blessings upon our lives, our community and your Holy Apostolic Universal Ecclesia. Through your Son our Lord Jesus Christ.

Title XVI – Proper of Mystery of the Eucharist

XVI.I – MYSTERY OF EUCHARIST

1. The most *Sacred Eucharistic Mystery of Christ*, also known as the Paschal Mystery and Lent and Eastertide, is a fixed liturgical season of 40 days and a maximum of 12 holy feast days, beginning on the *Feast of Divine Humility*, also known as *Ash Wednesday* (at mid February), then rising to the solemnity of *Good Friday* (1st Friday after or upon Spring Equinox) and concluding on the solemnity of *Easter Sunday* (First Sunday after Good Friday at end of March). Mystery of Eucharist

The liturgical season of the *Eucharistic Mystery of Christ* exists as a most important time for personal austerity and abstinence, reflection, meditation on the sacrifice of Christ and all Heroes and Saints of the community, as well as the deeper meditation on the paradoxes of life and eternal life and death and resurrection.

2. The Sacred Colour for the liturgical season of the *Eucharistic Mystery of Christ* is **red**, representing the ultimate sacrifice of Christ of his flesh and blood, his death and resurrection for the forgiveness of all the sins of humanity, of the past, now and forever. All Vestments used in relation to all feast days of the liturgical season and all dressings and fabrics used throughout the church during this period, should adhere to the colour of red. Sacred Colour of Season and Vestments

XVI.II – FEAST OF DIVINE HUMILITY

1. The Universal Feast of Divine Humility, also known as Ash Wednesday is mid February. Feast of Divine Humility

Entrance Antiphon: Prov. 15: 33

> Wisdom's instruction is to love the Lord with all your heart and mind; for humility comes before honour.

Magisterium: Luke Luke 18:9-14

> Jesus said, There are some who have such confidence in themselves, thinking they had won acceptance with God, and despised the rest of the world; to them I address this parable: Two men went up into the temple to pray; one was a doctor of law, the other a publican. The doctor of law stood upright, and made this prayer in his heart, I thank thee, God, that I am not like the rest of men, who steal and cheat and commit adultery, or like this publican here; for myself, I fast twice in the week, I give tithes of all that I possess. And the publican stood far off; he would not even

lift up his eyes towards heaven; he only beat his breast, and said, God, be merciful to me; I am a sinner. I tell you, this man went back home higher in God's favour than the other; everyone who exalts himself shall be humbled, and the man who humbles himself shall be exalted.

Good News: Matthew

Matt. 4:1-11

Now it happened that Jesus was led by the Holy Spirit away into the wilderness, to be tested and tempted. For forty days and forty nights he spent fasting and praying, and at the end of the final day was exceedingly hungry and weak of body. It was then that the tempter appeared in the form of a man, and said to him, If thou truly are the Son of God, bid these stones turn into loaves of bread. Jesus answered, *It is written, Man cannot live by bread only; there is life for him in all the words which proceed from the mouth of God.* Next, the Evil One took him into the holy city, and there set him down on the pinnacle of the temple, saying to him, If thou are truly the Son of God, cast thyself down to earth; for it is written, He has given charge to his angels concerning thee, and they will hold thee up with their hands, lest thou should chance to trip on a stone. Jesus said to him, But it is further written, Thou shall not challenge the Lord thy God to the test. Once more, the tempter took him to the top of an exceedingly high mountain, from where he revealed him all the kingdoms of the world and the glory of them, and said, I will give thee all these if thou will fall down and worship me. Then Jesus said to him, Away with thee, Satan; it is written, Thou shall worship the Lord thy God, and serve none but him. Then the tempter left him alone; and thereupon angels came and ministered to him.

Offertory Antiphon

O God and Divine Creator of all Wisdom and Vision, grant us the strength of humility to not boast of our accomplishments; and the courage of silence not to be beguiled by false promises of short cuts, and easy road or compromise without consequences. That it is your wisdom our life should be one of inner discernment and discovery; and that hardship and occassional discomfort are there to remind us and guide us, not to condemn or stop us. Through our Lord Jesus Christ, your Son, who lives and reigns with you in the unity of the Holy Spirit, one God, for ever and ever.

Prayer over the Offerings

May God and the Divine Creator accept and sanctify these humble gifts as symbols of the genuine personal offerings we make in respect and honour of your *Holy Feast of Divine Humility*. Through Christ our Light and Saviour.

Communion Antiphon — Psalm 69: 32

The humble shall see his truth, and be glad; for their hearts shall be filled the joy of life of those that know God.

Prayer after Communion

Heavenly Father and God of all Wisdom and Vision, we give thanks for the nourishment of your heavenly gifts of the Bread and Fruits of Eternal Spiritual Life. May our earnest participation in your *Holy Feast of Divine Humility* bring forth favourable blessings upon our lives, our community and your Holy Apostolic Universal Ecclesia. Through your Son our Lord Jesus Christ.

XVI.III – FEAST OF HOLY ABSTINENCE

1. The Universal Feast of Holy Abstinence, also known as Abstinence Sunday is the 1st Sunday after Ash Wednesday. — Feast of Holy Abstinence

Entrance Antiphon: — Prov. 27: 1

Do not boast about tomorrow, for only God and Heaven truly know what the day may bring.

Magisterium: Luke — Luke 14:25-35

Jesus said, If any man comes to me and proclaims he seeks to walk in my shoes, without first disowning his father and mother and wife and children and brethren and sisters, yes, and his own name and life too, then he can be no leader of mine. A man cannot be an exemplary of others unless he takes up his own cross willingly and follows after me. Consider, if one of you has a mind to build a tower, does he not first sit down and count the cost that must be paid, if he is to have enough to finish it? Is he to lay the foundation, and then find himself unable to complete the work, so that all who see it will fall to mocking him? For the world is a fickle place that destroys men for even the smallest of false accusations. What then of a king is setting out to join battle against another, does not first sit down and deliberate, whether with his army of ten thousand he can meet the onset of one who has twenty thousand? If he cannot, then, while the other is still at a distance, he dispatches envoys to ask for conditions of peace. And so it is with anyone who seeks to lead in my footsteps. None can truly be a servant of others, unless he takes leave of all that binds him and prevents him fully giving his life to others. Verily, salt is a good thing; but if the salt itself becomes tasteless, what is there left to give taste to it? It is of no use either to the soil or to the dung-heap; it will be thrown away altogether. Listen, you that have ears to hear.

Good News: Matthew

Matt. 6: 1-18

Jesus said, Be careful you do not perform acts of authentic charity before others, so as it to be seen by them, otherwise such actions mean nothing to God or to heaven. Therefore, when you do give alms to those in need, do not make a fanfare about it, as hypocrites do in the temples and in the streets, so that they may have the glory of the people. Verily, I say unto you, they have already received more than their fair share. Thus, when you do give alms to those in need, do it in a way that not even the left hand knows what the right hand is doing, so secret then is your authentic acts of charity be; and then my Father, seeing what is done in secret shall reward you openly. And when you pray, do not be like the hypocrites are. For they love to pray standing in the temples and at the corners of streets, so that they may be seen by everyone. Verily, I say unto you, they have already received more than their fair praise. Thus, when you pray, go into an inner room and when you have shut the door, pray to God in secret; and then my Father, seeing what is done in secret shall reward you openly. Moreover, when you pray, do not use vain repetitions, as the foolish do. For they think that they shall be better heard for much speaking of noise. Therefore, be not like these ignorant people, for your Father knows what things you have need of, before you ever ask him. Let this then be your prayer, Our Father, of All Creation, We beseech thee and honour your name; For your Rule be united as One, and your Laws be equal to All, on Earth as it is in Heaven; Grant us the means to sustenance, as we shall give alms to those in need. Save us from trickery and false oaths, as our vows and our oaths be true. Forgive us our debits and transgressions, as we shall forgive the debits and transgressions of others. Release us from any curse and ills, as we shall not curse nor wish ill upon another. Amen. Your heavenly Father will forgive you your transgressions, as you forgive your fellow men theirs. Yet if you do not forgive them, your heavenly Father will bind and hold you then to those punishments for your own transgressions. Again, when you fast, do not show it by gloomy looks, as the hypocrites do. They make their faces unsightly, so that men can see they are fasting; believe me, they have had more than their fair share. Instead, even at times of fasting, anoint thy head and wash thy face, so that your abstinence may not be known to others, but only to God, and then my Father, seeing what is done in secret shall reward you openly.

Offertory Antiphon

O God and Divine Creator of Infinite Patience and Discipline, whose discipline in not circumventing the laws of nature ensures the integrity of all existence, grant us the patience and self discipline to be patient before we speak; and to demonstrate resolute character in choosing to abstain from the things we like and enjoy from time to time, in order to appreciate your gifts more fully and the blessings we have been given. Through our Lord Jesus Christ, your Son, who lives and reigns with you in the unity of the Holy Spirit, one God, for ever and ever.

Prayer over the Offerings

May God and the Divine Creator accept and sanctify these humble gifts as symbols of the genuine personal offerings we make in respect and honour of your *Feast of Holy Abstinence*. Through Christ our Light and Saviour.

Communion Antiphon Psalm 33: 18-19

Behold, the Hand of God is upon those that respect him, upon those that trust in his mercy; To deliver their soul from death, and to keep them alive in times of famine.

Prayer after Communion

Heavenly Father and God of Infinite Patience and Discipline, we give thanks for the nourishment of your heavenly gifts of the Bread and Fruits of Eternal Spiritual Life. May our earnest participation in your *Feast of Holy Abstinence* bring forth favourable blessings upon our lives, our community and your Holy Apostolic Universal Ecclesia. Through your Son our Lord Jesus Christ.

XVI.IV – FEAST OF THE GOLDEN RULE OF LAW

1. The Universal Feast of the Golden Rule of Law, also known as Divine Law Sunday is the 2nd Sunday after Ash Wednesday. Feast of the Golden Rule of Law

Entrance Antiphon: Prov. 21: 3

To do what is merciful and just is more acceptable to God than any offering and sacrifice.

Magisterium: Luke Luke 11:5-13

Jesus said to his disciples, Let us suppose that one of you has a neighbour, to whom he goes at dead of night, and asks him saying Brother, lend me three loaves of bread; for a friend of mine has turned in to me after a journey, and I have nothing to offer him. And suppose the other answers, from within doors, Do not put me to such trouble; the door is locked, my children and I are in bed; I cannot bestir myself to grant thy request. I tell you, even if he will not bestir himself to grant it out of the obligation of charity to our neighbours, then the shameless asking awaking the whole neighbourhood will make him rise and give him all that he needs. And I say the same to you; do not be afraid to ask plainly, and the gift you need will come; seek, and you shall find; knock, and the door shall be opened to you. Everyone that asks, will receive in time, that his spirit ultimately seeks; and will find the deeper meaning; that knocks, will have the door of redemption opened to him. Among yourselves, if a father is asked by his son for bread, will he give him a stone? Or for a fish, will he give him a snake instead of a fish? Or if he is asked for an egg, will he give him a scorpion? Why then, if you, weak and unfaithful as you are, know well enough how to give your children what is good for them, is not your Father much more ready to give, from heaven through his gracious Spirit to those who ask him?

Good News: Matthew Matt. 7:1-12

Jesus said, Do not judge others, lest you yourself be judged. For with what judgement you have judged another, you shall be judged; and with what measures you make, it shall be measured to you the same. Behold! how is it that one can see the tiny splinter that is within the eye of your brother or sister, but cannot see the beam of wood that is in your own eye? You hypocrite! Take the beam out of your own eye first, and then you shall see clearly to cast out the tiny splinter in the eye of your brother or sister. Give not what is sacred to thieves and pirates. Do not cast pearls of wisdom before the wicked, or the wicked may trample them under foot and then turn on you and tear you to pieces. Ask, and it shall be given you; See and you shall find. Knock and it shall be opened unto you. For everyone that asks will receive; and that seeks, will find; that knocks will have it opened unto them. Is there any true father among you, whom if his daughter did ask for bread, would then give her a stone? Or if his son did ask for a fish, would then give him a serpent? Verily, if you, as imperfect as you are, know well enough how to give good gifts unto your children, how much more shall your Father in Heaven give as gifts you need to those that ask him? Therefore, all good things whatsoever you seek others should do for you, must you do so for them. For this is the Law and the Law of the Prophets.

Offertory Antiphon

O God and Divine Creator of all Law, grant us the persistence and desire to know your true Divine maxims of Law, so that we might be a witness to the truth of your laws and a defender of them against the oppression of those who seek to confuse and corrupt your laws. Through our Lord Jesus Christ, your Son, who lives and reigns with you in the unity of the Holy Spirit, one God, for ever and ever.

Prayer over the Offerings

May God and the Divine Creator accept and sanctify these humble gifts as symbols of the genuine personal offerings we make in respect and honour of your *Holy Feast of the Golden Rule of Law*. Through Christ our Light and Saviour.

Communion Antiphon

Psalm 19: 8

Verily, it is the perfect Divine Law of God, that restores the spirit of humanity back to life!The immutable wisdom and canons that may be simply learned and comprehended.

Prayer after Communion

Heavenly Father and God of all Law , we give thanks for the nourishment of your heavenly gifts of the Bread and

Fruits of Eternal Spiritual Life. May our earnest participation in your *Holy Feast of the Golden Rule of Law* bring forth favourable blessings upon our lives, our community and your Holy Apostolic Universal Ecclesia. Through your Son our Lord Jesus Christ.

XVI.V – FEAST OF DIVINE JUSTICE

1. The Universal Feast of Divine Justice, also known as Justice Sunday is the 3rd Sunday after Ash Wednesday. Feast of Divine Justice

Entrance Antiphon: Prov. 29: 4

A good leader gives a country stability through mercy and justice, but those who are greedy for bribes tear it down.

Magisterium: Matthew Matt. 21:33-44

Jesus spoke of another parable, saying: There was a rich man who planted a vineyard; he walled it in, and dug a wine-press and built a tower in it, and then let it out to some vine-dressers, while he went on his travels. When vintage-time drew near, he sent his own servants on an errand to the vine-dressers, to claim its revenues. Whereupon the vine-dressers laid hands upon his servants; one they beat, one they killed outright, one they stoned. And he sent other servants on a second errand, more than he had sent at first, but they were used no better. After that, he sent his own son to them; They will have reverence, he said, for my son. But when the vine-dressers found his son coming to them, they said among themselves, This is the heir; come, let us kill him, and seize upon the inheritance. And they laid hands on him, thrust him out from the vineyard, and killed him. And now, what will the owner of the vineyard do to those vine-dressers when he returns? They said, He will bring those wretches to a wretched end, and will let out the vineyard to other vine-dressers, who will pay him his due when the season comes. And Jesus said to them, Have you never read those words in the scriptures, The very stone which the builders rejected has become the chief stone at the corner; this is the Lord's doing, and it is marvellous in our eyes? I tell you, then, that the kingdom of God will be taken away from you, and given to a people who yields the revenues that belong to it. As for the stone, when a man falls against it, he will break his bones; when it falls upon him, it will scatter him like chaff.

Good News: Matthew Matt. 5:20-37

Jesus said, Verily, I caution you all that unless your acts of mercy and justice shall greatly exceed the mercy and justice of the scribes and doctors of law, then you shall not enter into the kingdom of heaven. For you have heard it said since ancient times, *Thou shalt not kill*; and whosoever commit murder shall be in danger of the harshest judgement: Yet I say unto you, that whosoever is belligerent against his neighbour without just cause be also in danger of harsh judgement; and whosoever condemn his brother as an idiot without fair cause be also in danger of harsh judgement; and anyone in a trusted position that does play another for a fool, must answer for such transgression with the harshest of punishment. Therefore, if you are bringing any gift before the altar of God and yet there exists at that time some just and fair grounds of complaint against thee, then leave the temple and go home; and be first reconciled with your brother and then come back and offer thy gift. Thus, seek to find common ground with any adversary without delay, whilst you can still meet and speak with him; lest your belligerence cause you to be delivered before a judge; and the judge deliver you to an officer and you be cast into prison. On that day, you shall no longer be at liberty until you have paid the last coin. You have also heard it said since ancient times, *Thou shalt not commit adultery*. Yet I say unto you, that whosoever casts their eyes on another man or woman in sacred union has already committed adultery in their heart. Therefore, if it be as if your right eye has offended thee, then pluck it out, and cast it from thee: for it is better that one of thy members be expelled than the whole body be condemned. And if it be as if your right hand has offended thee, then cut it off, and cast it far from thee: for it is better that one of thy members be sacrificed than the whole body be corrupted. You have heard it said, that whoever physically abuses his wife must give her the right of divorce. But I tell you that the man who inures his wife in holy matrimony is condemned twice, for also causing her to disavow heaven, even if she remarries under a lawful union. Again, you have heard it said since ancient times, *Thou shalt not make blasphemous oaths, but shall make all they proper oaths to God*. Yet I say unto you, do not make false promises at all; neither by heaven, nor by the earth, nor by the sacred city, nor even thy head. Therefore, let your word be your bond so that your Yea means yea and your Nay, means nay.

Offertory Antiphon

O God and Divine Creator of all Rights and Justice, grant us the wise discernment and courage to know and respect and defend our rights, against the dangers of tyranny that face every generation who forget to stand and be counted in the defence of your true justice. Through our Lord Jesus Christ, your Son, who lives and reigns with you in the unity of the Holy Spirit, one God, for ever and ever.

Prayer over the Offerings

May God and the Divine Creator accept and sanctify these humble gifts as symbols of the genuine personal offerings we make in respect and honour of your *Holy Feast of Divine Justice*. Through Christ our Light and Saviour.

Communion Antiphon — Psalm 89: 13-14

How mighty be his arms: how strong is the Hand of God, and how great be his reach. Justice and truth are the habitation of thy throne: mercy and love is your true face.

Prayer after Communion

Heavenly Father and God of all Rights and Justice, we give thanks for the nourishment of your heavenly gifts of the Bread and Fruits of Eternal Spiritual Life. May our earnest participation in your *Holy Feast of Divine Justice* bring forth favourable blessings upon our lives, our community and your Holy Apostolic Universal Ecclesia. Through your Son our Lord Jesus Christ.

XVI.VI – FEAST OF DIVINE SERVICE

1. The Universal Feast of Divine Service, also known as Obligation Sunday is the 4th Sunday after Ash Wednesday. — Feast of Divine Service

Entrance Antiphon: — Prov. 22: 8

Whoever sows injustice reaps calamity upon their office, for the rod they wield will be broken midst the fury against such evil.

Magisterium: Luke — Luke 19:11-28

While the disciples stood listening to Jesus, he went on and told them a parable; this was because he had now reached Jerusalem, and they supposed that the kingdom of God was to appear immediately. He told them, then, There was a man of noble birth, who went away to a distant country, to have the royal title bestowed on him, and so return. And he summoned ten of his servants, to whom he gave each a pound of coins, and said to them, Trade with this while I am away. But his fellow citizens hated him, and sent ambassadors after him to say, We will not have this man for our king. Afterwards, when he came back as king, he sent for the servants to whom he had entrusted the money, to find out how much each of them had gained by his use of it. The first came before him and said, Lord, thy pound has made ten pounds. And he said to him, Well done, my true servant: since thou hast been faithful over a very little, thou shalt have authority over ten cities. The second came and said, Lord, thy pound has made five pounds; and to him he said, Thou too shalt have authority, over five cities. Then another came and said, Lord, here is thy pound; I have kept it laid up in a handkerchief. I was afraid of thee, knowing how exacting a man thou art; thou dost claim what thou didst never venture, dost reap what thou didst never sow. Then he said to him, Thou false servant, I take thy judgement from thy own lips. Thou knew that I was an exacting man, claiming what I never ventured and reaping what I never sowed; then why didst thou not put my money into the bank, so that I might have recovered it with interest when I came? Then he gave orders to those who stood by, Take the pound away from him, and give it to the man who has ten pounds. No, but I tell you, if ever a man is rich, gifts will be made to him, and his riches will abound; if he is poor, even the little he has will be taken from him. But as for those enemies of mine, who refused to have me for their king, bring them here and punish them in my presence. And when he had spoken thus, he went on his way, going up to Jerusalem.

Good News: Matthew — Matt. 5:1-19

When Jesus saw how great was the multitude following him, he went up on to the mountain-side; and his disciples came about him and sat down; before he began speaking to them; and teaching them, saying, Blessed are the poor: for theirs is the kingdom of heaven. Blessed are they that mourn: for they shall see their beloved again. Blessed are the humble: for they shall become the stewards of the earth. Blessed are they who hunger and thirst for justice: for they shall see justice served. Blessed are the merciful: for they shall obtain divine mercy and forgiveness. Blessed are the true of heart: for they shall see God. Blessed are the peace-makers; for they shall be called the sons and daughters of God. Blessed are those who suffer and die in true witness to their trust in God; for they are the greatest heroes of heaven. Blessed are you, when men revile you, and persecute you, and speak all manner of evil against you falsely, because of me. Rejoice and be exceedingly glad, for great is your reward in heaven: for so persecuted were the prophets that came before you. You are the salt of the earth; yet if salt loses its taste, what is there left to give taste to it? There is no more to be done with it, but throw it out of doors for men to tread it under foot. You are the light of the world; but a city cannot be hidden if it is built on a mountain-top. A lamp is not lit to be put away under a bushel measure; it is put on the lamp-stand, to give light to all the people of the house; and your light must shine so brightly before men that they can see your good works, and glorify your Father who is in heaven. Do not think that I have come to destroy the laws or the writings of the prophets; I have not come to destroy, but to restore the law and fulfil. Verily, I say unto you, better the world pass away sooner than one clause or title of the true law of Heaven disappear, until all be fulfilled. Whosoever therefore shall break or corrupt one of these commandments, or shall teach men so to do, then he shall be called an enemy of heaven: but whosoever keeps them and teaches others to keep these commandments will be accounted in the kingdom of heaven as the greatest.

Offertory Antiphon

O God and Divine Creator of all Talents and Creativity, may we never forget the ultimate source of all our talents and creative abilities; and grant us the fortitude and honesty of self to serve in your name those who are less fortunate than us and in need of our love, charity and support. Through our Lord Jesus Christ, your Son, who lives and reigns with you in the unity of the Holy Spirit, one God, for ever and ever.

Prayer over the Offerings

May God and the Divine Creator accept and sanctify these humble gifts as symbols of the genuine personal offerings we make in respect and honour of your *Holy Feast of Divine Service*. Through Christ our Light and Saviour.

Communion Antiphon — Psalm 90:16-17

Let thy work appear unto thy servants, and thy glory unto your children. Let the beauty of God be upon us that we may establish your works through our hands with your blessing.

Prayer after Communion

Heavenly Father and God of all Talents and Creativity, we give thanks for the nourishment of your heavenly gifts of the Bread and Fruits of Eternal Spiritual Life. May our earnest participation in your *Holy Feast of Divine Service* bring forth favourable blessings upon our lives, our community and your Holy Apostolic Universal Ecclesia. Through your Son our Lord Jesus Christ.

XVI.VII – DIVINE NEW COVENANT

1. The Universal Feast of the Divine New Covenant, also known as Pi Day is always March 14th and the Feast of the Last Blood Sacrifice. — Divine New Covenant

Entrance Antiphon: — Prov. 2: 6

For Christ gives us Divine Wisdom. From his mouth come knowledge and understanding of the Divine.

Magisterium: Luke — Luke 17:20-36

Upon the persistence of the doctors of law, asking when the Kingdom of Heaven on Earth was to come and all scripture be fulfilled, Jesus did say, The Kingdom of Heaven shall come unnoticed in plain sight of the eyes of men and women. There will be no saying look! it is here, or see! it is there, for behold, the Kingdom of God is within you. Jesus then said to his disciplines, The time will come when those that follow you shall long to witness but for a day, the presence of the Son of Man and yet when it happens they shall not see him. And they shall say to one another, look! he is here, or see! he is there. Yet let no man or woman be tricked to follow the falsities. Verily, the Son of Man, when his time comes, will be like the lightning which lightens from one border of heaven to the other. But before that time, he must undergo many sufferings, and be rejected by this generation. For as it was in the days of Noah, so shall it be also in the days of the Son of Man. In those days, they did eat and drink to excess while many starved; and they rejected the fidelity of holy matrimony for wickedness and debauchery, until the days that Noah entered into the ark and the floods did come and destroyed them all. Likewise also, as it was in the days of Lot; when men and women did engage in every vice and evil, until the day that Lot went out of Sodom and it rained fire and brimstone from heaven and destroyed them all. Even thus shall it be in the days when the Son of Man is revealed. In these days to come, if a man is on the house-top and his goods are in the house, let him not come down to take them with him; and if a man is in the fields, he too must beware of turning back, lest he suffer the same fate as the wide of Lot. Whosoever shall seek to save his life shall lose it; and whosoever shall lose his life shall preserve it. I tell you, in these days, there shall be two men in beds; when one shall be taken and the other shall be left. Two women shall be grinding together, the one shall be taken and the other left. Two workers shall be in the field; the one shall be taken and the other left.

Good News: Matthew

Matt. 7:13-29

Jesus said, Enter through the true gate: For wide is the gate and broad is the way that leads to self destruction; and many; and those that choose such a path are many indeed. Yet, how small is the gate and how narrow is the road that leads to a genuine life of joy, and how few are there that seek it! Beware of false prophets that come to you in the clothing of sheep, but inwardly are ravenous wolves. For you shall know them by their fruits. Can grapes be plucked from thorns? or figs from thistles? So it is that every heroic and virtuous tree brings forth good fruit; but a corrupt tree brings forth fruit that is worthless. A good tree cannot bring forth evil fruit. Neither can a corrupt tree bring forth good fruit. Every tree that brings forth wicked and evil fruit must be hewn down and cast into the fire. Therefore, by their fruits you shall know them. The kingdom of Heaven will not give open entrance to every one who calls themselves a follower of Christ. Only those who obey and do the will of my Father the Divine Creator are assured easy entry into Heaven. For many shall say to me when their final hour comes, Master, Master, was it not in your name we prophesied? Was it not in thy name that we performed many miracles? Whereupon I will tell them openly, You were never friends of mine; depart from me, you that traffic in falsities until you have learned your lessons in perdition and finally change your ways. Whoever, then, hears these commandments of mine and carries them out, is like a wise man who built his house upon rock; and the rain fell and the floods came and the winds blew and beat upon that house, but it did not fall; it was founded upon rock. But whoever hears these commandments of mine and does not carry them out is like a man or woman, who built their house upon sand; and the rain fell and the floods came and the winds blew and beat upon that house, and it collapsed. Afterwards, when Jesus had finished these sayings, the multitudes found themselves amazed at his teaching. For he taught them, not like their scribes and doctors of law, but like one who had Divine Authority.

Offertory Antiphon

O God and Divine Creator of the Divine New Covenant of Light, who through the Testament of your son ended all forms of ritual blood sacrifice and heralded a new age of a Society of Light, grant us the wisdom of discernment to understand your Divine Revelations and honour your Divine Word. Through our Lord Jesus Christ, your Son, who lives and reigns with you in the unity of the Holy Spirit, one God, for ever and ever.

Prayer over the Offerings

May God and the Divine Creator accept and sanctify these humble gifts as symbols of the genuine personal offerings we make in respect and honour of your *Holy Feast of the Divine New Covenant*. Through Christ our Light and Saviour.

Communion Antiphon

Psalm 89: 2-4

The Mercy and forgiveness of God shall be built up for ever. The faithfulness of the people shall be established in the very heavens. God has made a new covenant with all people as promised through the Son of Man. The seed of new life is established forever as a new kingdom on Earth for all generations.

Prayer after Communion

Heavenly Father and God of the Divine New Covenant of Light, we give thanks for the nourishment of your heavenly gifts of the Bread and Fruits of Eternal Spiritual Life. May our earnest participation in your *Holy Feast of the Divine*

New Covenant bring forth favourable blessings upon our lives, our community and your Holy Apostolic Universal Ecclesia. Through your Son our Lord Jesus Christ.

XVI.VIII – PALM SUNDAY

1. Palm Sunday is the Sunday before Good Friday. Palm Sunday

Entrance Antiphon: Prov. 14: 11

The citadel of the wicked will eventually be destroyed, but the tent of the upright will flourish.

Magisterium: Zechariah Zechariah 9:9

Rejoice greatly, O sons and daughter of the Lord! Shout aloud, O sons and daughter of Jerusalem! Behold, your king is coming to you; righteous and having salvation is he, humble and mounted on a donkey, on a colt, the foal of a donkey.

Good News: Matthew Matt. 21:1-15

When they were near Jerusalem, and had reached Bethany, close to the Mount of Olives, Jesus sent two of his disciples on an errand, saying *Go into the village that faces you and the first thing you will find there will be a she-ass tethered, and a foal at her side; untie them and bring them to me. And if anyone speaks to you about it, tell him, My Lord has need of them, and they will let you have them without more questions.* All this was so ordained, to fulfil the word spoken by the prophet: Tell the daughter of Sion, Behold, thy king is coming to thee, humbly, riding on an ass, as a colt whose mother has borne the yoke. The two disciples went and did as Jesus told them; and returned with the she-ass and its colt, and saddled them with their garments, and bade Jesus mount. Most of the multitude awaiting the arrival of Jesus into the city did spread their garments along the way, while others strewed the way with branches cut down from the trees. And the multitudes that went before him and that followed after him cried aloud, Hosanna for the son of David, blessed is he who comes in the name of the Lord, Hosanna in heaven above. When Jesus reached Jerusalem, the whole city was in a stir; Even strangers asked who is this? and the multitude answered, This is Jesus, the prophet from Nazareth, in Galilee. Jesus then went into the temple of God, and was enraged and drove out from it all those who sold and bought there; and overthrew the tables of the bankers and money changers, and the stalls of the people selling animals for sacrifice; As the merchants scattered, Jesus did cry out, saying, *Behold! It is written, My house shall be kept as a house of prayer, and you have made it into a den of thieves.*

Offertory Antiphon

O God and Divine Creator of all Sanctity and Authority, grant us the courage and willingness to defend the sanctity of your sacred places against those who would pollute them with the exchange of money and other sordid acts. Grant us the skill of vigilance so that your holy places shall never again be corrupted under our watch. Through our Lord Jesus Christ, your Son, who lives and reigns with you in the unity of the Holy Spirit, one God, for ever and ever.

Prayer over the Offerings

May God and the Divine Creator accept and sanctify these humble gifts as symbols of the genuine personal offerings we make in respect and honour of your *Holy Feast of Palm Sunday*. Through Christ our Light and Saviour.

Communion Antiphon Psalm 67: 3-4

Let the people praise thee, O God; let all the people praise thee. O let the nations be glad and sing for joy: for thou shall judge the people righteously, and govern all nations upon earth.

Prayer after Communion

Heavenly Father and God of all Sanctity and Authority, we give thanks for the nourishment of your heavenly gifts of the Bread and Fruits of Eternal Spiritual Life. May our earnest participation in your *Holy Feast of Palm Sunday* bring forth favourable blessings upon our lives, our community and your Holy Apostolic Universal Ecclesia. Through your Son our Lord Jesus Christ.

XVI.IX – HOLY TUESDAY

1. Holy Tuesday is the Tuesday before Good Friday. Holy Tuesday

Entrance Antiphon: Prov. 11: 3

Integrity of the faithful guides them through rocky waters, but the unfaithful are destroyed by their duplicity.

Magisterium: Luke

Luke 22: 1-37

Now, as the holiest week of Jerusalem since the time of the Persians, called the Paschal did draw near, the priests and doctors of law of the temple became even more agitated how they might kill Jesus without causing the people to turn against them. Yet greed and perfidy had found its way into the heart of Judas, who was also called Iscariot, one of the twelve, and he went off secretly and conspired with the chief priests and the temple guard how he might betray Jesus unto them. They gladly consented to pay him a handsome sum of money, and Judas in turn promised to find the earliest opportunity to betray Jesus unto them, in the absence of the multitude. Soon after, upon the holy week of Paschal and four days before the most solemn day of blood, being the ancient celebration of the sacrifice of the paschal victim as the lamb, Jesus did send Peter and John on an errand, saying: *Go into the city and make ready for us a room for the paschal meal*. The disciples did reply, saying: Lord, where shall we go and prepare for thee? And Jesus said to them, *Behold! when you enter into the city, there shall you meet a man, bearing a pitcher of water; follow him into the house where he enters; and there you shall say to the head servant, The Master sends word to thee. Where is the room where I am to eat the paschal meal with my disciples? And he shall show you a large upper room that is furnished. It is there you are to make ready*. So they went, and found all as he had told them, and so made ready for the paschal meal. But three days before the most solemn feast, Jesus came to the room and sat down with his disciples said to them, *I have long considered this time and of sharing this paschal meal with you before my passion. Verily, I tell you, I shall not share such a meal as one body again, until all be revealed through the kingdom of God*. And he took a cup, and gave thanks, and said, *Take this and share it among you; For I say unto you, I shall not drink of the fruit of the vine again, until the kingdom of God shall come*. Then Jesus took bread, and gave thanks and broke it, and gave it to them, saying, *This is my body, that is given for you; Do this in remembrance of me*. When supper was near ended, Jesus took the cup again and said, Behold! This cup is a symbol of a new testament, sealed by my blood that shall be shed for you. Alas, even now, the hand of him that shall betray me, is with me at this table. Verily, the Son of Man must depart as it has been ordained; yet woe upon those who betray my words. Thereupon, they began enquiring among themselves, who of them could do such a thing, and strife erupted between them as to whom had accounted for their greatest loyalty. But Jesus said unto them, *The highest lords over men claim to be kings and those that exercise authority under them are called benefactors. With you it is not to be so; for he that claims to be the greatest by seniority, let him be the one with the youngest rank; and he that seeks to give commands then let him be a servant. Tell me, who is greater, the man who sits at table, or the man who serves him? It is not the man who sits at table?; and yet I am here among you as your servant. You are the ones who have stayed with me throughout my temptations. Thus, I appoint unto you a kingdom, as my Father has appointed all his kingdoms unto me; and that you are given a place to eat and drink at my table in my kingdom; and be empowered to administer as one body all the tribes of the People of God.* At these words, the disciples were dumbfounded, before Jesus then turned to Peter and said, *Simon, behold the Evil One has claimed power over you all, so that he can sift you like wheat. Yet I have prayed for thee, that thy faith may not fail; when, after a while, thou hast come back to me, it is for thee to be the support of thy brothers and sisters.* Peter did say, Lord, I am ready to go with thee, both into prison and even unto death. But Jesus did answer, *I tell thee, Peter, by cock-crow this morning thou wilt thrice have denied knowledge of me.* Jesus then said to his disciples, *Did you go in want of anything, when I sent you out without purse, or wallet, or shoes?* They replied that they did not. Jesus then continued and said, *the day will come soon enough when a man need take hold of his purse with him, and likewise those scripts in his name; and if he has no sword, let him sell his garment and buy one. For I say unto you, these things that are written are yet to be accomplished in me, as is the reckoning of all transgressors. For all that has been written of me shall be fulfilled in the end.*

Offertory Antiphon

O God and Divine Creator of all Wisdom, grant us the serenity of docility to the mission of your Holy Spirit; and to trust in the strength of our faith and in your love that everything in life happens for a higher purpose; and that sometimes from the greatest betrayals by others may rise the greatest triumphs of spirit. Through our Lord Jesus Christ, your Son, who lives and reigns with you in the unity of the Holy Spirit, one God, for ever and ever.

Prayer over the Offerings

May God and the Divine Creator accept and sanctify these humble gifts as symbols of the genuine personal offerings we make in respect and honour of your *Feast of Holy Tuesday*. Through Christ our Light and Saviour.

Communion Antiphon — Psalm 116: 13-14

I will take the cup of salvation, and call upon the name of God our Divine Creator. I will pay my vows unto God in the presence of all his faithful.

Prayer after Communion

Heavenly Father and God of all Wisdom, we give thanks for the nourishment of your heavenly gifts of the Bread and Fruits of Eternal Spiritual Life. May our earnest participation in your *Feast of Holy Tuesday* bring forth favourable blessings upon our lives, our community and your Holy Apostolic Universal Ecclesia. Through your Son our Lord Jesus Christ.

XVI.X – HOLY WEDNESDAY

1. Holy Wednesday is the Wednesday before Good Friday. — Holy Wednesday

Entrance Antiphon: — Prov. 15: 8

God our Father detests the sacrifice of the wicked, but is pleased with the prayers of the upright.

Good News: Matthew — Matt. 26:36-75

In the evening, Jesus did come with them to the entrance of a place called Gethsemani; and said to his disciples, Sit down here, while I enter and pray quietly. And he took with him only Peter and the two sons of Zebedee into the gardens and soon became overwhelmed with sorrow and dismay, saying to them, *My soul is exceedingly sick with sorrow, even unto welcoming death if it comes quickly. Stay with me and do not leave me.* Jesus then walked a little further, before falling upon his face in prayer in deep lament, and said, *O my Father, if it be possible, let this cup pass from me; if only thy would will it, and not for my own, let it be so.* After a while, he returned to his disciples, to find them asleep; and he said to Peter, *Had you no strength, then, to watch with me even for an hour? Watch and pray, that you may not enter into temptation; for the spirit indeed is willing, but the flesh is weak.* Jesus then went back again, and prayed a second time, saying, *O my Father, if it be your will this cup may not pass away from me, except my choice to drink it, then thy will be done.* And returning once more he found his disciples still asleep, for their eyes were heavy; and he left them, and went away again, and prayed the third time, saying the same words. On returning to the sleeping disciples, he said unto them, *You sleep on now and take your rest, and yet the hour is at hand the Son of Man is betrayed into the hands of blasphemers and heretics. Rise up, let us be on our way; already, he who has betrayed me is close at hand.* And all at once, while he was speaking, Judas, who was one of the twelve, came near; accompanied by a company of the temple guard, who had been sent by the chief priests and the elders of the people. The traitor had appointed them a signal; It is none other, he told them, than the man whom I shall greet with a kiss; hold him fast. No sooner, then, had Judas come near to Jesus than he said, Hail, Master, and kissed him. Jesus said to him, *My brother, on what awful errand hast thou come?* Then they came forward and laid their hands on Jesus, and held him fast. And at that, one of those who were with Jesus lifted a hand to draw his sword, and struck one of the high priest's servants with it, cutting off his ear. Whereupon Jesus said to him, *Put thy sword back into its place; for all those who take up the sword against heaven will perish by the sword. Dost thou doubt that if I call upon my Father, even now, he will send more than twelve legions of angels to my side? But how, were it so, should the scriptures be fulfilled, that have prophesied all must be as it is?* And Jesus said to the multitude at that hour, *You have come out to my arrest with swords and clubs, as if I were some murderous marauder; and yet I used to sit teaching in the temple close to you, day after day, and you never laid hands on me.* All this was so ordained, to fulfil what was written by the prophets. And now all his disciples abandoned him, and fled. And those who had arrested Jesus led him away into the presence of the high priest, Caiphas, where the scribes and the doctors of law had assembled. Yet Peter followed him at a long distance, as far as the high priest's palace; where he went in and sat among the servants, to see the end. The chief priests and doctors of law and all the Council tried to find false testimony against Jesus, such as would compass his death. But they could find none, although many came forward falsely accusing him; until at last two false accusers came forward who declared, This man said, I have power to destroy the temple of God and raise it again in three days. Then the high priest stood up, and asked him, Hast thou no answer to make to the accusations these men bring against thee? Jesus was silent; and the high priest said to him openly, I adjure thee by the living God to tell us whether thou art the Christ, the Son of God? Jesus answered, *Thy own lips have said it. And moreover I say unto you; In the hereafter, you shall see the Son of Man again, when he is seated at the right hand of power midst the clouds of heaven.* Enraged, the high priest tore his garments, and cried out, He has blasphemed; what further need have we of witnesses? Mark well, you have heard his blasphemy for yourselves. What is your finding? And they answered, The penalty is death. The priests and servants then blindfolded Jesus and then began spitting upon his face and buffeting him and smiting him on the cheek, saying mockingly as they did so, Show thyself a prophet, O Christ; tell us who it is that struck thee. Meanwhile, Peter sat in the court without; and there a maid-servant came up to him, and said, Thou too wast with Jesus the Galilean. Whereupon he denied it before all the company; I do not know what thou meanest. And he went out into the porch, where a second maid-servant saw him, and said, to the bystanders, This man, too, was with Jesus the Nazarene. And he made denial again with an oath, I know nothing of the man. But those who stood there came up to Peter soon afterwards, and said, It is certain that thou art one of them; even thy speech betrays thee. And with that he fell to calling down curses on himself and swearing, I know nothing of the man; and thereupon the cock crew. Then Peter remembered the word of Jesus, how he had said, Before the cock crows, thou wilt three times disown me; and he went out, and wept bitterly.

Offertory Antiphon

O God and Divine Creator of all Love, Mercy and

Forgiveness, who forgave the disciples of your son for their betrayal, by granting them the strength of the Holy Spirit to become the greatest of heroes, grant us your strength and wisdom so that we may see it is not our failings to your Divine Mission that matters as much as our willingness to change our ways and forgive and love others as you forgive and love us. Through our Lord Jesus Christ, your Son, who lives and reigns with you in the unity of the Holy Spirit, one God, for ever and ever.

Prayer over the Offerings

May God and the Divine Creator accept and sanctify these humble gifts as symbols of the genuine personal offerings we make in respect and honour of your *Feast of Holy Wednesday*. Through Christ our Light and Saviour.

Communion Antiphon — Psalm 7: 2

O Lord my God, my confidence is in thee. Save me from all my pursuers, and grant me deliverance.

Prayer after Communion

Heavenly Father and God of all Love, Mercy and Forgiveness, we give thanks for the nourishment of your heavenly gifts of the Bread and Fruits of Eternal Spiritual Life. May our earnest participation in your *Feast of Holy Wednesday* bring forth favourable blessings upon our lives, our community and your Holy Apostolic Universal Ecclesia. Through your Son our Lord Jesus Christ.

XVI.XI – HOLY THURSDAY

1. Holy Thursday is the Day before Good Friday. — Holy Thursday

Entrance Antiphon: — Prov. 1: 27-29

When fear comes as desolation, and destruction appears as a whirlwind; and when distress and anguish rises upon the unfaithful, then they shall call upon the Lord and find no answer, for they hated knowledge and did not choose to learn the wisdom of the Divine.

Magisterium: John — John 18:28-40

The temple guards and high priests did lead Jesus away from the house of Caiphas to the hall of judgement of the Roman Governor. It was morning, and after the priests and doctors of law arrived, they protested to the Romans they could not enter the judgement hall themselves on account of sacred paschal customs, so the Governor Pontius Pilate was forced to come out to meet them. On seeing Jesus, Pilate said to the priests, What accusation do you bring against this man? The priests then handed Pilate a scroll of the accusations, but were hesitant in their reply saying, We would not have given this man up to thee, if he had not been a malefactor. Yet Pilate was not convinced and said to them, If he be so condemned as you say, then take him yourselves and punish him according to your laws. Whereupon the high priests said, Under Roman Law, we no longer have the power to put any man to death. Thus, in that moment, the revelation of Christ was fulfilled when he prophesied that by unclean hands even the Son of Man shall be falsely condemned. So Pilate ordered Jesus be taken into his custody before he returned to the judgement hall, and called Jesus to appear before him and said unto him, Are you the Messiah King they speak of? Jesus replied, saying, *Does thou say this of thy own accord, or is it on account of what others have told thee?* Pilate then answered, Am I a doctor of your laws? It is by the hands of your own priests and people, who have given thee up to me. Therefore, tell me what be the offence hast thou committed? Jesus said, *My kingdom, does not belong to this world. If my kingdom were one that belonged to this world, my forces would be fighting, to prevent my falling into the hands of my enemies; but no, my kingdom does not take its origin from here.* Thou art a king, then? Pilate asked. And Jesus answered, *It is thy own lips that have called me a king. What I was born for, what I came into the world for, is to bear witness of the truth. Whoever belongs to the truth, listens to my voice.* Pilate then said to him, What is truth? Yet Jesus did not answer, and so Pilate wrestled with himself until he finally summonsed the priests and doctors of law to return to him, and told them, I can find no fault in him at all, though he remains bound in my custody. Thus you have a custom that I should release unto you one deserving of mercy: would you have me release a man of depravity and vicious cruelty, or release this man? Whereupon there was at first silence, before the priests agreed among themselves and called out: Release Barabbas, though it was known that Barabbas was a notorious marauder and murderer.

Offertory Antiphon

O God and Divine Creator of all History and Lessons, who revealed through the suffering of your son at the unjust hands of corrupt human laws, the unstoppable and transformative power of your love through the lessons of history, grant us the trust and certainty of faith that every moment and every action of our loves has consequences and is a learning opportunity for ourselves and others. Through our Lord Jesus Christ, your Son, who lives and reigns with you in the unity of the Holy Spirit, one God, for ever and ever.

Prayer over the Offerings

May God and the Divine Creator accept and sanctify these humble gifts as symbols of the genuine personal offerings we make in respect and honour of your *Feast of Holy Thursday*. Through Christ our Light and Saviour.

Communion Antiphon — Psalm 71: 4

Deliver me, O my God, out of the hand of the wicked, out of the hand of the unrighteous and cruel.

Prayer after Communion

Heavenly Father and God of all History and Lessons, we give thanks for the nourishment of your heavenly gifts of the Bread and Fruits of Eternal Spiritual Life. May our earnest participation in your *Feast of Holy Thursday* bring forth favourable blessings upon our lives, our community and your Holy Apostolic Universal Ecclesia. Through your Son our Lord Jesus Christ.

XVI.XII – GOOD FRIDAY

1. Good Friday, is the 1st Friday after or upon Spring Equinox. — Good Friday

Entrance Antiphon: — Prov. 11: 4

Wealth is worthless upon the day of death. Only virtue and good works delivers one from perdition.

Magisterium: John — John 19:1-42

After the crowd called out for the release of Barabbas, the Roman Governor Pontius Pilate ordered Jesus to be scourged. So the Roman Soldiers took him away and whipped him, before forcing upon his head a crown they had woven out of thorns and cloaking him in a scarlet robe. As the soldiers tortured and mocked Jesus, they did come up to him and say, Hail the Messiah King and strike him on the face before returning him to the Governor. Pilate then stepped out before the crowd again and said, See, I am bringing him out to you, to show that I cannot find any fault in him. Then, as Jesus came out, wearing the crown of thorns and the scarlet cloak, Pilate said to the assembled, See, here is the man. When the chief priests and the doctors of the law saw Jesus, they cried out, Crucify him, crucify him. Yet Pilate answered them back, saying, Take him yourselves then and crucify him; For I cannot find any fault in him. The chief priests and their followers answered saying, We have our own law, and by our law he must die, for pretending to be the Son of God. When Pilate heard this from them, he became more fearful than ever and withdrew back into the palace and asked Jesus, From whence hast thou come? Yet Jesus gave no answer. Frustrated, Pilate spoke to Jesus again, saying, has thou no word for me? Does thou not know that I have power to crucify thee and power to release thee? Jesus answered saying, *Verily, you would not have any power over me at all, if it had not first been granted to thee from above*. After this reply, Pilate was even more desperate for having Jesus released, yet the priests and the crowd of their followers began chanting Death to the enemy of Caesar! When Pilate heard the chant of the crowd, he ordered Jesus be brought out again, as Pilate then sat down on the imperial judgement seat. It was now about the sixth hour, on the eve of the solemn paschal feast. Pilate then addressed the assembled crowd and priests and their officers, saying Behold! Here is truly your Messiah. But the crowd cried out even louder, Crucify him! crucify him! Pilate then replied, saying, What you ask of me then, is to condemn your own king? Yet the priests quickly replied, saying We have no king, except Caesar, before the crowd began chanting Caesar! Thereupon, exhausted and perplexed, the Roman Governor lowered his baton and Jesus was taken away by the soldiers to be crucified. Not long after, Jesus was led out, carrying his own cross, to the place named after a skull called Golgotha. There they crucified him, and with him two others, one on each side with Jesus in the midst. And in contempt for the actions of the priests and doctors of the law, Pilate ordered a proclamation be affixed upon the the cross, saying: Jesus of Nazareth, the Messiah King of the People. This proclamation was read by many of the priests and their followers, since the place where Jesus was crucified was close to the city; and it was written in multiple languages. Upon hearing of the proclamation, the chief priests pleaded with Pilate saying, Thou should not write, The Messiah King; thou should write, This man said, I claim to be the Son of God. Pilate did answer saying, What I have written, I have written. The soldiers, once they had crucified Jesus, took up his garments, that they divided into four shares, one share for each soldier. Then they took up his cloak, that was without seam, woven from the top throughout; so they said to one another, Better we not to tear it; instead let us cast lots to decide whose it shall be. This was in fulfilment of the passage in scripture which says, They divide my spoils among them; casting lots for my clothing. So it was then the manner whereby the soldiers occupied themselves. Meanwhile, only Mary the mother of Jesus, with her sister, Mary the wife of Cleophas, Mary Magdalen and only one other disciple, had come to bear witness and stand beside the Cross. And Jesus, seeing the heart and courage of his mother, and the disciple, whom he loved, standing with her, said to his mother, *Woman, this is thy son*. Then he said to the disciple, *Brother, this is thy mother*. And from that hour the disciple took Mary into his own safe keeping. And now Jesus knew well that all was achieved which the scripture demanded for its accomplishment; and he said, I am thirsty. There was a jar there full of vinegar; so they filled a sponge with the vinegar and put it on a stick of hyssop, and brought it close to his mouth. Jesus drank the vinegar, and said, It is achieved. Then he bowed his head, and yielded up his spirit. The priests and doctors of the law would not let the bodies remain crucified on the paschal feast, for fear all the people would see Jesus as the sacrificial lamb; and since it was now the eve of the paschal feast, they asked Pilate that the bodies might have their legs broken, and be taken away. And so the soldiers came and broke the legs both of the one and of the other that were crucified with him; but when they came to Jesus, and found him already dead, they did not break his legs, but one of the soldiers opened his side with a spear; and immediately blood and water flowed out. He who saw it has borne his witness; and his witness is worthy of trust. He tells what he knows to be the truth, that you, like him, may learn to believe. This was so ordained to fulfil what is written, You shall not break a single bone of his. And again, another passage in scripture says, They will look upon the man whom they have pierced. After this Joseph of Arimathea, who was a disciple of Jesus, asked Pilate in secret to let him take away the body of Jesus. Pilate gave him leave; so he came and took Jesus' body away; and with him was Nicodemus, the same who made his first visit to Jesus by night; he brought with him a mixture of myrrh and aloes, of about a hundred pounds' weight. They took Jesus' body, then, and wrapped it in winding-cloths with the spices; that is how the Jews prepare a body for burial. In the same quarter where he was crucified there was a garden, with a new tomb in it, one in which no man had ever yet been buried. Here, since the tomb was close at hand, they laid Jesus, because of the time of the solemn feast.

Offertory Antiphon

O God and Divine Creator of all Compassion, Love and Healing, grant us the humility and clarity of conscience to never forget the real and manifest suffering you willingly chose to endure, so that we might be saved. May we never forget your beloved martyrs and heroes whose exploits of bravery and faith serve as a living beacon of light for each and every generation and that to be true to your Divine Word requires us to live a life of personal sacrifice and death to what is false and deliberately ignorant and corrupt. Through our Lord Jesus Christ, your Son, who lives and reigns with you in the unity of the Holy Spirit, one God, for ever and ever.

Prayer over the Offerings

May God and the Divine Creator accept and sanctify these humble gifts as symbols of the genuine personal offerings we make in respect and honour of your *Holy Feast of Good Friday*. Through Christ our Light and Saviour.

Communion Antiphon — Psalm 31: 5

Into thine hand I commit my spirit: thou hast redeemed me, O God of truth.

Prayer after Communion

Heavenly Father and God of all Compassion, Love and Healing, we give thanks for the nourishment of your heavenly gifts of the Bread and Fruits of Eternal Spiritual Life. May our earnest participation in your *Holy Feast of Good Friday* bring forth favourable blessings upon our lives, our community and your Holy Apostolic Universal Ecclesia. Through your Son our Lord Jesus Christ.

XVI.XIII– EASTER SUNDAY

1. Easter Sunday, also known as Resurrection Day is the first Sunday on or after after Spring Equinox. Easter Sunday

Entrance Antiphon: Prov. 21: 31

The strongest army may be prepared for battle, but victory always rests with the holy writ of Heaven.

Good News: John John 20: 1-7

Early in the morning on the first day of the week, while it was still dark, Mary Magdalen braved to walk to the tomb of Jesus, yet found it unguarded and the large stone moved away from the mouth of the tomb. So she came running to Simon also known as Peter and the other disciples, saying, They have carried the Lord away, and I fear where they have his body. Upon this, Peter and John set out, and made their way to the tomb running side by side, until John outran Peter, and reached the tomb first. He looked in and saw the linen cloths lying there, but he did not go in. Simon Peter, coming up after him, went into the tomb and saw the linen cloths lying there, and also the veil which had been put over Jesus' head, not lying with the linen cloths, but still wrapped round and round in a place by itself. Then John, who had reached the tomb first, also went in, and saw this, yet struggled to comprehend, for they still had not yet mastered what was written of Christ, that he was to rise from the dead. The disciples returned home fearful of being discovered, whilst Mary Magdalen chose to remain outside the tomb, weeping. As she bent down, still weeping, and looked into the tomb; two angels clothed in white appeared sitting there, one at the head, and the other at the feet, where the body of Jesus had lain. They said to her, Woman, why art thou weeping? At first fearful, Mary replied, saying Because my Lord has gone, and I do not understand why you have taken him. Saying this, she turned round, and saw Jesus standing there, without knowing at first that it was him. Jesus said to her, Woman, why are you weeping? For whom are you searching? She supposed at first she was looking at another angel and said to him, If it is the will of God you must carry him away, pray tell me where thou has put his body, so that I might make my last farewell. Jesus then smiled and said to her, Mary can you not truly see me? And with that, her eyes were opened and she lept up to kiss his feet, saying Master. Then Jesus said to her, Do not cling to me thus. Return to my brethren and tell them what you have seen and that I am risen; and to remove into Galilee; where they shall see me there.

Offertory Antiphon

O God and Divine Creator of all Light and Redemption, who raised your son from death to become the Light of Redemption through his Ressurection, grant us the certainty of Trust in your Testament that we are redeemed through his life, sacrifice, death and resurrection. Through our Lord Jesus Christ, your Son, who lives and reigns with you in the unity of the Holy Spirit, one God, for ever and ever.

Prayer over the Offerings

May God and the Divine Creator accept and sanctify these humble gifts as symbols of the genuine personal offerings we make in respect and honour of your *Most Holy Feast of Resurrection Day*. Through Christ our Light and Saviour.

Communion Antiphon — Psalm 50: 4-6

He shall call to the heavens from above, and to the earth, that he may judge his people. Let all the saints be gathered unto him; and all who have sealed his new covenant of mercy and forgiveness by their sacrifice. For the heavens shall declare his glory according to his Will.

Prayer after Communion

Heavenly Father and God of all Light and Redemption, we give thanks for the nourishment of your heavenly gifts of the Bread and Fruits of Eternal Spiritual Life. May our earnest participation in your *Most Holy Feast of Resurrection Day* bring forth favourable blessings upon our lives, our community and your Holy Apostolic Universal Ecclesia. Through your Son our Lord Jesus Christ.

Title XVII – Proper of Mystery of Transcendent Christ

XVII.I – MYSTERY OF TRANSCENDENT CHRIST

1. The most *Sacred Transcendent Mystery of Christ*, is a fixed liturgical season of 44 days and a maximum of 8 holy feast days, beginning on the *Feast of Authentic Revelation* (first Sunday after Easter Sunday), then rising to the solemnity of *Ascension Day* (First Thursday within 40 days since Easter Sunday); and concluding on the solemnity of *Pentecost Sunday* (First Sunday within 50 days since Easter Sunday (end of May). Transcendent Mystery of Christ

   The liturgical season of the *Transcendent Mystery of Christ* exists as a time of deep learning and spiritual wisdom, courage and willingness to push beyond the boundaries of fear, prejudice, narrow judgement and selfishness to explore the supernatural mysteries of the transcendent Christ as the singularity of all human beings that have ever lived or will ever live, as the embodiment and personification of the Divine and son of the Divine and the extraordinary potential of all human beings.

2. The Sacred Colour for the liturgical season of the *Transcendent Mystery of Christ* is **gold**, representing the illumination of the Risen Christ with the gift of the Holy Spirit in the emancipation of the mind, spirit and body; and the renewal of the Universal Ecclesia. All Vestments used in relation to all feast days of the liturgical season and all dressings and fabrics used throughout the church during this period, should adhere to the colour of gold. Sacred Colour of Season and Vestments

---

XVII.II – FEAST OF AUTHENTIC REVELATION

1. The Universal Feast of Authentic Revelation, also known as Revelation Sunday is the first Sunday after Easter Sunday. Feast of Authentic Revelation

   Entrance Antiphon: Prov. 30: 5

   > Every word of authentic revelation is flawless. It is a shield for those who take refuge in God.

   Magisterium: Mark Mark 4:1-9

   > Jesus returned to the sea-side; and a great multitude gathered before him, so that he stepped into a boat, and sat there on the sea, while all the multitude sat on the land, at the sea's edge. And he taught them for a long time, but in parables, saying, Listen all of you, for here is the sower gone out to sow. And as he sowed, some grains chanced to fall beside the path, so that the birds came and ate them up. And others fell on rocky land, where the soil was shallow; these sprang up all at once, because they had not

sunk deep in the ground: and when the sun rose they were parched; for they had taken no root, and so they withered away. Some fell among thorns, so that the thorns grew up and smothered them, and they gave no crop. And others fell where the soil was good, and these sprouted and grew, and yielded a harvest; some of them thirtyfold, some sixtyfold, some a hundredfold. Listen, then all who have ears to hear.

Good News: Mark

Mark 4:10-20

When the disciples were sure they could speak with Jesus alone, they asked him the meaning of the parable of the sower and the seeds on different ground. And Jesus said to them, It is granted to you to understand the deepest secrets of knowledge of the kingdom of God, yet for others it shall remain as if simple stories: so they watch and watch, yet never see; and listen and listen, yet never hear, until the day they turn their back on sinfulness and ignorance and all is forgiven them. Jesus then said to them, Alas, even you do not understand this parable? And yet are you not the apostles who given the deepest secrets of knowledge to understand all parables? Therefore, what the sower sows is the word of our Father the Divine Creator. Those by the way-side are those who have the word sown in them, but no sooner have they heard it than greed and avarice comes, and takes away this word that was sown in their hearts. In the same way, those who take in the seed in rocky ground are those who entertain the word with joy as soon as they hear it, and yet have no foundation of learning in themselves; they last for a time, but afterwards, when tribulation or persecution arises over the word, their faith is soon shaken and lost. And there are others who take in the seed in the midst of thorns and weeds; they are those who hear the word, but allow the cares of this world and the deceitfulness of riches and their other addictions to smother the word, so that it remains fruitless. And those who take in the seed in good soil are those who hear the word and welcome it in their hearts and yield a harvest, one grain thirtyfold, one sixtyfold, one a hundredfold. Jesus then said to them, Is a lamp brought in to then be hidden away, or under a bed and not in the lamp-stand? What is hidden, is hidden only so that it may be revealed; what is kept secret, is kept secret only that it may come to light. Jesus then said to them, Listen, all you that have ears to hear; Look, all you that have eyes to see. Behold! The measure that you give is the measure you shall receive.

Offertory Antiphon

O God and Divine Creator of all Authentic Revelation, who revealed so much of your knowledge and true nature through your Son and your greatest prophets and saints, grant us the discernment and good sense to see and trust what is your authentic Revelation against those who would seek to beguile and betray each generation with false claims and fears; and that we may help others develop the same ability to distinguish the truth from falsities. Through our Lord Jesus Christ, your Son, who lives and reigns with you in the unity of the Holy Spirit, one God, for ever and ever.

Prayer over the Offerings

May God and the Divine Creator accept and sanctify these humble gifts as symbols of the genuine personal offerings we make in respect and honour of your *Holy Feast of Authentic Revelation*. Through Christ our Light and Saviour.

Communion Antiphon Psalm 66: 6

He turned the sea of iniquity into sacred land, so that all did survive the flood unto the New Kingdom; and here we do rejoice in him.

Prayer after Communion

Heavenly Father and God of all Authentic Revelation, we give thanks for the nourishment of your heavenly gifts of the Bread and Fruits of Eternal Spiritual Life. May our earnest participation in your *Holy Feast of Authentic Revelation* bring forth favourable blessings upon our lives, our community and your Holy Apostolic Universal Ecclesia. Through your Son our Lord Jesus Christ.

XVII.III – FEAST OF THE ARCHANGELS

1. The Universal Feast of the Archangels, also known as Angelic Sunday is the first Sunday after Revelation Sunday. Feast of the Archangels

Entrance Antiphon: Prov. 1: 2-6

To know wisdom and instruction; to perceive the words of understanding; To receive the instruction of wisdom, equality, discernment and justice; To give honestly to the less fortunate, to the young man knowledge and discretion. A wise man will hear, and will increase learning; and a man of understanding shall attain unto wise counsels: To understand a proverb, and the interpretation; the words of the wise, and their solemn sayings.

Magisterium: Mark

Mark 5:1-14

So Jesus and his disciples came to the shore of the northern inland sea, in the country of the Gerasa. And as soon as Jesus had disembarked, a strange and fearsome looking man came out from some nearby rock tombs uttering profanities and curses. Some locals came up to Jesus and told him this man be possessed and had made his dwelling among the tombs, and nobody could keep him bound any longer, even with chains. They said that he had been bound with fetters and chains often before, but had torn the chains apart and broken the fetters, and nobody had the strength to control him. Thus he spent all his time, night and day, among the tombs and the hills, crying aloud and cutting himself with stones. When Jesus approached him, the man ran up and fell at his feet, and cried with a loud voice, Why does thou torment me Nazarene? I adjure thee in the name of your God, let us be. Jesus then said, *Speak your name*, but the man fell into laughter. Jesus said to him again, *Speak your name*, or I shall condemn you by your silence. But the man fell silent. Finally Jesus in a loud voice called out, *In the name of God the Father and all the Angels and Saints in Heaven*, before the man cried out: My name is Legion. We are many. Do not force us from this world Christ. This be the only home we know. There, at the foot of the hills, was a great herd of swine feeding; and the spirits entreated him, Send us into the swine, let us make our lodging there. With that, Jesus gave them leave; and the unclean spirits came out, and went into the swine; whereupon the herd rushed down at full speed into the sea, some two thousand in number, and the sea drowned them. The swine-herders fled, and told their news in the city and in the country-side; so that many came out to see what had befallen; and when they reached the place, they found the former possessed man sitting there, clothed and restored to his wits, and they were overcome with fear.

Good News: Luke

Luke 7:24-35

Once the messengers of John the Baptist had gone away, Jesus took occasion to speak of the Baptist to the multitudes present and said, What was it that you expected to see when you went out into the wilderness in search of meaning? Was it a reed trembling in the wind? If not, then what was it you went out to see? Was it for a man clothed in the finest garments? Behold! those who are adorned in such expensive apparel and delicate lives are to be found in the palaces and courts of rulers. Who was it, then, that you went out to see? A prophet? Yes, and something much more than a prophet. This is the man of whom it is written in scripture, *Behold, I am sending before thee an angel of mine who is to prepare the way for thy coming*. For I say unto you, there is no greater prophet than John the Baptist among all the sons of women, save the one that is the least servant of all of the kingdom of God. It was not the academics and educated who listened to him, but the common folk that honoured the Will of the Divine Creator by receiving the gift of baptism through John. Yet the academics and doctors of law, by refusing to listen to and act upon the true word of God, have frustrated such Divine Mercy offered unto them. Jesus then said, Behold! How then shall I compare the men and women of this generation? What are they like? They are like children sitting in a marketplace, calling out to one another and saying, We have dedicated music to you, yet we have not danced; we have prepared a mourning to you, yet we have not wept. For John the Baptist came neither eating meat nor drinking strong wine; and yet this generation claims he was possessed by some demon. Yet, the Son of Man comes eating and drinking; and yet the wilfully ignorant and arrogant say he is a gluttonous fool and alcoholic; and a friend of criminals and the wicked! Verily, in the end, Divine Wisdom is vindicated by all her children.

Offertory Antiphon

O God and Divine Creator of all Heaven and Earth, continue to grant your angels the mandate to help and support your faithful, through your Divine Covenant, so that your One Holy and Apostolic Universal Ecclesia may be defended from all spiritual and temporal forces. Through our Lord Jesus Christ, your Son, who lives and reigns with you in the unity of the Holy Spirit, one God, for ever and ever.

Prayer over the Offerings

May God and the Divine Creator accept and sanctify these humble gifts as symbols of the genuine personal offerings we make in respect and honour of your *Holy Feast of the Archangels*. Through Christ our Light and Saviour.

Communion Antiphon — Psalm 91: 5-7

We shall not be afraid for any terror by night; nor for the arrow that may fly by day; nor for the pestilence that hides in darkness; nor for the destruction that condemns at noonday. Verily, though a thousand fall at thy side, and ten thousand at thy right hand; but no harm shall come to us.

Prayer after Communion

Heavenly Father and God of all Heaven and Earth, we give thanks for the nourishment of your heavenly gifts of the Bread and Fruits of Eternal Spiritual Life. May our earnest participation in your *Holy Feast of the Archangels* bring forth favourable blessings upon our lives, our community and your Holy Apostolic Universal Ecclesia. Through your Son our Lord Jesus Christ.

XVII.IV – FEAST OF THE APOSTLES

1. The Universal Feast of the Apostles, also known as Apostolic Sunday is the second Sunday after Revelation Sunday. — Feast of the Apostles

Entrance Antiphon: — Prov. 10: 25

When the storm and tempest have passed, the wicked shall be no more; yet the faithful stand firm forever.

Magisterium: Matthew — Matt.8:18-27

And now, seeing how great were the multitudes about him, Jesus gave the word for crossing to the other side of the sea. Whereupon one of the scribes of the temple came to him, and said, Master, I will follow thee wherever thou you going: But Jesus told him, *Foxes live with foxes; and birds of the air flock together; Thus all creatures are named for what are and known by the company they keep*. And another said to him, Lord, I wish to serve thee, but give me leave to go home and bury my father before I shall return. But Jesus said to him, *Alas, if you would truly serve me, then you would denounce your family on earth for your family in heaven and leave the dead to bury their dead.* Jesus then took ship, and his disciples followed him. And suddenly a great storm arose on the sea, so that the waves rose high over the ship; but he lay asleep. And his disciples came and roused him, crying, Lord, save us, we are sinking. But Jesus said to them, *Why are you faint-hearted, men of little faith?* Then he rose up, and checked the winds, and the sea, and there was deep calm. So that all asked in amazement, What kind of man is this, who is obeyed even by the winds and the sea?

Good News: Matthew — Matt. 10:1-15

Jesus called his remaining disciples to him, and gave them as Apostles the authority to cast out unclean spirits, and to heal every kind of disease and infirmity. These are the names of the twelve apostles; first, Simon, also called Peter, then his brother Andrew, James the son of Zebedee and his brother John, Philip and Bartholomew, Thomas and Matthew the publican, James the son of Alphaeus, and Thaddaeus, Simon the Cananean, and Judas Iscariot, the traitor. Jesus did then give them instructions, saying: Do not go into the places of those who do not profess to trust in the one God and seek to convert them, nor enter any city or town in strange lands. Go rather to the lands of the scattered flock that belong to the People of God and share with them that the true Kingdom of Heaven is at hand. Behold! You are empowered to heal the sick, raise the dead from perdition, cleanse the lepers and cast out unclean spirits: Thus, give as you have received such sacraments, without payment. Provide neither gold nor silver for your purses, nor scripts of credit or promise for your journey. Bring neither an extra coat or shoes, or staff; for the good labourer shall be confident of his sustenance. Whenever you enter a city or a village, enquire who in it is the most humble and heroically virtuous and make your lodging there until you continue your journey. When you enter such a house, you are to make blessings upon it and its inhabitants. If the house is worthy, let your peace come upon it; but if it be not worthy, let your peace return to you. And whosoever shall not receive you, nor hear your words, when you depart out of that house, or city or village, shake off the dust from your feet. Verily, I say unto you, the lands of Sodom and Gomorrha shall appear to have been more tolerable than for such a place in the days of judgement.

Offertory Antiphon

O God and Divine Creator of all Faiths, who empowered the Apostles through your Holy Spirit to be transformed from men and women of fear and doubt, to titans and heroes of history, grant us the illumination of the Holy Spirit in our lives so that we may overcome any doubt or fear in our trust in your Divine Mission and our eternal life. Through our Lord Jesus Christ, your Son, who lives and reigns with you in the unity of the Holy Spirit, one God, for ever and ever.

Prayer over the Offerings

May God and the Divine Creator accept and sanctify these humble gifts as symbols of the genuine personal offerings we make in respect and honour of your *Holy Feast of the Apostles*. Through Christ our Light and Saviour.

Communion Antiphon — Psalm 25: 10-11

The humble will he guide in judgement: and the merciful will he teach his way. All the paths of God are mercy and love unto such as keep his covenant and his testimonies.

Prayer after Communion

Heavenly Father and God of all Faiths, we give thanks for the nourishment of your heavenly gifts of the Bread and Fruits of Eternal Spiritual Life. May our earnest participation in your *Holy Feast of the Apostles* bring forth favourable blessings upon our lives, our community and your Holy Apostolic Universal Ecclesia. Through your Son our Lord Jesus Christ.

XVII.V – FEAST OF THE DISCIPLES

1. The Universal Feast of the Disciples is the third Sunday after Revelation Sunday. — Feast of the Disciples

Entrance Antiphon: — Prov. 13: 8

A treasure in this world holds a rich man to ransom, whereas one without such wealth cannot be controlled by such fear of loss.

Magisterium: Matthew — Matt.9:9-13

As he passed further on his way, Jesus saw a man called Matthew sitting at work in the customs-house, and said to him, Follow me; and Matthew rose from his place and followed him. And afterwards, when he was taking a meal in the house, many publicans and sinners were to be found at table with him and his disciples. The doctors of law saw this, and asked his disciples, How comes it that your master eats with publicans and sinners? Jesus heard it, and said, It is not those who are in health that have need of the physician, it is those who are sick. Go home and find out what the words mean, It is mercy that wins favour with me, not sacrifice. I have come to call sinners, not the just.

Good News: Matthew Matt.10:16-33

Jesus said, Remember, I send you forth like sheep in the midst of wolves: be you therefore wise as serpents and harmless in appearance as doves. Beware of those who claim to be experts of law and doctrine; for they will betray you over to their courts of judgement; and have you scourged in their temples of false piety. For you shall be brought before governors and false priests on my account, that they might trick you into giving false testimony against me and the people. But when they deliver you up, be not anxious as to how or what you shall say or how to say it, for the words you need shall be given unto you when the time comes. Through a true heart, it is not you who speaks, it shall be the true Spirit of the Law of the Father that shall speak through you in their false courts. Brothers will be falsely given up to condemnation by their brothers; and children shall be wickedly betrayed by their father and mothers; and even disturbed children will falsely rise up against their parents and guardians and will cause great torment. And you will be hated and mocked by many people, because you stand resolute to my true words. Such men and women of heroic virtue are already saved, who endure to the last. And if you are persecuted in one place, then take refuge in another. I promise you, the Son of Man will come before your mission unto all the cities and towns of the People of God is fulfilled. A disciple is no better than his master, a servant than his lord. It is enough that the disciple be like his master, the servant like his lord. If they have blasphemed and cursed the master of the house to be Beelzebub, then how much worse shall they seek to curse and shame those of the same house? Do not, then, be afraid of them. What is veiled will all be revealed, what is hidden will all be known. What I have said to you under cover of darkness, you are to utter in the light of day; what has been whispered in your ears, you are to proclaim on the house-tops. And there is no need to fear those who seek to kill the body, but have no means of killing the mind and soul; but rather guard against one who speaks in such falsities to infect and condemn the mind and soul to its own hell. Are not sparrows sold two for a penny? And yet not one of them shall fall to the ground without the presence of your Father and Divine Creator. Verily, the very hairs of your head are all numbered and valued. Fear not therefore, for you are greatly loved by God. Whosoever therefore shall confess my true words before men and women, shall I then confess and stand as their surety before my Father in Heaven. And whoever corrupts my words and disowns me before men and women, shall I then disown before our Heavenly Father.

Offertory Antiphon

O God and Divine Creator of all Courage and Compassion, grant us the heart of your disciples, to see Christ in the face of every person we meet who is suffering or in need and the courage to cross the road and make a real difference in the lives of others, even if others tell us to walk by and ignore the suffering and pain in our communities. Through our Lord Jesus Christ, your Son, who lives and reigns with you in the unity of the Holy Spirit, one God, for ever and ever.

Prayer over the Offerings

May God and the Divine Creator accept and sanctify these humble gifts as symbols of the genuine personal offerings we make in respect and honour of your *Holy Feast of the Disciples*. Through Christ our Light and Saviour.

Communion Antiphon Psalm 46: 1-2

God is our refuge and strength, in times of trouble. We shall not fear, though the earth trembles and the mountains be carried into the midst of the sea.

Prayer after Communion

Heavenly Father and God of all Courage and Compassion, we give thanks for the nourishment of your heavenly gifts of the Bread and Fruits of Eternal Spiritual Life. May our earnest participation in your *Holy Feast of the Disciples* bring forth favourable blessings upon our lives, our community and your Holy Apostolic Universal Ecclesia. Through your Son our Lord Jesus Christ.

XVII.VI – FEAST OF ST. PETER, ROCK OF AGES

1. The Universal Feast of St. Peter, Rock of Ages, also known as *Foundation Stone Sunday* is the fourth Sunday after Revelation Sunday.

Feast of St. Peter, Rock of Ages

Entrance Antiphon:

Prov. 15: 25

The Lord tears down the house of the proud, but he keeps the widow's boundary stones in place.

Magisterium: Matthew

Matt.14:22-33

Jesus prevailed upon his disciples to take ship and cross to the other side before him, leaving him alone to send the multitudes home. When he had finished sending them home, he went up by himself on to the hill-side to pray alone as twilight had come. Meanwhile the disciples were already half-way across the sea, hard put to it by a howling wind and rising waves against them. As the disciples prayed for deliverance, by the fourth quarter of the night, Jesus came to them, walking upon the sea. When they saw him walking on the sea, the disciples were terrified and said, It is an apparition, and cried out for fear. But all at once Jesus spoke to them and said, *Take courage and have no fear, for you called and I am with thee*. And Peter answered him, Master, if it is thyself, bid me come to thee over the water. Jesus replied, *Come*; and Peter let himself down out of the ship and walked over the water to reach Jesus. Then, seeing how strong the wind was, he lost courage and began to sink; whereupon he cried aloud, Lord, save me. And Jesus at once stretched out his hand and caught hold of him, saying to him, *Why did thou hesitate, man of little faith?* So they went on board the ship, and thereupon the wind dropped. And the crew of the ship came and said, falling at his feet, You are indeed the Son of Man.

Good News: Matthew

Matt. 16:13-26

Then Jesus came into the neighbourhood of Caesarea Philippi; and there he asked his disciples, saying, What do men say of the Son of Man? Who do they think he is? They replied and said to him, Some say you are John the Baptist, others say you are Elijah, others again think you are Jeremiah or one of the other prophets. Jesus then said to them, And what of you all? Who do you think that I am? Then Simon Peter answered, saying, You are Christ, the Son of the living God. And Jesus answered Peter, saying, Blessed are you, Simon son of Jonah. For it was not flesh and blood that revealed this to thee, but the Spirit of my Heavenly Father. Behold! Verily, I say unto thee Simon, that you are the one I have called Peter meaning rock; and upon this rock I will build my Ecclesia as my living body; and no kingdom or force or army shall prevail against it. For I will give unto thee the very keys to united Kingdom of Heaven; and whatsoever you shall bind on Earth shall be bound in all of Heaven; and whatsoever you shall loose on Earth shall be loosed in Heaven. Jesus then strictly forbade the disciples from speaking that he was the Christ until the appointed time. From that time onwards Jesus began to make it known to his disciples that he must go up to Jerusalem, and there, with much ill usage from the chief priests and lawyers and scribes, must be put to death, and rise again on the third day. Whereupon Simon Peter, drawing him to his side, began remonstrating with him; Never, Lord, he said; no such thing shall befall thee. Whereupon Jesus did turn round and say to Simon Peter, Get behind me adversary! You shall not be the stone that blocks my path. For these thoughts of yours are of a man and not Divine. Jesus then said to the disciples, If any man has a mind to come my way, let him renounce self, and take up his cross, and follow me. The man who tries to save his life shall lose it; it is the man who loses his life for my sake that will secure it. How is a man the better for it, if he gains the whole world at the cost of losing his own soul? For a man's soul, what price can be high enough?

Offertory Antiphon

O God and Divine Creator of all Compassion and Greatness, who called upon Saint Peter to willingly be the foundation stone upon which your church will stand for all ages, grant us the perseverance and humility to listen to your calling in how we may best be of service to our family, our community and our planet. Through our Lord Jesus Christ, your Son, who lives and reigns with you in the unity of the Holy Spirit, one God, for ever and ever.

Prayer over the Offerings

May God and the Divine Creator accept and sanctify these humble gifts as symbols of the genuine personal offerings we make in respect and honour of your *Holy Feast of St. Peter, Rock of Ages*. Through Christ our Light and Saviour.

Communion Antiphon — Psalm 18: 3

The Lord my God is my rock, my fortress and my saviour. He is the foundation stone of my protection. He is my shield and the power that saves me; and my place of sanctuary.

Prayer after Communion

Heavenly Father and God of all Compassion and Greatness, we give thanks for the nourishment of your heavenly gifts of the Bread and Fruits of Eternal Spiritual Life. May our earnest participation in your *Holy Feast of St. Peter, Rock of Ages* bring forth favourable blessings upon our lives, our community and your Holy Apostolic Universal Ecclesia. Through your Son our Lord Jesus Christ.

XVII.VII – FEAST OF THE ASCENSION OF CHRIST

1. The Universal Feast of the Ascension of Christ, also known as Ascension Day is the Thursday approximately forty days after Easter Sunday. Feast of the Ascension of Christ

Entrance Antiphon: — Prov. 8: 12

Wisdom dwells together with prudence and the possession of knowledge with discretion.

Magisterium: Matthew — Matt 23:1-12

Jesus addressed himself to the multitudes, and to his disciples and said, Behold! The priests, scribes and doctors of law have established themselves higher than even the place that Moses used to teach. Do not abandon your faith in law or justice; but be careful what they tell you. For they worship and trust nothing and will tell you one thing and do another. Verily, they impose such burdens upon the shoulders of honest and hard working men and women, that too heavy to be borne; yet they themselves curse heaven by falsely claiming a birth right to not stir a finger to lift them or bestow any mercy or forgiveness. They act, always, so as to be the enslavers of the people of God. Yet, they boldly write their profanities and heresies within the texts they carry, and deep within the hem of their garments. Their heart is set on taking the chief places at table of peace while being the source of sowing war. They yearn to have their hands kissed and being called great titles among fellow men, while they curse them as beasts and creatures in secret. Verily, none shall have the birthright to claim to be king, but one who is proven the living embodiment of humility, virtue and courage; and None are to claim the title of Master, unless they have first experienced enough failure and trials of life to be able to truly stand in the shoes of the least of their brethren; and None may be called father but one who sacrifices his life in service of mercy, love and compassion to all others as his children. Behold! Among you, the greatest of all is to be the servant of all; for the man who exalts himself will be humbled, and the man who humbles himself will be exalted.

Good News: Acts Acts 1:2-12

Until the appointed day when the Christ was taken up to united Heaven, he did give clear commandments through the Holy Spirit unto those whom he had chosen. He revealed many infallible proofs of his living presence after his period of his terrible suffering; and throughout the course of the forty days did reveal further revelations as to the Kingdom of Heaven and upon the Earth. Christ, being assembled together with them, did say: *Do not fear, nor seek to escape into the wilderness away, but remain in the city and the presence of your enemies. Behold! the Father is sending you a great gift, in fulfilment of the promise that I have spoken. For whereas John baptised with water, you shall be baptised with the illumination of the Holy Spirit not many days from hence.* The Companions of Jesus did then ask saying, Lord, does this mean you now seek to destroy this world and restore the dominions of God to the People? But Christ said, *It is not for you to know the times or the seasons whereby the Heavenly Father of all Creation does put in motion through his own authority. It is enough you shall soon receive the great gift and powers of the Holy Spirit with all courage and discernment; and shall go forth as witnesses of the Good News from Jerusalem unto all the regions and then to the ends of the Earth. Amen.* When he had said this, they saw him lifted up, and a cloud caught him away from their sight. And as they strained their eyes towards heaven, to watch his journey, all at once two men in white garments were standing at their side. One of the angels did then speak and said, Sons of Light, why do you stand here waiting and looking to the sky? He who is, who was and who will ever be has returned to Heaven; and by the Covenant of Heaven and unity of all his people you shall know his return. After the angels had gone, the disciples agreed to overcome their fears and return to Jerusalem as they had been instructed.

Offertory Antiphon

O God and Divine Creator of all Truth and Covenants, who promised through before the ascension of your Son, that he would one day physically return to us, though not in the same way or time or place as we expected, grant us the clearness of thought and vision of sight that we may truly comprehend your Divine Covenant in fulfilment of your promise of the return of Christ through the restoration of His Divine Liturgy and the New Evangelisation of His Church as His Living Body on Earth for ever and ever. Through our Lord Jesus Christ, your Son, who lives and reigns with you in the unity of the Holy Spirit, one God, for ever and ever.

Prayer over the Offerings

May God and the Divine Creator accept and sanctify these humble gifts as symbols of the genuine personal offerings we make in respect and honour of your *Holy Feast of the Ascension of Christ*. Through Christ our Light and Saviour.

Communion Antiphon — Psalm 67: 5-6

Let the people praise thee, O God; let all the people praise thee. Then shall the earth yield her increase; and God shall bless us through our unity.

Prayer after Communion

Heavenly Father and God of all Truth and Covenants, we give thanks for the nourishment of your heavenly gifts of the Bread and Fruits of Eternal Spiritual Life. May our earnest participation in your *Holy Feast of the Ascension of Christ* bring forth favourable blessings upon our lives, our community and your Holy Apostolic Universal Ecclesia. Through your Son our Lord Jesus Christ.

XVII.VIII – FEAST OF THE NEW EVANGELISATION

1. The Universal Feast of the New Evangelisation, also known as Evangelisation Sunday is the Sunday before Pentecost. Feast of the New Evangelisation

Entrance Antiphon: Prov. 3: 13-14

Blessed are those who find wisdom, those who gain understanding, for it is more profitable than silver and yields better returns than gold.

Magisterium: Luke Luke 7: 1-10

When Jesus had finished speaking with the people, he and the disciples travelled north to the Roman garrison town of Capernaum near the edge of the inland sea in Galilee. When Jesus arrived, the Centurion of the garrison, sent two of his servants to plead for him to come and heal the head steward of his house, saying though he be a Roman, and a symbol of the oppression of the people, he was fair and just to all men. But when Jesus was nearing the Roman barracks, the Centurion himself came out and fell to his face in front of Jesus, saying: Do not put thyself to any trouble, Lord, he said; I am not worthy to receive thee under my roof. Jesus called for him to get up, before the Centurion continued and said, I did not presume to come to thee myself, that is why I sent my servants. For I trust that my servant will be healed if thou will only speak a word of command. I too know what it is to obey authority; I have soldiers under me, and I say, Go, to one man, and he goes, or, Come, to another, and he comes, or, Do this, to my servant, and he does it. When Jesus heard these words, he embraced the Centurion, before turning to multitude and said, Verily, I have not found faith like this, even midst the holiest shrines. And as Jesus was speaking, a messenger came to summons Centurion back to his house, and when he returned, he found the servant who had been sick fully recovered.

Good News: John John 17: 1- 19

Thus Jesus spoke to his disciples, and then, lifting up his eyes to heaven, he said, Heavenly Father, my hour is soon to come. Give strength unto your Son, so that he may honour and give glory unto thee. Verily, just as you have given him the form of living flesh, so that he should reveal the gift of eternal life to as many of the living as may listen, the gift of eternal life is found in trusting absolutely that you are the only true God and Divine Creator of all existence and that these be your words as witnessed by your son Jesus Christ, whom you sent. For I have glorified thee upon the Earth. I have revealed your works of mercy and justice as you anointed me to do. Now, O Father, grant me your mercy and strength in the same glory that I had with thee before even the world began. For I have Revealed your true nature of love and forgiveness to all the men and women you entrusted to me, chosen out of the world. All belong to thee and through thy gift have become a singular embodiment in me and I have kept true to your word. Now, they have learned to discern all the gifts you have given through me as coming from thee. I have given them the Good News that you gave to me; and they have received it, and recognise it for truth that such Divine Wisdom comes from thee; and have found faith to trust that it was thou who did send me. I pray not for the present world, but for all those living beings in it that belong to thee. For all I have is yours and all they are is personified in me, and through their heroic virtue and unity your glory is achieved. Now as the hour comes quickly that I shall be no more in the world, they shall remain in the world as witnesses to thee. Father of all Creation, keep them true to thy Will, that none may be condemned or lost, so that all scripture might be fulfilled. As long as I was with them, it was for me to keep them true to thy name, thy gift to me; and I have watched over them, so that only one has been lost, he whom perdition claims for its own, in fulfilment of the scripture. Now, as I soon return to thee; and while I am still in the world I am telling them this, so that there be no fear or misunderstanding, but that they might have joy fulfilled in themselves. I have given them the message of your Good News; and the world does hate them, because they are not of the world, even as I am not of the world. I pray not that you take them away from this world, but that you keep them safe from the corruptions of evil. Verily, they do not belong to the world, as I, too, do not belong to the world. Keep them sanctified, then, through the truth; for it is thy word that is truth. Thou did send me into the world on thy errand, and I now do send them into the world on your errand; and I affirm my mission before that hour, so that all people may be saved through the truth.

Offertory Antiphon

O God and Divine Creator of all Mission and Renewal, who through the working of the Holy Spirit did command all faithful clergy of all Christian denominations to unite and renew the faith through a Divine Mission of New Evangelisation, grant us the inspiration and enthusiasm to participate in a meaningful way to the renewal of the Universal Ecclesia with the Living Liturgy of Christ. Through our Lord Jesus Christ, your Son, who lives and reigns with you in the unity of the Holy Spirit, one God, for ever and ever.

Prayer over the Offerings

May God and the Divine Creator accept and sanctify these humble gifts as symbols of the genuine personal offerings we make in respect and honour of your *Holy Feast of the New Evangelisation.* Through Christ our Light and Saviour.

Communion Antiphon — Psalm 33:4-6

For the word of God is just; and all his works are done in truth. He loves mercy and forgiveness for the earth is full of the goodness of God. By the mind of God were the heavens made; and by his breath all that exists therein.

Prayer after Communion

Heavenly Father and God of all Mission and Renewal, we give thanks for the nourishment of your heavenly gifts of the Bread and Fruits of Eternal Spiritual Life. May our earnest participation in your *Holy Feast of the New Evangelisation* bring forth favourable blessings upon our lives, our community and your Holy Apostolic Universal Ecclesia. Through your Son our Lord Jesus Christ.

XVII.IX – PENTECOST SUNDAY

1. The Pentecost Sunday is the fifty days after Easter Sunday. — Pentecost Sunday

Entrance Antiphon: — Prov. 29: 18

Where there is no trust in authentic revelation, people cast off all restraint; but blessed is the one who heeds wisdom's instruction.

Magisterium: Luke — Luke 24: 36-49

While the disciples were speaking of all that had happened, the Risen Christ appeared in the flesh and stood in the midst of them, and said, *Peace be with you. Do not be in fear. Peace I give unto all of you.* Yet, the disciples could not contain themselves and cowered down, full of fear, thinking they were witnessing an apparition. Christ then said, *Why are you so troubled? Why do you permit any such doubt to arise in your hearts? See the wounds of my hands and feet. Be totally assured, that it is myself. Touch me, see me as your own evidence. For a spirit has not flesh and bones, as you see that I have.* As he spoke in this manner, he revealed his hands and his feet and allowed the disciples to touch him. Yet many still hesitated to trust their own eyes, ears or minds, so Christ said: *Have you anything here to eat?* So they put before him a piece of roast fish, and a honeycomb; and after blessing the meal, he took these and ate in their presence and shared his meal with them. Christ then said, *Verily, this is what I revealed to you, while I still walked in your company; how all that was written of me in the scripture and laws of the prophets, and in the psalms, must be fulfilled.* He then enlightened their minds further, to make them understand the scriptures. Jesus said, *So it was written that Christ as the Paschal Lamb should suffer, and should rise again from the dead on the third day; so that the transgressions of humanity of the past, the present and future are forgiven by God the Divine Father. Of this, you are the first witnesses. Behold, I am sending down upon you the gift which was promised by my Father; and you must wait in the city until you are clothed with such power from on high.*

Good News: Acts Acts 2:1 - 4

When the day of Pentecost came round, while the Apostles were all gathered together in unity of purpose, all at once a thunderous sound came from the heavens and a strong wind began blowing, and filled the whole house where they were sitting. Then appeared to them
a blinding ball of light, as bright as the sun, that parted and came to rest above each of them, like tongues of fire. And each of them were all filled with the Holy Spirit, and began to speak in strange languages and great wisdom, as the Spirit gave utterance to each of them.

Offertory Antiphon

O God and Divine Creator of all Light and Illumination, grant us the gift of the Holy Spirit in our lives, that we may be living beacons of your faith and renewal so that all may see the wonder of your unity of all Christianity as the Living Body of your Son on Earth. Through our Lord Jesus Christ, your Son, who lives and reigns with you in the unity of the Holy Spirit, one God, for ever and ever.

Prayer over the Offerings

May God and the Divine Creator accept and sanctify these humble gifts as symbols of the genuine personal offerings we make in respect and honour of your *Holy Feast of Pentecost Sunday*. Through Christ our Light and Saviour.

Communion Antiphon

Psalm 51: 10-12

Create in me a clean heart, O God; and renew the good spirit within me. Cast me not away from thy presence; and take not thy holy spirit from me. Restore unto me the joy of thy salvation; and uphold me with thy light.

Prayer after Communion

Heavenly Father and God of all Light and Illumination, we give thanks for the nourishment of your heavenly gifts of the Bread and Fruits of Eternal Spiritual Life. May our earnest participation in your *Holy Feast of Pentecost Sunday* bring forth favourable blessings upon our lives, our community and your Holy Apostolic Universal Ecclesia. Through your Son our Lord Jesus Christ.

Title XVIII – Proper of Mystery of Sacred Heart of Christ

XVIII.I – MYSTERY OF SACRED HEART OF CHRIST

1. The most *Sacred Heart Mystery of Christ*, is a fixed liturgical season of 44 days and a maximum of 7 holy feast days, beginning on the feast of the *Living Body of Christ*, also known as *Corpus Christi Sunday* (first Sunday after Pentecost Sunday), then rising to the solemnity of *Holy Matrimony Day* (4th Sunday after Corpus Christi); and concluding on the solemnity of *Sacred Heart Sunday* (last Sunday of June). Sacred Heart Mystery of Christ

The liturgical season of the *Sacred Heart Mystery of Christ* exists as a time of celebration and joy at the abundance of love of the Divine and the institutions of the sacraments at the heart of our society, exemplified by the sacrament of Holy Matrimony between men and women.

The Sacred Colour for the liturgical season of the *Sacred Heart Mystery of Christ* is **pink**, representing the People of God as the Universal Ecclesia as the living flesh and living Body of Christ. All Vestments used in relation to all feast days of the liturgical season and all dressings and fabrics used throughout the church during this period, should adhere to the colour of pink.

XVIII.II – FEAST OF THE LIVING BODY OF CHRIST

1. The Universal Feast of the Living Body of Christ, also known as Corpus Christi Sunday is the 1st Sunday after Pentecost Sunday. Feast of the Living Body of Christ

Entrance Antiphon: Prov. 1: 33

> Those who hearken unto the Crucified and Living Christ shall dwell safely, and be quiet from fear of evil.

Magisterium: John John 9:1-12

> And Jesus saw, as he passed on his way, a beggar who had been blind from his birth. Whereupon his disciples asked him, Master, was this man guilty of sin, or was it his parents, that he should have been born blind? Jesus answered, *Verily, No man be afflicted by the sins of his parents. Behold! Such a doctrine be an abomination against God. Instead, it was so that the actions of God might declare themselves to others through him. While the Light in this world lasts, I must work in the service of him who sent me; the night is coming, when there is no working any more. As long as I am in the world, I am the Light of the World.* With that, he spat on

the ground, and made clay with the spittle; then he spread the clay on the eyes of the blind beggar, and said to him, Away with thee, and by your own faith then wash thyself in the purification pools. So he went to the purification pools of the temple and washed himself and his full sight and strength was restored. And the people in the temple who witnessed the miracle were in awe and asked him, Are you not that blind beggar that sat on the street corner begging for alms? And the man replied, Yes, I am he. They then asked him, By what miracle that thy eyes have been opened and your strength restored? And he answered, By faith in words of the man called Jesus, who anointed my eyes and called me to wash in these clear pools. Yet upon news of what had happened, the priests of the temple ordered the man given his sight and dignity be arrested, for defiling the purifications that the priests and doctors of the law regarded their doctrines and rules as more sacred than the wonders of God.

Good News: John

John 6:35-59

The disciples said to him, My Lord, help us that we may better understand. And Jesus said unto them, *Behold I am the bread of life: He that comes to me shall never hunger; and he that trusts in me shall never thirst. But Lo, I say unto you, that you have seen me and my works and still do not fully trust in me. All that the Father has entrusted to me is kept safe for thee, and all who come to me I will never abandon. For I came down from heaven, not only of my own will, but the will of him who sent me. And it is by the will of the Father of all Creation and Existence that I have been sent, so that none be lost, but all be given eternal life by the sacrifice upon my last day. And this be the Will of Light of him that sent me, that everyone who trusts in the Son, even if they do not see him, may have everlasting life and I will raise everyone up at the last days of this world.* The zealous followers of the customs and traditions then began to complain between themselves, because of the words that Jesus had said that he is the true bread that comes down from heaven. And they said to one another, Is this not just a man? the son of a carpenter? whose father and mother we know? How then can he account for his words when he said, I came down from heaven? Jesus therefore answered them, saying, *Murmur not behind my back. Most solemnly I tell you, No one comes to me, except by the Will of the Father who has sent me, so that I may raise them up by my last day. For it is written by the prophets, And they shall be all taught the true knowledge of God. Behold! Every man and woman therefore that shall come to know the authentic laws of the Divine and the true nature of God our Father, it shall be because Christ is their teacher. No living being can seek and find the true knowledge of the Father, except from he that is the singular embodiment of God the Father. Verily, I say unto you again, one who trusts in my words completely shall have everlasting life, for I am that bread of life. Your fathers, who ate manna in the desert, died none the less; yet the bread that comes down from heaven is such that one who eats of it never dies. I am the singular embodiment as the bread of knowledge that has come down from heaven. If anyone eats of this bread, he shall live for ever. And now, what be the symbol of the living bread that I am called to soon give? It is my flesh that I give for the life of the world and to end all blood sacrifices.* The followers of the orthodox and customary ways since the times of the Persians then fell into a rage, saying? How can this man claim to be the lamb of god? Or that he shall end the customs of blood sacrifice of the paschal feast? Whereupon Jesus said to them, Verily, I say unto you, unless one makes their own life and works a worthy sacrifice according to the laws of the Father, then you shall have no eternal life in spirit. *Verily, one who sacrifices the flesh and blood of others shall not enjoy the fruits of eternal life. Nor shall he be raised up at the last day. For the practice of flesh and blood sacrifice is an abomination before the true laws of God the Father of all Creation. Yet he who eats of my knowledge, and drinks of my truth, lives continually in me, and I in him. As is it the living Father of all existence that has sent me and I live according to the true laws of the Father, anyone who so eats of my knowledge does so by living life according to my knowledge. Such is the bread of knowledge of Divine Law that has come down from heaven. For it is not as it was with your fathers, who ate manna and died none the less. For anyone who eats this bread will live eternally.*

Offertory Antiphon

O God and Divine Creator of all Prophecy and Fulfilment, who promised at the end of times that the world would be reborn and renewed an the presence of you Son will be with us forever, grant us the strength and vision to complete your Divine Mission of unifying all Christians, whilst respecting their unique culture and historical differences into the one Living Body of Christ. Through our Lord Jesus Christ, your Son, who lives and reigns with you in the unity of the Holy Spirit, one God, for ever and ever.

Prayer over the Offerings

May God and the Divine Creator accept and sanctify these humble gifts as symbols of the genuine personal offerings we make in respect and honour of your *Holy Feast of the Living Body of Christ*. Through Christ our Light and Saviour.

Communion Antiphon — Psalm 56: 4

In God I will praise his word; in God I have put my trust; for I will not fear what flesh can do unto me.

Prayer after Communion

Heavenly Father and God of all Prophecy and Fulfilment, we give thanks for the nourishment of your heavenly gifts of the Bread and Fruits of Eternal Spiritual Life. May our earnest participation in your *Holy Feast of the Living Body of Christ* bring forth favourable blessings upon our lives, our community and your Holy Apostolic Universal Ecclesia. Through your Son our Lord Jesus Christ.

XVIII.III – FEAST OF DIVINE LOVE

1. The Universal Feast of Divine Love is the first Sunday after Corpus Christi. — Feast of Divine Love

Entrance Antiphon: — Prov. 10: 12

Hatred is the fuel of conflict, but true love is the balm that heals even the deepest wounds.

Magisterium: John — John 9:13-23

The temple guard now brought the previously blind and frail beggar before the priests, scribes and doctors of the law of the Temple, and they said to him: Surely, you must know your offences as to your imprisonment? For you broke our laws on our ordained holy day of the week and defiled the purification pools of the temple. The man replied, I do not know your laws, because you refuse to teach me and all those you choose to discard as beneath you, so how can you justify charging me for breaking laws, I myself have never been allowed to see by you, because you refused to tell me what they are? Frustrated, the priests then asked him. Did this man Jesus then order you to defile the laws and doctrines of our temple? Say this and you a free of any culpability. But the man replied, he did not command me, only that I show my faith in God. Whereupon an argument erupted between the priests and the doctors of law of the temple, saying, This man Jesus can be no messenger from God, for he does not observe our laws and doctrines. Others asked, How can a man do such miracles like this and yet be a sinner. Thus there was a division of opinion among them until they questioned the former blind man again, saying, What account does thou give of him? Did he say unto you he was Christ? or some messenger of God? The man said, He did not. But his actions speak louder than words, for truly he must be a prophet on account of the wonders some of you have even witnessed. Division again erupted among the priests until it was agreed to call for the parents of the man who had recovered his sight, before they would trust even themselves his story that he had been blind, and that he had had his sight restored to him. And they questioned them, Is this your son, who, you say, was born blind? How comes it, then, that he is now able to see? His parents answered them, We can tell you that this is our son, and that he was blind when he was born; we cannot tell how he is able to see now; we have no means of knowing who opened his eyes for him. Ask the man himself; he is of age; let him tell you his own story. The priests sent the parents away, but kept the man prisoner, for fear now that news of the miracles of Jesus would spread further. And the priests, scribes and doctors of law agreed among themselves, that anyone who acknowledged Jesus as the Christ, or defied any of their doctrines, should be forbidden from the temple.

Good News: John John 3:16-21

Jesus said, For God our Father of all Creation so loves the world, that He has offered up his only-begotten Son to the people as the last paschal lamb, so that all who trust in the true laws and knowledge of the Divine shall have eternal life. Verily, God did not send the Son of Man into the world to condemn life; but so that all living beings be reborn anew through him into a new world of peace and unity. He that trusts in him, can never be condemned; but he who does not trust in the true revelations of God condemns themselves, because they deny the presence and authority of the Son of Man. For this be the sign of self condemnation: that the Light comes into the world, yet some men love the darkness more than the light, because their deeds do not cease to be evil. For everyone that continues to do evil hates the Light and turns away from the Light out of fear and ignorance that they shall be condemned for eternity for their past deeds. But he that knows and lives the truth comes to the Light, so that new good deeds may be made manifest and any past evil deeds be forgiven and washed clean before the eyes of God.

Offertory Antiphon

O God and Divine Creator of all Love and Mercy, who demonstrates every day and in every generation your unconditional Love and Mercy upon the human species and life on Earth, grant us the gift of an open heart and mind to the needs of others, that through love we may in a concrete and meaningful way heal, inspire and improve the quality and standard of life for all within our communities, not simply a precious few. Through our Lord Jesus Christ, your Son, who lives and reigns with you in the unity of the Holy Spirit, one God, for ever and ever.

Prayer over the Offerings

May God and the Divine Creator accept and sanctify these humble gifts as symbols of the genuine personal offerings we make in respect and honour of your *Holy Feast of Divine Love*. Through Christ our Light and Saviour.

Communion Antiphon — Psalm 5: 12

For all those who trust in God there is joy and everlasting triumph; welcome protection they have from thee, those who are true lovers of thy truth.

Prayer after Communion

Heavenly Father and God of all Love and Mercy, we give thanks for the nourishment of your heavenly gifts of the Bread and Fruits of Eternal Spiritual Life. May our earnest participation in your *Holy Feast of Divine Love* bring forth favourable blessings upon our lives, our community and your Holy Apostolic Universal Ecclesia. Through your Son our Lord Jesus Christ.

XVIII.IV – FEAST OF HOLY UNION

1. The Universal Feast of Holy Union is the second Sunday after Corpus Christi. Feast of Holy Union

Entrance Antiphon: Prov. 12: 26

The righteous choose their friends carefully, but the way of the wicked leads them astray.

Magisterium: John John 9:24-34

The priests and doctors of the law summonses temple guard to bring to them the now healthy man who had once been blind and frail, and said to him, Friend we do not wish to torment you further. We know this man Jesus is a sinner and has no respect for our laws or customs. Speak plainly about him and then be on your way. The man replied, Sinner or not all I know is that once I was blind, and now I can see; I was lame and know I can walk. One of the priests then asked him, saying, But what was it he did to thee? By what means of spell did he open thy eyes? And he answered them, I have told you already, and you would not listen to me. Why must you hear it over again? Would you too become his disciples? Upon this, they covered him with abuse, saying, only fools have such faith in men, no matter what they do. We are disciples of the laws of Moses. For we are certain that God spoke to Moses, yet we know nothing of this man that does not obey our doctrines, nor whence he comes. The man then answered, I be not an educated man like all of you, but these things I know: You say you cannot tell when he comes, and yet he opened my eyes and restored my strength; and I have heard you say repeatedly that by your laws and doctrines, God does not answer the prayers of sinners, but condemns them to damnation; and that it is only when a man is devout and follows your doctrines that his prayers shall be answered. Yet that a man should open the eyes of one born blind is something unheard of since the world began. Verily, if this man did not come from God, he would have no powers at all. Upon such a speech, all the priests, scribes and doctors of the law were astounded before they said, Are we to have lessons from thee, all steeped in sin from thy birth? And they cast him out from their presence and set him free.

Good News: Mark

Mark 12:18-34

Jesus was approached by a question from some religious conservatives, who did reject the truth of a living and merciful God that raises all people to eternal life. They asked him, saying, Master, the laws of Moses prescribe for us that if the brother of a man dies but he leaves a widow with no children, then it be lawful the brother should marry his widow and beget children in the name of his dead brother; and now if there were seven brothers: and first did take a wife, and dying left no children; and the second married her, and also died without leaving any children; and then the third likewise until all seven had married her according to the law and no children were born, before the widow seven times also died, then in any resurrection from death, when they shall rise to eternal life, whose wife shall she be of them? for the seven all had her as wife under the laws of the prophets? Jesus then said to them, *Is this not the source of your woe, that you do not comprehend the true laws of the Divine Creator, nor the nature of God? For when the spirits of the dead rise, they neither marry in civil union, nor are given in holy matrimony; but are as free and pure as the angels that are in Heaven. As for the bodies of the dead and the spirits of the dead, have you never properly read the scriptures of the prophets and of Moses and how God did speak to him, saying I am the God of Abraham and all the prophets of existence? Yet it is for the living, not the dead, that such laws of an old covenant were made by God. Thus, you are wrong, then, altogether.* One of the scribes of the temple that witnessed the test to try and trick Jesus and upon hearing the answer then asked him, saying: Lord, what be then the first commandment of all? Jesus answered him and said, *Verily, the first commandment of all is: there is no God but God the Father of all Creation and all Existence; and thou shall love thy Father with all thy heart, with all thy mind and with all thy spirit; and with all thy strength. Behold, this is the first commandment above all others.* Upon hearing these words, the scribe bowed his head to Jesus and said, Master, I know you speak the truth: for there is only one God, and there is none other but he, who is a loving God: And to love him in return with all our heart, and with all our discernment and with all our spirit and strength, and to love our neighbour as ourselves, is worth more to God than all the burnt offerings and sacrifices ever made at the temple. When Jesus heard the answer of the scribe, he reached out and said unto him, *Verily, you are not far from the love of your Heavenly Father and the reward of eternal life*. Thereafter, no man on that day, dared ask Jesus another question.

Offertory Antiphon

O God and Divine Creator of all People and Relations, who continues to admonish each and every generation not to misrepresent the Will of Christ and condemn others because of their differences, grant us the heart and wisdom to see your Divine Word in others and accept the rights of people to form unions and associations through the distinct Rite of Union that neither harms Divine Law, nor diminishes the sanctity of the separate Holy Rite of Matrimony. Through our Lord Jesus Christ, your Son, who lives and reigns with you in the unity of the Holy Spirit, one God, for ever and ever.

Prayer over the Offerings

May God and the Divine Creator accept and sanctify these humble gifts as symbols of the genuine personal offerings we make in respect and honour of your *Holy Feast of Holy Union*. Through Christ our Light and Saviour.

Communion Antiphon — Psalm 50: 14-15

Let us offer unto God thanksgiving; and pay thy vows unto the most High: And call upon him in the days of our trouble: For he shall I will deliver those who honour their promises.

Prayer after Communion

Heavenly Father and God of all People and Relations, we give thanks for the nourishment of your heavenly gifts of the Bread and Fruits of Eternal Spiritual Life. May our earnest participation in your *Holy Feast of Holy Union* bring forth favourable blessings upon our lives, our community and your Holy Apostolic Universal Ecclesia. Through your Son our Lord Jesus Christ.

XVIII.V – FEAST OF AUTHENTIC FIDELITY

1. The Universal Feast of Authentic Fidelity, also known as Fidelity Sunday is the third Sunday after Corpus Christi. — Feast of Authentic Fidelity

Entrance Antiphon: Prov. 3: 7-8

Do not be lustful in your own eyes; respect what is sacred and shun evil. This will bring health to your body and nourishment to your spirit.

Magisterium: Luke Luke 17: 11-17

A time came when Jesus was on his way to Jerusalem, and was passing between Samaria and Galilee; and as he was going into a village, ten men that were lepers cried out from a distance, saying: Jesus, Master, have pity on us. He then approached them, embracing them and then said, *Go and present yourselves to the priests*; and thereupon, as they went, they were made clean. Later, one of them, finding that he was cured, came back, praising God aloud, and threw himself at the feet of Jesus with his face to the ground, to thank him; and this man was a Samaritan. Jesus answered and said, *Were not all ten made clean? And the other nine, where are they? Not one has come back to give God the praise, except this stranger*. And he said to the cured man, *Arise and go on thy way, thy faith has brought thee cure even unto the next life*.

Good News: Matthew Matt. 19:16-26

A young man in fine clothes came to Jesus and said, Master, how many good works of mercy and charity must I do in order to have eternal life? Jesus said to him, *Why does thou come to me asking of accounting for goodness? God is love and perfect credit of mercy and forgiveness. Thus, if thou have a mind to enter into eternal life, simply keep the commandments of God the Father as revealed to you through all the prophets*. The man did reply and said, Do you mean the commandments of our forefathers, or the revelation you have spoken? Jesus said, *Thou shalt do no murder, Thou shalt not commit adultery, Thou shalt not steal, Thou shalt not bear false witness, Honour thy father and thy mother, and Thou shalt love thy neighbour as thyself*. The young man then said, Though I be fortunate in wealth, all these laws I have kept from my youth. What do I lack? Jesus said to him, *If thou hast a mind to be perfect in the eyes of God, go home and sell all that belongs to thee; give it to the poor, and so the treasure thou has shall be in heaven; then come back and follow me*. But when the young man heard these words, he departed in sorrow, for he had great possessions. Then

Jesus said to his disciples, *Verily I say unto you, that a rich man by his own burdens shall not enter the Kingdom of Heaven easily. And once again I say unto you, it is easier for a camel to pass through a gate of the eye of the needle, than for a rich man to enter the gates of the kingdom of heaven.* At hearing this, the disciples were thrown into bewilderment, saying to themselves, if so many are addicted to holding wealth and possessions who then can possibly be saved? But Jesus fastened his eyes on them, and said to them, *To men such a change of heart and mind seem impossible; but with God all things are possible.*

Offertory Antiphon

O God and Divine Creator of all Trust and Virtue, who through your son gave us your Testament of the Light of Christ through the *Good News* of your Divine Mission to the Universal Ecclesia, grant us the fortitude and discipline to honour our duty as custodians of gifts and resources of value, so that we neither waste what we have been given, nor breach your trust in each and every one of us. Through our Lord Jesus Christ, your Son, who lives and reigns with you in the unity of the Holy Spirit, one God, for ever and ever.

Prayer over the Offerings

May God and the Divine Creator accept and sanctify these humble gifts as symbols of the genuine personal offerings we make in respect and honour of your *Holy Feast of Authentic Fidelity*. Through Christ our Light and Saviour.

Communion Antiphon — Psalm 56: 10-12

In God will I praise his word: through obeying his laws will I praise his word. In God have I put my trust: I will not be afraid what man can do unto me. My vows are upon me, O God: I will render praises unto thee.

Prayer after Communion

Heavenly Father and God of all Trust and Virtue, we give thanks for the nourishment of your heavenly gifts of the Bread and Fruits of Eternal Spiritual Life. May our earnest participation in your *Holy Feast of Authentic Fidelity* bring forth favourable blessings upon our lives, our community and your Holy Apostolic Universal Ecclesia. Through your Son our Lord Jesus Christ.

XVIII.VI – FEAST OF HOLY MATRIMONY

1. The Universal Feast of Holy Matrimony, also known as Matrimony Sunday is the 4th Sunday after Corpus Christi. Feast of Holy Matrimony

Entrance Antiphon: Prov. 19: 14

Houses and wealth are inherited, but a patient spouse is a gift from heaven.

Magisterium: Matthew Matt.25:1-12

Jesus said, When that day comes, the kingdom of heaven will be like ten virgins, who went to bring the bridegroom and his bride home, taking their lamps with them. Five of these were foolish, and five were wise; the five foolish, when they took their lamps, did not provide themselves with oil, but those who were wise took oil in the vessels they carried, as well as the lamps. The bridegroom was long in coming, so that they all grew drowsy, and fell asleep. And at midnight the cry was raised, Behold, the bridegroom is on his way; go out to meet him. Thereupon all these virgins awoke, and fell to trimming their lamps; and now the foolish ones said to the wise, Share your oil with us, our lamps are burning low. But the wise ones answered, How if there is not enough for us and for you? Better that you should find your way to the merchants, and buy for yourselves. And so, while they were away buying it, the bridegroom came; those who stood ready escorted him to the wedding, and the door was shut. Afterwards those other virgins came, with the cry, Lord, Lord, open to us. And he answered, Believe me, I do not recognise you. Be on the watch, then; the day of it and the hour of it are unknown to you.

Good News: Mark Mark 10:1-12

When Jesus sat down to teach, the multitudes gathered around him once more. Then some of the doctors of law came to Jesus to try and put him to the test by asking him, whether it is right for a man to strike his wife? He answered them, What command did Moses give you? And the doctors of the law said, Moses ruled that a man be free from punishment if he strikes his wife, so long if he then give her the right of a writ of divorce. Jesus answered them, It was because of the hardness of your hearts that Moses wrote you this precept of civil union. But from the beginning of creation, God the Divine Creator made them male and female. For this cause shall a man leave his father and mother and separate from them unto one wife; and the two thus shall become one flesh under God in holy matrimony. Why then, since they are no longer two, but one flesh, what God has joined, let not man put asunder. After the doctors of law had left and when they were in a house, his disciples asked him further about the same question, whereupon Jesus told them: There be no divorce in heaven, for if a man and a woman divorce and remarry in civil union, though it be lawful in the courts, they each be joined in holy matrimony only once.

Offertory Antiphon

O God and Divine Creator of all Sacraments and Holy Rites, who through your son instituted the sacred Rite of Holy Matrimony solely between a consenting man and woman, without excluding the ability of others to form associations through the Rite of Union, grant us the courage to restore the significance and importance of Holy Matrimony as the foundation stone of the nuclear family and the sustainable future and harmony of a loving society. Through our Lord Jesus Christ, your Son, who lives and reigns with you in the unity of the Holy Spirit, one God, for ever and ever.

Prayer over the Offerings

May God and the Divine Creator accept and sanctify these humble gifts as symbols of the genuine personal offerings we make in respect and honour of your *Holy Feast of Holy Matrimony*. Through Christ our Light and Saviour.

Communion Antiphon Psalm 103: 18-19

To such as keep his covenant, and to those that remember his commandments to do them. God has prepared his Kingdom of heaven; and his kingdom shall rule over all the Earth.

Prayer after Communion

Heavenly Father and God of all Sacraments and Holy Rites, we give thanks for the nourishment of your heavenly gifts of the Bread and Fruits of Eternal Spiritual Life. May our earnest participation in your *Holy Feast of Holy Matrimony* bring forth favourable blessings upon our lives, our community and your Holy Apostolic Universal Ecclesia. Through your Son our Lord Jesus Christ.

XVIII.VII – FEAST OF IMMACULATE HEART OF MARY

1. The Universal Feast of Immaculate Heart of Mary, also known as Immaculate Heart Sunday is the Sunday before Feast of Sacred Heart. Feast of Immaculate Heart of Mary

Entrance Antiphon: Prov. 22: 1

A kind and generous heart is more desirable and longer lasting than a good name or any great riches.

Magisterium: Luke Luke 7: 11-17

And now it happened that Jesus was going into a city called Naim, attended by his disciples and by a great multitude of people. And as he drew near the gate of the city, a dead man was being carried out to his burial; the only son of a widow; followed by a crowd of mourners. When Christ saw the distraught mother and widow, he had pity on her, and said, *Mother, do not weep*. Then he went up and put his hand on the bier; and those who were carrying it stood still. And he said, *Man, I say to thee in the name of the Father of all Creation and Existence, rise up*. And the dead man sat up, and spoke; and Jesus gave him back to his mother. The crowd of onlookers were all overcome with awe, and said, praising God, A great prophet has risen up among us; God has visited his people. And this story of this miracle was spoken throughout the whole region and even unto surrounding countries.

Good News: John John 19: 23-28

The soldiers, once they had crucified Jesus, took up his garments, that they divided into four shares, one share for each soldier. Then they took up his cloak, that was without seam, woven from the top throughout; so they said to one another, Better we not to tear it; instead let us cast lots to decide whose it shall be. This was in fulfilment of the passage in scripture which says, They divide my spoils among them; casting lots for my clothing. So it was then the manner whereby the soldiers occupied themselves. Meanwhile, only Mary the mother of Jesus, with her sister, Mary the wife of Cleophas, Mary Magdalen and only one other disciple, had come to bear witness and stand beside the Cross. And Jesus, seeing the heart and courage of his mother, and the disciple, whom he loved, comforting her, Jesus said to his mother, *Woman, this is thy son*. Then he said to the disciple, *Brother, this is thy mother*. And from that hour the disciple took Mary into his own safe keeping. And now Jesus knew well that all was achieved which the scripture demanded for its accomplishment.

Offertory Antiphon

O God and Divine Creator of all Sanctity and Mercy, who chose to recognise the extraordinary humility and docility to the Holy Spirit of Mary, by elevating her love and heart to become a Divine aspect of your love as the Immaculate Heart of our Mother Mary, grant us through her most holy intercession that we might seek to live our lives in humility and willing docility to the creativeness and inspiration of the Holy Spirit. Through our Lord Jesus Christ, your Son, who lives and reigns with you in the unity of the Holy Spirit, one God, for ever and ever.

Prayer over the Offerings

May God and the Divine Creator accept and sanctify these humble gifts as symbols of the genuine personal offerings we make in respect and honour of your *Holy Feast of the Immaculate Heart of Mary*. Through Christ our Light and Saviour.

Communion Antiphon Psalm 141: 3-4

Set a watch, O God, before my mouth; keep the door of my lips. Incline not my heart to any evil thing, to practise wicked works with men that work iniquity: and let me not eat of their dainties.

Prayer after Communion

Heavenly Father and God of all Sanctity and Mercy, we give thanks for the nourishment of your heavenly gifts of the Bread and Fruits of Eternal Spiritual Life. May our earnest participation in your *Holy Feast of the Immaculate Heart of Mary* bring forth favourable blessings upon our lives, our community and your Holy Apostolic Universal Ecclesia. Through your Son our Lord Jesus Christ.

XVIII.VIII – FEAST OF THE SACRED HEART OF JESUS

1. The Universal Feast of the Sacred Heart of Jesus, also known as Sacred Heart Sunday. Feast of the Sacred Heart of Jesus

Entrance Antiphon: Prov. 3: 3-4

Let love and faithfulness never leave you; bind them around your neck, write them on the tablet of your heart. Then you will win favour and a good name in the sight of God and man.

Magisterium: Matthew Matt.17:14-20

When Jesus and his disciples reached the front of the multitude, an older man with a young boy came up and knelt before him and said: Lord have pity on my son, who is a lunatic and suffers great affliction of mind. He will often throw himself into a fire of trouble, and often into difficult water. I brought him here to thy disciples, but they have not been able to cure him. Jesus answered him, saying, *Ah, faithless and misguided generation, how long must I be with you? How long must I suffer your lack of judgement and comprehension?* Jesus then ordered the boy be brought before him, before saying: *Awaken and be rid of dull mind! For I love and forgive you!* With those words, the dullness and idiocy came out of him and the boy was cured. Afterwards, when they were alone, the disciples came to Jesus and asked, Why was it that we could not cast it out? Jesus said to them, B*ecause you had no faith nor reasoning. I promise you, if you have faith, though it be but like a grain of mustard seed, you have only to say to this mountain, Remove from this place to that, and it will remove; nothing will be impossible to you. Verily, there is no way of exorcising such ignorance or spirits except by knowledge and faith.*

Good News: John John 14: 6-21

Jesus said to his disciples, I am the way, the truth, and the life: no man comes to truly know the Father, except through me. If you have come to know the truth of my words, then you have come to know the true nature of our Divine Father. From now henceforth you have the means of discernment of what is or is not true revelation. At these words, Philip the disciple said to Jesus, Lord, grant us that we too may see the Father, that is all we ask. Jesus then said unto him, How long has my time been with you, and yet you still do not recognise me Philip? Verily, I say to you that he that has seen my works, has seen the true nature of the Father; and yet you say unto me, show us the Father? Is it that you doubt that I am in the Father and the Father is in me? Is it not clear by the words that I reveal to you are not just my own, but the words of God our Father who dwells continually in me and through my works. If you cannot trust my word, when I tell you that I am in the Father and the Father is in me, then let all the fulfilment of scriptures you have heard and the many miracles you have witnessed be my warrant. Listen to me when I tell you that one who has learned to trust in me, will be able to do what I do; nay he will be able to accomplish even greater things yet. Soon I shall return to our Heavenly Father, so whatever request you make of the Father in my name, will be received, so that through the Son, the Father of all Creation may be glorified; and every petition you make of me in my own name, I myself shall receive and grant you what is needed. If you have any love for God, you must keep my commandments. And I ask the Father that he give you comfort and spiritual protection all the days of your life. It shall be the Spirit of Light and the bringer of Divine Truth, whom the world cannot receive, because they neither know him or can discern him. But you shall be granted the power to recognise him, as he will be continually at your side and shall dwell within you. Behold, I shall not abandon you, nor leave you without spiritual company. It is only a little while now, before this world shall see me no more; but you shall see me, because I shall live on and you too will have eternal life. When that day comes, you will learn for yourselves the singular mystery that I am in the Father and you are in me as I am in you. Verily, he that loves God, keeps my commandments; and he who trusts in me is loved by me and the Father of all Creation; and I will reveal my love to him.

Offertory Antiphon

O God and Divine Creator of all Love, Mercy and Transformation, who through your son demonstrated such love and devotion to all life on Earth, that you brought forth an unbreakable sacred Covenant between Heaven and Earth, that none be condemned, nor the Earth be destroyed; and that the Revelation of the end of time and beginning of new life be when the Kingdom of Heaven be brought forth onto Earth according to your Divine Testament and Will, grant us the courage to bear witness to the Light of Christ and the Divine Mission of New Evangelisation to transform our hearts, our communities and our planet to a place of love and living harmony. Through our Lord Jesus Christ, your Son, who lives and reigns with you in the unity of the Holy Spirit, one God, for ever and ever.

Prayer over the Offerings

May God and the Divine Creator accept and sanctify these humble gifts as symbols of the genuine personal offerings we make in respect and honour of your *Holy Feast of the Sacred Heart of Jesus*. Through Christ our Light and Saviour.

Communion Antiphon

Psalm 19: 2

See how the skies proclaim the glory of God, how the vault of heaven reveals his perfection!

Prayer after Communion

Heavenly Father and God of all Love, Mercy and Transformation, we give thanks for the nourishment of your heavenly gifts of the Bread and Fruits of Eternal Spiritual Life. May our earnest participation in your *Holy Feast of the Sacred Heart of Jesus* bring forth favourable blessings upon our lives, our community and your Holy Apostolic Universal Ecclesia. Through your Son our Lord Jesus Christ.

Title XIX – Proper of Mystery of Mercy & Redemption

XIX.I – MYSTERY OF MERCY & REDEMPTION

1. The most *Sacred Mercy & Redemption Mystery of Christ*, is a fixed liturgical season of 44 days and a maximum of 8 holy feast days, beginning on the feast of *Divine Mercy* (first Sunday after *Sacred Heart Sunday*), then rising to the solemnity of *Assumption Day* (August 15th); and concluding on the solemnity of *Redemption Sunday* (first Sunday after Assumption Day near end of August). Mystery of Mercy & Redemption

The liturgical season of the *Redemption Mystery of Christ* exists as a time of thanksgiving, penance, confession, blessing and reconciliation with God in knowing the Divine Mercy, Forgiveness and Redemption of each person and each institution and the entirety of the Christian and Jewish family.

The Sacred Colour for the liturgical season of the *Redemption Mystery of Christ* is **white**, representing the purification of sin, the absence of blemish of humanity in the mind and face of God and the authenticity of penance and reconciliation of all the people of God through faith in the Crucified and Risen Christ. All Vestments used in relation to all feast days of the liturgical season and all dressings and fabrics used throughout the church during this period, should adhere to the colour of white.

XIX.II – FEAST OF DIVINE MERCY

1. The Universal Feast of Divine Mercy, also known as Divine Mercy Sunday is the 1st Sunday after Sacred Heart Sunday. Feast of Divine Mercy

Entrance Antiphon: Prov. 19: 17

> Whoever is kind to the poor also gives to Christ, and he will reward them for what they have done.

Magisterium: Luke Luke 10:30-37

> Jesus gave a certain Parable and said; A Levite man who was on his way down from a City to a distant town fell in with robbers, who stripped him and beat him, and went off leaving him half dead. And a priest, who chanced to be going down by the same road, saw him there and passed by on the other side. And a Levite also came upon him and recognised him, yet passed by on the other side. But a complete stranger and Samaritan, who was on his travels, saw him and took pity at the sight; he went up to him and bound up his wounds, pouring oil and wine into them, and so mounted him upon his own beast and brought him to

an inn, where he took care of him. And the next day he took out two silver pieces, which he gave to the inn-keeper, and said, Take care of him, and on my way home I will give thee whatever else is owing to thee for thy pains. Jesus then asked, Of these three, who proved himself a better neighbour to the man who had fallen in with robbers? Was it his fraternal brother or the stranger? And they said, It is the one that showed mercy upon him. Then Jesus said, Go thy way, and do thou likewise.

Good News: Matthew

Matt. 5:33-48

Jesus said, You have heard it said since ancient times, *Thou shalt not make blasphemous oaths, but shall make all thy proper oaths to God*. Yet I say unto you, do not make false promises at all; neither by heaven, nor by the earth, nor by the sacred city, nor even thy head. Therefore, let your word be your bond so that your Yea means yea and your Nay, means nay. Verily, you have heard it said since ancient times, *An eye for an eye and a tooth for a tooth*. But I tell you that you should not seek retribution for the sake of vengeance against some injury; for if a man strikes thee on thy right cheek, resist only against evil, else forgive him. And if he is ready to seek relief by the courts against thee over thy coat, resist only perfidy and malice, else let him have it; And if he compels thee to attend him on a mile's journey, resist only oppression and slavery, else go two miles with him of thy own accord. Give to him who asks, and if a man would borrow from thee, resist only impostors and liars, else do not turn away. You have heard that it was said, Thou shall love thy neighbour and hate thy enemy. But I tell you, Love and comprehend your enemies; and try to do good to those who hate you, pray for those who persecute and insult you, so that you may be true sons and daughters of your Father in heaven, who makes his sun rise on the evil and equally on the good, his rain fall on the just and equally on the unjust. If you just love those who love you, what title have you to a reward? Will not the publicans do as much? If you greet none but your brethren, what are you doing more than others? Will not the very heathen do as much? But you are to be perfect, as your heavenly Father is perfect.

Offertory Antiphon

O God and Divine Creator of all Mercy and Forgiveness,

grant us the wisdom and decency to forgive others for their transgressions against us, as you forgive us for our transgressions; and to be courageous enough to admit our transgressions to others and seek their forgiveness, so we live our lives without harm and without fear or regret. Through our Lord Jesus Christ, your Son, who lives and reigns with you in the unity of the Holy Spirit, one God, for ever and ever.

Prayer over the Offerings

May God and the Divine Creator accept and sanctify these humble gifts as symbols of the genuine personal offerings we make in respect and honour of your *Holy Feast of Divine Mercy*. Through Christ our Light and Saviour.

Communion Antiphon — Psalm 107: 1-2

Give thanks unto God, for he is good: For his mercy and forgiveness endures forever. Let the redeemed of God acknowledge his mercy, and all whom he has redeemed from the hands of wickedness.

Prayer after Communion

Heavenly Father and God of all Mercy and Forgiveness, we give thanks for the nourishment of your heavenly gifts of the Bread and Fruits of Eternal Spiritual Life. May our earnest participation in your *Holy Feast of Divine Mercy* bring forth favourable blessings upon our lives, our community and your Holy Apostolic Universal Ecclesia. Through your Son our Lord Jesus Christ.

XIX.III – FEAST OF SACRED ANIMAL LIFE

1. The Universal Feast of Sacred Animal Life, also known as Animals Day is the first Sunday after the Feast of Divine Mercy. — Feast of Sacred Animal Life

Entrance Antiphon: — Prov. 12: 10

The merciful care for the needs of their animals, but even the kindest acts of the wicked are cruel.

Magisterium: Luke — Luke 15:1-7

When they found all the publicans and common folk coming to listen to him, the doctors of law and scribes were indignant, saying: Here is a man, that entertains sinners, and eats with them. Whereupon Jesus told them this parable: If any of you owns a hundred sheep, and has lost one of them, does he not leave the other ninety-nine in the wilderness, and go after the one which is lost until he finds it? And when he does find it, he sets it on his shoulders, rejoicing, and so goes home, and calls his friends and his neighbours together; Rejoice with me, he says to them, I have found my sheep that was lost. So it is, I tell you, in heaven; there will be more rejoicing over one sinner who repents, than over ninety-nine souls that are justified, and have no need of repentance.

Good News: Luke Luke 12: 37-48

Jesus said, Blessed are those servants, whom their master will find as good and faithful stewards when he comes. I promise you, the master will prepare the feast himself, and make his servants sit down to celebrate, and he shall minister to them as their servant. Whether he returns in the second quarter of the night or in the third, blessed then are those servants if he finds them alert. Be sure of this; if a good steward of the house had known at what time the thief was coming, he would have kept watch, and not allowed the house to be in disrepair. You too, then, must stand ready. For the Son of Man shall return at an hour when you are not expecting him. Whereupon Simon Peter said to Jesus, Lord, why has thou addressed this parable to us, or to all men? And Jesus answered, saying, Behold!, a faithful and wise steward, is one whom God the Father of all Creation entrusts with the care of the Earth and all the animals and life upon the Earth; and to respect life and to give them their allowance of food and habitat with mercy and justice. Blessed then is that servant who is found performing his duty when the Son of Man returns. I promise you, he will delegate him with even more authority. But if that servant says in his heart, My lord is long in coming, and falls into being cruel to animals and life; and torturing and killing men and women; and eating and drinking himself to excess, then on some day when he expects nothing, at an hour when he is all unaware, his lord will come, and will cut him off and throw him into prison, and assign over his flesh and spirit to those forces and armies that guard against the enemies of Heaven. Yet, it is the servant who knew of the Will of Light, and yet did not make ready for Him, or refused to do his Will, that shall be greatly punished and stripped of power and condemned, while those who did not know, even if they rejected the truth shall be treated more lightly. Verily, much will be asked of the man to whom much is given; and more will be expected of him who claims to serve in my name, because he is entrusted with more.

Offertory Antiphon

O God and Divine Creator of all Creation, who imagined the Universe into being with such beauty that life was able to emerge in the right conditions in our Solar System and throughout our Galaxy and beyond, grant us the intelligence and respect of all life, especially animal life; and remember that all animals that have the capacity to dream also have the capacity of a soul; and that we take care of animals to avoid causing needless harm or cruelty. Through our Lord Jesus Christ, your Son, who lives and reigns with you in the unity of the Holy Spirit, one God, for ever and ever.

Prayer over the Offerings

May God and the Divine Creator accept and sanctify these humble gifts as symbols of the genuine personal offerings we make in respect and honour of your *Holy Feast of Sacred Animal Life*. Through Christ our Light and Saviour.

Communion Antiphon — Psalm 8-10

Thou has put all life under his dominion and good stewards: and all the domesticated and wild animals and beasts; and all birds in the sky, and the fish in the sea and everything that lives. O God, how the beauty and majesty of your gift of life fills all the earth!

Prayer after Communion

Heavenly Father and God of all Creation, we give thanks for the nourishment of your heavenly gifts of the Bread and Fruits of Eternal Spiritual Life. May our earnest participation in your *Holy Feast of Sacred Animal Life* bring forth favourable blessings upon our lives, our community and your Holy Apostolic Universal Ecclesia. Through your Son our Lord Jesus Christ.

XIX.IV – FEAST OF DIVINE CHARITY

1. The Universal Feast of Divine Charity, also known as Benevolence Sunday is the second Sunday after the Feast of Divine Mercy. — Feast of Divine Charity

Entrance Antiphon: — Prov. 14: 31

Whoever oppresses the poor shows contempt for their

Maker, but whoever is kind to the needy honours God.

Magisterium: Luke

Luke 12:13-21

One of the multitude said to Jesus, Master, our father left us a substantial estate. Bid then my brother give me my due share of my inheritance. And Jesus answered him, What justice is served in yielding to such addiction to entitlement fuelled by a sense of avarice and greed? How can any sentence made from two wrongs be put right in heaven? Look at yourself and not the faults of your brother and keep clear of covetous desires. For the purpose of life of a man or woman is not to accrue more and more possessions than is needed. And Jesus then told them a parable, There was a rich man whose lands yielded a heavy crop: and he debated in his mind, What am I to do, with no room to store my crops in? Should, I sell the excess at a discount and lessen my profit, or even give some to those in hunger? Instead, the rich man decided to pull down his barns and build even greater ones, telling himself, Now I shall be able to store all my harvest and all the goods that are mine; and now my soul is at ease, for I have goods in plenty laid up for many years to come; take thy rest now, eat, drink, and make merry. And in seeing such hubris, God called upon his angels to reap his soul that night whilst he was asleep. Thus, so it is with any man or woman who in hubris and arrogance against heaven seeks to lay up treasure for themselves on Earth, yet with no credit with God.

Good News: Matthew

Matt.18:21-35

Then Peter came to Jesus and asked him saying, Lord, how often must I see my brother do me wrong, and still forgive him; as much as seven times? Jesus said to him, I tell thee to forgive, not seven wrongs, but seventy times seven. Here then is an image of the kingdom of heaven; there was a king who resolved to enter into a reckoning with his servants, and had scarcely begun the reckoning, when one was brought before him who was ten thousand talents in his debt. He had no means of making payment; whereupon his master gave orders that he should be sold, with his wife and children and all that he had, and so the debt should be paid. With that the servant fell at the feet of his king and said, Have patience with me, and I will pay thee in full. And his master, moved with pity for him, let the servant go and discharged him of his debt. So this servant went out, and met with a fellow servant of his, who owed him a hundred pieces of silver; whereupon he caught hold of him and took him by the throat, and said, Pay me all thou owe me. His fellow servant went down on his knees in entreaty; Have patience with me, he said, and I will pay thee in full. But the other refused; he went away and committed him to prison for such time as the debt was unpaid. The rest of the servants were full of indignation when they saw this done, and went in to tell the king what had happened. And so the unforgiving servant was summoned to give an account to his lord and master, who said to him, I remitted all that debt of thine, thou wicked servant, upon your entreaty; was it not then thy duty to show mercy and forgiveness on thy fellow servant, as I had mercy on thee? And his master, then handed over all the property and powers of the wicked servant to others and thrust him into the deepest and darkest prison and struck him from the rolls of the house as if he had never existed. So it is thus that my heavenly Father will deal with you, if brother does not forgive brother with all his heart.

Offertory Antiphon

O God and Divine Creator of all Mercy, Charity and Sacred, grant us the strength of discipline and quality of personal character that we commit to regular concrete acts of charity and volunteer assistance in our community to assist those who are disabled or who are suffering, or who are hungry or homeless. Through our Lord Jesus Christ, your Son, who lives and reigns with you in the unity of the Holy Spirit, one God, for ever and ever.

Prayer over the Offerings

May God and the Divine Creator accept and sanctify these humble gifts as symbols of the genuine personal offerings we make in respect and honour of your *Holy Feast of Divine Charity*. Through Christ our Light and Saviour.

Communion Antiphon — Psalm 82: 3-4

God commands we defend the poor and fatherless: do justice to the afflicted and needy. Deliver the poor and needy from hunger: and free them from the chains of the wicked.

Prayer after Communion

Heavenly Father and God of all Mercy, Charity and Sacred

Gifts , we give thanks for the nourishment of your heavenly gifts of the Bread and Fruits of Eternal Spiritual Life. May our earnest participation in your *Holy Feast of Divine Charity* bring forth favourable blessings upon our lives, our community and your Holy Apostolic Universal Ecclesia. Through your Son our Lord Jesus Christ.

XIX.V – FEAST OF ATONEMENT

1. The Universal Feast of Atonement, also known as Atonement Sunday is the third Sunday after the Feast of Divine Mercy. Feast of Atonement

Entrance Antiphon: Prov. 23: 4-5

Let yourself not be exhausted in pursuit of riches, nor blinded in trusting your own cleverness. Cast but a glance at riches, and they are gone, for they will surely sprout wings and fly off to the sky like an eagle.

Magisterium: Luke Luke 16: 19-31

Jesus spoke a parable, saying: There was a rich man once, that was clothed in purple and gold, and feasted sumptuously every day. And there was a beggar, called Lazarus, who lay at his gate, covered with sores, wishing that he could be fed with the crumbs which fell from the rich man's table, but none was ready to give them to him; the very dogs came and licked his sores. Time went on; the beggar died, and was carried by the angels to Abraham's bosom; the rich man died too, and found his grave in purgatory. And there, in his suffering, he lifted up his eyes, and saw Abraham far off, and Lazarus in his bosom. And he said, with a loud cry, Father Abraham, take pity on me; send Lazarus to dip the tip of his finger in water, and cool my tongue; I am tormented in this flame. But Abraham said, My son, remember that thou didst receive thy good fortune in thy life-time, and Lazarus, no less, his ill fortune; now he is in comfort, thou in torment. And, besides all this, there is a great gulf fixed between us and you, so that there is no passing from our side of it to you, no crossing over to us from yours. Whereupon he said, Then, father, I pray thee send him to my own father's house; for I have five brethren; let him give these a warning, so that they may not come, in their turn, into this place of suffering. Abraham said to him, They have Moses and the prophets; let them listen to these. They will not do that, father Abraham, said he; but if a messenger comes to them from the dead, they will repent. But Abraham answered him, If they do not listen to Moses and the prophets, they will be unbelieving still, should one rise from the dead.

Good News: Luke

Luke 11: 37-52

At the time when Jesus was teaching, one of the doctors of law invited him to his house for the mid-day meal; so he went in and sat down at table. Before the meal, the host while watching Jesus did ask him why he had not performed the ritual purification and washing before his meal? And Jesus did say to him, You who are obsessed in the observance of endless laws and doctrines and are content to cleanse the outward part of cup and dish, while all within is running with avarice and wickedness. How foolish! Did not he who made the outward part also make the inward too? If it were truly your intent to be purified, then you would atone for your hypocrisy and give alms out of the store you have and at once all that is yours becomes clean. Woe upon you, you hypocrites of Divine Law, that you demand a purity tax upon meat and flour and all manner of herbs, yet ignore your obligations to deliver to the people the mercy and justice and love of God. These are the laws of heaven that ought to have been done by you; instead you ignore the true law of God and obsess yourself in false doctrines. Woe upon you, you hypocrites of Divine Law, for loving the first seats in the temples more than God, and to have your hands kissed in the market-place more than perform your obligations; Woe upon you, you hypocrites of Divine Law, for you are like the spirits and apparitions of the dead that men do converse with, without knowing they are of no substance. And here one of the scribes at the meal answered Jesus saying, Master, in speaking this way, you also bring the clerks and scribes that serve the doctors of law into contempt. And he replied, saying: Woe upon you too, you hypocrites of Divine Truth, for loading men and women with deeds and contracts too heavy to be borne; wicked burdens that you yourselves will not touch with one finger. Woe upon you, you hypocrites of Divine Truth, for building up the tombs of the prophets, when it be the same prophets who were murdered by your fathers; Truly you bear witness and approve of the deeds of your fathers for you refuse to write the truth and restore the law. Atone while you still have the chance. Behold! the very scriptures you pretend to uphold warns you, I will send my prophets and my apostles to them, and there will be some they will kill and persecute; and so the wicked and hypocrites shall be answerable to atone for all the blood of prophets and apostles that has been shed since the beginning of the world, from the blood of Abel to the blood of Zachariah before they even see the gates of heaven. Yes, I tell you even the generations of hypocrites to come will be held answerable to atone for it. Woe upon you, you hypocrites of Divine Truth, for hiding away the keys of knowledge of heaven, even though you may not enter yourselves. For your hindrances against the People of God shall be removed.

Offertory Antiphon

O God and Divine Creator of all Mercy, Compassion, grant us the courage to admit our faults and transgressions; and atone for our actions; and be willing and committed to concrete change, for the sake of those that love us, our families and our community that depend on us. Through our Lord Jesus Christ, your Son, who lives and reigns with you in the unity of the Holy Spirit, one God, for ever and ever.

Prayer over the Offerings

May God and the Divine Creator accept and sanctify these humble gifts as symbols of the genuine personal offerings we make in respect and honour of your *Holy Feast of Atonement*. Through Christ our Light and Saviour.

Communion Antiphon — Psalm 86: 4-5

Help us, O God of our salvation, for the glory of thy name: and deliver us, and purge away our sins, for thy name's sake.

Prayer after Communion

Heavenly Father and God of all Mercy, Compassion and Forgiveness, we give thanks for the nourishment of your heavenly gifts of the Bread and Fruits of Eternal Spiritual Life. May our earnest participation in your *Holy Feast of Atonement* bring forth favourable blessings upon our lives, our community and your Holy Apostolic Universal Ecclesia. Through your Son our Lord Jesus Christ.

XIX.VI – FEAST OF DIVINE RECONCILIATION

1. The Universal Feast of Divine Reconciliation, also known as Reconciliation Sunday is the fourth Sunday after the Feast of Divine Mercy.

Feast of Divine Reconciliation

Entrance Antiphon:

Prov. 25: 21

If your enemy is hungry, give him food to eat; if he is thirsty, give him water to drink.

Magisterium: Luke

Luke 15: 11-32

Jesus did then speak in parable, saying, There was a certain man who had two sons. And the younger of these said to his father, Father, give me that portion of the estate which falls to me. So he divided his property between them. Not many days afterwards, the younger son put together all that he had, and went on his travels to a far country, where he wasted his fortune on riotous living. Then, when all was spent, a great famine arose in that country, and he found himself in want; whereupon he went and attached himself to a citizen of that country, who put him on his farm, to feed swine. He would have been glad to fill his belly with husks, such as the swine used to eat; but none was ready to give them to him. Then he came to himself, and said, How many hired servants there are in my father's house, who have more bread than they can eat, and here am I perishing with hunger! I will arise and go to my father, and say to him, Father, I have sinned against heaven, and before thee; I am not worthy, now, to be called thy son; treat me as one of thy hired servants. And he arose, and went on his way to his father. But, while he was still a long way off, his father saw him, and took pity on him; running up, he threw his arms round his neck and kissed him. And when the son said, Father, I have sinned against heaven and before thee; I am not worthy, now, to be called thy son, the father gave orders to his servants, Bring out the best robe, and clothe him in it; put a ring on his hand, and shoes on his feet. Then bring out the calf that has been fattened, and kill it; let us eat, and make merry; for my son here was dead, and has come to life again, was lost, and is found. And so they began their merry-making. The elder son, meanwhile, was away on the farm; and on his way home, as he drew near the house, he heard music and dancing; whereupon he called one of the servants and asked what all this meant. He told him, Thy brother has come back, and thy father has killed the fattened calf, glad to have him restored safe and sound. At this he fell into a rage, and would not go in. When his father came out and tried to win him over, he answered his father thus, Think how many years I have lived as thy servant, never transgressing thy commands, and thou hast never made me a present of a kid, to make merry with my friends; and now, when this son of thine has come home, one that has swallowed up his patrimony in the company of harlots, thou hast killed the fattened calf in his honour. He said to him, My son, thou art always at my side, and everything that I have is already thine; but for this merry-making and rejoicing there was good reason; thy brother here was dead, and has come to life again; was lost, and is found.

Good News: Luke Luke 7:36-50

One of the doctors of law invited Jesus to a meal at his home; so Jesus accepted and he went into the house and took his place at table. And there was an infamous woman in the same city, who, upon hearing that Jesus was to be at a meal in the house, did find a way to enter, carrying a priceless alabaster box of ointment. As soon as she saw Jesus at the table, she fell upon her face and began weeping, before washing his feet with her tears and drying them with her hair, kissing them and then anointing them with the ointment. His host, the doctor of law, was troubled at the display of utter humiliation by the woman, before Jesus raised his hand to let her be, and the host did say, Is this not a sign? Surely if one be the Son of Man, then he would know what kind of wicked and sinful woman touches him? Jesus answered him saying, *Simon the words I wish to say to you now, I cannot, but shall speak thus as my Father wishes. There was a creditor who had two debtors; one owed him five hundred pieces of silver, the other fifty. Neither had means of paying the creditor before default, and yet he gave them both their discharge. And now tell me, who is the one of these two that loves him the more?* Simon the doctor of law did reply, saying, The one surely who had the greater debt discharged, whereupon Jesus said to him. *Thou has judged rightly.* Then, he turned and reached out to the woman, summonsing her to arise, and said, *Simon do you not see this woman? For I came into thy house and thou gave me no water for my feet, yet she has purified my feet with her tears and wiped them with her hair. Thou gave me no kiss of greeting, yet she has not ceased kissing my feet since she entered. Verily, thou did not pour oil on my head, yet she has anointed my feet with priceless ointment. Wherefore I say unto thee, her sins, even though they are many, are forgiven. For she has greatly humbled herself in love to the one who comes from the Father. Yet, I say most solemnly, to one who does little to humble themselves or show any love to our Heavenly Father, the same shall be given.* Then Jesus said to the woman, *Go in peace. Thy sins are forgiven.* The woman departed and the fellow guests thereupon began speaking among themselves, saying Who be this man, that he have the authority even to forgive sins? And that he have the power to change the hearts of the wicked and give them peace?

Offertory Antiphon

O God and Divine Creator of all Healing, Growth and Wisdom, grant us the courage and good sense to acknowledge our transgressions and hurt of other people, especially those that once loved us and depended on us; and seek to make known our genuine remorse and to make concrete atonement for our actions, so we may help them heal and overcome the scars we may have caused. Through our Lord Jesus Christ, your Son, who lives and reigns with you in the unity of the Holy Spirit, one God, for ever and ever.

Prayer over the Offerings

May God and the Divine Creator accept and sanctify these humble gifts as symbols of the genuine personal offerings we make in respect and honour of your *Holy Feast of Divine Reconciliation*. Through Christ our Light and Saviour.

Communion Antiphon Psalm 79: 1

Help us, O God of our salvation, for the glory of thy name: and deliver us, and purge away our sins, for thy name's sake.

Prayer after Communion

Heavenly Father and God of all Healing, Growth and Wisdom, we give thanks for the nourishment of your heavenly gifts of the Bread and Fruits of Eternal Spiritual Life. May our earnest participation in your *Holy Feast of Divine Reconciliation* bring forth favourable blessings upon our lives, our community and your Holy Apostolic Universal Ecclesia. Through your Son our Lord Jesus Christ.

XIX.VII – FEAST OF DIVINE ILLUMINATION OF CHRIST

1. The Universal Feast of Divine Illumination of Christ, also known as Sacred Fire Sunday or Bonfire Sunday is the fifth Sunday after the Feast of Divine Mercy. Feast of Divine Illumination of Christ

Entrance Antiphon: Prov. 9: 10

The love of God is the beginning of wisdom, and knowledge of the Holy One is understanding.

Magisterium: Matthew Matt. 12:22-30

Then they brought to him a man possessed, who was both blind and dumb; whom Christ cured, returning to him both speech and sight. The multitudes were filled with amazement; Can this, they asked, be no other than the Son of Man? But the zealots and religious fanatics said, when they heard of it, It is only through the power of Beelzebub, the prince of the devils, that this false prophet casts the devils out. Whereupon Christ, who knew what was in their thoughts, said to them, Behold! no kingdom can truly be at war with itself without being laid waste. No city or house that is at war with itself can stand firm. If you claim that it is Satan who casts Satan out, then Satan is at war with himself, and does this not expose the illness of your minds? If it is through Beelzebub that I cast out devils, by what means then did the beloved prophets of your laws cast them out? It is for these heroes and saints of yours, then, to pronounce judgement on you and your wilful ignorance. But if, when I cast out devils, I do it through the Spirit of God, then it must be that the kingdom of God has already appeared among you. For how is anyone to gain entrance into the house of a strong man and plunder his goods without first making the strong man his prisoner? Then he can plunder his house at will. Verily, he who is not with me, is against me; and he who does not gather his store safely with me, scatters his future to the winds.

Good News: Matthew Matt. 17:1-13

Jesus took Peter and James and his brother John with him, and led them up on to a high mountain where they were alone. And he was transfigured then in their presence, with his face shining like the sun, and his garments becoming white as the purest snow; and the disciples were forced to shield their faces before all at once they had sight of Moses and Elijah conversing with Jesus. Then Peter called out in a loud voice, saying, My Lord, we praise thee as your witnesses; if it pleases thee, let us make three seats in this place, one for thee, one for Moses and one for Elijah. Even before Simon Peter had finished speaking, a shining cloud overshadowed them. And a powerful and booming voice did appear to come from the cloud and said, *This is my beloved Son, in whom I am well pleased; to him, then, listen*. The disciples, when they heard the powerful voice, fell on their faces, overcome with fear; but Jesus came near and raised them with his touch and said, *Arise, and do not be afraid, for I am with thee always*. And they lifted up their eyes, and saw no man there but only Jesus. And as they were coming down from the mountain, Jesus warned them, saying, *Do not tell anyone of what you have seen, until the Son of Man has risen from the dead*. And his disciples asked him and said, Tell us Lord, why is it that the scribes speak of the prophecy that Elijah must come before the Messiah? Jesus then answered, saying, V*erily, Elijah is a symbol for the righteous before the true laws of God and the restoration of Divine Law. But I tell you this, that the voice of Elijah in the wilderness has already appeared to them and they refuse to acknowledge him and blaspheme against Heaven, just as the Son of Man shall suffer at the hands of hypocrites*. Then the disciples understood that he had been speaking to them of John the Baptist.

Offertory Antiphon

O God and Divine Creator of all Light and Revelation, grant us the light of inspiration and illumination of your most Holy Spirit, so that we may go forward in respect and concrete actions to fulfilling your Divine Testament in the Light of your Son. Through our Lord Jesus Christ, your Son, who lives and reigns with you in the unity of the Holy Spirit, one God, for ever and ever.

Prayer over the Offerings

May God and the Divine Creator accept and sanctify these

humble gifts as symbols of the genuine personal offerings we make in respect and honour of your *Holy Feast of Divine Illumination of Christ*. Through Christ our Light and Saviour.

Communion Antiphon — Psalm 84: 11

God is our sun and shield: the Lord our God grants us his grace and glory so we be unconquerable in the face of evil. Thus, nothing shall prevent the greater glory of God through his sons and daughters of light.

Prayer after Communion

Heavenly Father and God of all Light and Revelation, we give thanks for the nourishment of your heavenly gifts of the Bread and Fruits of Eternal Spiritual Life. May our earnest participation in your *Holy Feast of Divine Illumination of Christ* bring forth favourable blessings upon our lives, our community and your Holy Apostolic Universal Ecclesia. Through your Son our Lord Jesus Christ.

XIX.VIII – FEAST OF THE ASSUMPTION OF BLESSED MARY

1. The Universal Feast of the Assumption of Blessed Mary, also known as Assumption Day is the August 15th. — Feast of the Assumption of Mary

Entrance Antiphon: — Prov. 4: 23-25

Above all else, guard your heart, for everything you do flows from it. Keep your mouth free of perversity; keep corrupt talk far from your lips. Let your eyes look straight ahead; fix your gaze directly before you.

Magisterium: Matthew — Matt.15:21-28

Jesus and his disciples withdrew to the coast of the great sea and the ancient lands of the Phoenician traders and the cities of Tyre and Sidon. And here a noble woman and land owner, a Caananite by birth, cried aloud to Jesus, saying, Have pity on me Lord, thou Son of the Prophets. My only daughter is cruelly troubled by evil spirits. But Jesus gave her no word in answer and continued on his journey. His disciples later came to him and pleaded with him, saying, Rid us of this woman, for she continues to follow us and torment us with her wailing. Jesus then answered and said, *My mission is not only to find the lost of the People of God*. Then the woman came up and said, falling at his feet, Lord, please help me. He answered, *It is an abomination before God to take the bread for hungry children and throw it to the gods, as your ancestors have done*. The woman replied, Ah yes, Lord. That is why the dogs in my house are well fed, for they feed on the crumbs that fall from the tables of my servants. And at that, Jesus answered her, *Woman, your great faith redeems even the souls of your ancestors. Behold, let thy will be granted*. And from that hour her daughter was cured.

Good News: Luke

Luke 11: 29-33

The multitudes gathered round Jesus, and he began speaking to them thus, saying: It is indeed a wicked and unfaithful generation that prays for a sign from God and yet refuses to open their eyes to it and see it. Jonah was the sign given to such previous generations of the wicked. But, the sign given to this generation shall be the Son of Man. Verily, for future generations the sign shall be when the Queen of Heaven awakens the Southern Spirit to bring final judgement against the wicked and unfaithful; and shall leave them without excuse. For she has traversed to the ends of the earth to open the hearts and wisdom of kings; and behold they shall witness a wisdom greater than even the wisest of kings. The previous generations and this generation shall rise up with the future generations upon the end of the old world; and they shall be without excuse. For as much as they did penance in the time of Jonah for their iniquities, behold! a far greater Light shall appear! Nobody lights a lamp, and then puts it away in a cellar or under a bushel measure; it is put on the lamp-stand, so that its light may be seen by all who come in. Thy body has the eye for its lamp; and if thy eye is clear, the whole of thy body will be lit up. When it is diseased with arrogance and ignorance, or hate, or envy or greed, then the whole of thy body will be in darkness. Take good care then, that this principle of light that is in thee is the true Light of the Spirit, not the false light of darkness. Then, if thy whole body is in the true Light of the Spirit, with no part of it in darkness, it will all be lit up as if by a bright lamp enlightening thee.

Offertory Antiphon

O God and Divine Creator of all Existence, who chose to protect from any form of corruption the immaculate heart and life of our Mother Mary, grant us through her most sacred intercession the humility and discipline to honour and respect the most holy Mother of all humanity through the respect and honour of all women, especially in steadfastly rejecting all forms of deliberate and wicked ignorance that degrades the image and sanctity of women. Through our Lord Jesus Christ, your Son, who lives and reigns with you in the unity of the Holy Spirit, one God, for ever and ever.

Prayer over the Offerings

May God and the Divine Creator accept and sanctify these humble gifts as symbols of the genuine personal offerings we make in respect and honour of your *Holy Feast of the Assumption of Blessed Mary*. Through Christ our Light and Saviour.

Communion Antiphon — Psalm 36: 5-6

Thy mercy, O God is in the heavens; and thy faithfulness reaches unto the clouds. Thy love is like the greatest mountains; and thy mercy is like the deepest sea: O Lord, you preserve humanity and all life.

Prayer after Communion

Heavenly Father and God of all Existence, we give thanks for the nourishment of your heavenly gifts of the Bread and Fruits of Eternal Spiritual Life. May our earnest participation in your *Holy Feast of the Assumption of Blessed Mary* bring forth favourable blessings upon our lives, our community and your Holy Apostolic Universal Ecclesia. Through your Son our Lord Jesus Christ.

XIX.IX – FEAST OF DIVINE REDEMPTION

1. The Universal Feast of Divine Redemption, also known as Redemption Day is the first Sunday after Assumption Day. — Feast of Divine Redemption

Entrance Antiphon: — Prov. 2: 12 - 15

Wisdom will save you from the ways of wicked men, from men whose words are perverse, who have left the straight paths to walk in dark ways, who delight in doing wrong and rejoice in the perverseness of evil, whose paths are crooked and who are devious in their ways.

Magisterium: John — John 11:1-44

Now a certain man was very ill, named Lazarus, of

Bethany, the town of Mary and her sister Martha. It was the same Mary that had anointed the Lord with ointment, and wiped his feet with her hair, whose brother Lazarus was sick. Therefore his sisters sent unto him, saying, Lord, behold, he whom thou loves is sick. When Jesus heard the news, he said, *This sickness is not unto death, but for the glory of God the Father and his Son*. Jesus did love Martha, her sister, and Lazarus. Yet, after hearing the news, he waited for two days in the same place where he was. Only then did he say to his disciples, *It is time*. But his disciples were fearful and said, Master the priests and the zealots seek reason to stone thee and yet you wish to travel to their doorstep? Jesus answered, *Are there not twelve hours in the day? If any man walk in the day, he does not stumble, because he sees the Light of this world. But if a man walk in the darkness, he stumbles, because there is no light in him. Our brother Lazarus is at rest now; I am going there to awake him*. Then his disciples replied, saying: If he is resting, should we not disturb him? For the disciples had supposed he meant the rest that comes with sleep, so Jesus spoke to them plainly and said, *Lazarus is Dead. And for your sakes I am glad that I was not there, for the time has now come to witness and see the power of your faith*. Whereupon, Thomas, also known as the twin did say to his fellow disciples, Let us delay our voyage with the Master, for I do not understand but fear that he means to call us to die with him. Then when Jesus arrived, he found that the body of Lazarus had been entombed for four days; and a large mourning party had gathered to Bethany from the nearby city of Jerusalem, to comfort Martha and Mary. Martha, when she heard that Jesus had come, went out to meet him, while Mary sat in the house. Martha then said to Jesus, Lord, if thou had of been here when I called for your help, my beloved brother would not have died. Now he is dead and my grief is overwhelming. Jesus replied, *Martha he will soon rise again*. Martha then said to him, I know of your teaching that my brother shall rise again at the resurrection of all spirits, when the last day comes, but alas my faith is sorely tested. Jesus said unto her, *Behold! I am the resurrection and the light: he who lives and entrusts in me can never die. Martha do you trust me?* Martha, replied, Yes Lord. I have faith and trust that you are the Christ and the Son of Man who came into this world as foretold to save all of us. And with that she went back and called her sister Mary aside; The Master is here, she said, and bids thee come. With these words, Mary rose up and went out to meet him as he was still a little distance from the house. Many of the mourners also followed and when Mary reached Jesus she fell at his feet and began wailing, saying: Master, if you had of been here as you had promised, my brother would not be dead. And when Jesus saw her distress and the grief of the mourners accompanying her, he himself was moved to deep grief and said, *Verily, it is not the will of God that any suffer such pain or loss. Where have you taken my brother?* Mary and the mourners then took Jesus to the tomb of Lazarus, before Jesus asked for a moment to express his own grief and they stepped back, leaving him alone, before Jesus wept. Some who were watching said to themselves, See, he truly did care for him; while others asked, If he could open the eyes of the blind and cure the sick, why could he not have prevented the death of Lazarus? Jesus then walked forward to the stone over the mouth of the tomb and said, *Remove the stone*. But Martha came forward and pleaded with him, saying, My Lord, in your grief I pray you protect his dignity; for he has been gone for four days and I fear the foulness of death will consume us. Jesus said to her, *Have I not told thee and you promised to hold firm to your faith?* So the stone was removed and Jesus lifted his eyes to heaven and said, *Father, I thank thee for hearing my prayers. For myself, I know that thou hear me at all times, but I say this for the sake of the multitude here present, that they may learn to trust it is thou who has sent me.* And with that he cried in a loud voice, Come out, Lazarus, to my side. Whereupon the dead man came out, his feet and hands tied with linen strips, and his face muffled in a veil. Jesus then said, *Loose him and let him go free.*

Good News: John

John 8:1-11

Jesus meanwhile went to the gardens at the mount of Olives to pray. In the morning he appeared again and joined his disciples to go to the temple. But before he could depart, news had spread of his presence and a crowd had gathered, so he sat down there and began to teach them. And several of the scribes and doctors of law heard the news of Jesus teaching outside the city to a multitude, so they brought to him a woman in their custody who had been found guilty by the temple court of committing adultery. In full view of the crowd and Jesus, they said, Master, this woman has been condemned by our laws and doctrines of adultery. The law of Moses prescribes that for such a wicked offence, the guilty be stoned death. Yet, as you are seen by many to be a good judge and teacher of law, what then be thy sentence? There was deathly quiet as the multitude did await the reply of Jesus to the scribes and lawyers. Yet he did not speak. Instead he bent down and began writing on the ground with his finger, before reaching over and gathering some stones and handing them to the scribes and doctors of law. Jesus then said to them, *Behold! Whoever of you is free from sin, shall cast the first stone*. Then Jesus bent down again and collected more rocks, handing them to the others nearby, saying the same words, before bending down again and writing on the ground. And soon, one by one, the crowd began to disperse, beginning with the scribes and doctors of law, until finally Jesus was left alone with the woman, still standing in front of him. Then Jesus stood up and walked over to her and said, *Woman, where are thy accusers? Has no one condemned thee?* The woman replied, No one, Lord. And Jesus said to her, *Neither do I condemn thee: go and sin no more.*

Offertory Antiphon

O God and Divine Creator of all Mercy and Redemption, who through the Testament and New Covenant of your Son revealed your true nature to be Divine Love, Mercy and Redemption, and not condemnation and harsh judgement, grant us the courage and integrity to resolutely confront and challenge those who continue to defile and misrepresent the Divine Word of Christ through hate, fear and condemnation, by being exemplars of your love, mercy and forgiveness to all others, including those who would commit unspeakable acts of evil in your name. Through our Lord Jesus Christ, your Son, who lives and reigns with you in the unity of the Holy Spirit, one God, for ever and ever.

Prayer over the Offerings

May God and the Divine Creator accept and sanctify these humble gifts as symbols of the genuine personal offerings we make in respect and honour of your *Holy Feast of Divine Redemption*. Through Christ our Light and

Saviour.

Communion Antiphon — Psalm 111: 7-9

The works of his hands are virtue and justice; all his commandments are sure. They stand fast for ever and ever, and are done in truth and mercy. He sent redemption unto his people: he has commanded his new covenant for ever: holy and reverend is his name.

Prayer after Communion

Heavenly Father and God of all Mercy and Redemption, we give thanks for the nourishment of your heavenly gifts of the Bread and Fruits of Eternal Spiritual Life. May our earnest participation in your *Holy Feast of Divine Redemption* bring forth favourable blessings upon our lives, our community and your Holy Apostolic Universal Ecclesia. Through your Son our Lord Jesus Christ.

Title XX – Proper of Mystery of Apostolic Life

XX.I – MYSTERY OF APOSTOLIC LIFE

1. The most *Sacred Apostolic Mystery of Christ*, is a variable liturgical season approximately 78 to 85 days and a maximum of 13 holy feast days, beginning on the *Feast of the One True Apostolic Universal Ecclesia of Christ*, also known as *Ecumenical Sunday* (first Sunday after Redemption Sunday), then rising to the solemnity of All Saints Day (1st November); and concluding on the solemnity of Mission Sunday (2nd Sunday after All Saints Day).

Mystery of Apostolic Life

The liturgical season of the *Apostolic Mystery of Christ* exists as a time of promise, courage, strength, faith, oath and vow to the Christian Mission of living, demonstrating and proclaiming the Good News of the Risen Christ and the continual Revelation found through the actions of people working together for common and ethical purposes and unifying as the living flesh of Christ.

The Sacred Colour for the liturgical season of the *Apostolic Mystery of Christ* is **green**, representing the the fruitful and vibrant life of the community of the people of God and the Universal Ecclesia, the sacredness of life and the journey of Apostolic Life for all living and departed souls. All Vestments used in relation to all feast days of the liturgical season and all dressings and fabrics used throughout the church during this period, should adhere to the colour of green.

XX.II – FEAST OF THE ONE TRUE APOSTOLIC UNIVERSAL ECCLESIA

1. The Universal Feast of the One True Apostolic Universal Ecclesia of Christ, also known as Ecumenical Sunday is the first Sunday after Redemption Sunday.

Feast of the One True Apostolic Universal Ecclesia

Entrance Antiphon: Prov. 24: 3-4

By wisdom a house is built, and through understanding it is established; through knowledge its rooms are filled with rare and beautiful treasures.

Magisterium: Matthew Matt.13:44-52

Jesus said, The knowledge of the kingdom of heaven is like a treasure hidden in a field; a man has found it and hidden it again, and now, for the joy it gives him, is going home to sell all that he has and buy that field. Again, the knowledge of the kingdom of heaven is as if a trader were looking for rare pearls: and now he has found one pearl of great cost, and has sold all that he had and bought it. Again, the knowledge of the Covenant of Heaven is like a net that was cast into the sea, and enclosed fish of every kind at once; when it was full, the fishermen drew it up, and sat down on the beach, where they stored all that was worth keeping in their buckets, and threw the useless kind away. So it will be when the world is brought to an end and a new world begun; God shall grant his Divine Mercy to all, but those of the living who refuse to cease their wicked and evil ways, of wars for money and unjust enrichment shall be struck like diseased limbs and cast away like weeds; and there will be weeping, and gnashing of teeth until they have earned their redemption. Have you grasped all this? Yes, Master, they said to him. And Jesus said to them, Every scholar, then, whose learning is of the knowledge of the Covenant of Heaven must be like a rich man, who knows how to bring both new and old things out of his treasure-house.

Good News: John

John 15: 1- 17

I am the true vine, and it is my Father who tends to my body. Every branch that yields no fruit in me, he cuts away; and every branch that yields fruit, he trims clean, so that it may yield more fruit. You are now clean and united with me through the truth of Divine Law revealed unto you. Verily, you live in me and I live in you. For as much as a branch that does not live in unity with the vine can yield no good fruit of itself; no more can those that shall follow you, if they do not live as one united body according to my words. I am the one true vine and you are my branches. For if men and women live united in me, and I in them, then they will yield abundant fruit. Yet if they choose to separate from me, then they shall have no power from heaven to do anything. Verily, if a man does not live united with my one true body, he can only be like a branch that is cast off and decays away. Behold, the Father shall ensure such a dead branch is picked up and thrown into the fire, to burn there. Yet as long as you live on united in me as one of my many branches, and my words live on in you, then you will be able to make what request you will, and have it granted. Verily, all shall be fulfilled and the true nature of my Heavenly Father shall be glorified, if you yield abundant fruit, and prove yourselves my disciples. I have bestowed my love upon you, just as my Father has bestowed his love upon me; live on, then, in my love. You will live on in my love, if you keep my commandments, just as it is by keeping my Father's commandments that I live on in his love. All this I have told you, is so that my joy may be yours, and the measure of your joy may be filled up. This is my commandment, that you should love one another, as I have loved you. This is the greatest love a man can show, that he should lay down his life for his friends; and you, if you do all that I command, you are my friends. I do not wish to speak of you any more as my servants; for a servant is one who despite such loyalty and love, still remains at a distance; whereas I have made known to you all that my Father has told me; and so I call you my Brothers and Sisters of Light. Just as you chose to follow me, it was I and the Father that also chose you from the beginning. The task therefore I have appointed you is to go out and unite my branches and tend to them, so that they bear good fruit; fruit that will endure; so that every request you make of the Father in my name may be granted you. These are the directions I give you, that you should love one another.

Offertory Antiphon

O God and Divine Creator of all Christians and Jews, grant all Christianity and Jewish clergy and leaders and all organisations and groups with wisdom and inspiration to see the true wonder and beauty of your promise of unity and respect of individual history and culture; and that every challenge and difficult of growth and experience of the fulfilment of your Divine Mission has been necessary to come to this moment of choice and unity. Through our Lord Jesus Christ, your Son, who lives and reigns with you in the unity of the Holy Spirit, one God, for ever and ever.

Prayer over the Offerings

May God and the Divine Creator accept and sanctify these humble gifts as symbols of the genuine personal offerings we make in respect and honour of your *Holy Feast of the One True Apostolic Universal Ecclesia of Christ*. Through Christ our Light and Saviour.

Communion Antiphon — Psalm 80: 14

Be with us always, we beseech thee, O God. Bring forth your holy spirit from heaven and behold the restoration of life to the one true Vine.

Prayer after Communion

Heavenly Father and God of all Christians and Jews, we

give thanks for the nourishment of your heavenly gifts of the Bread and Fruits of Eternal Spiritual Life. May our earnest participation in your *Holy Feast of the One True Apostolic Universal Ecclesia of Christ* bring forth favourable blessings upon our lives, our community and your Holy Apostolic Universal Ecclesia. Through your Son our Lord Jesus Christ.

XX.III – FEAST OF THE NEW KINGDOM OF HEAVEN ON EARTH

1. The Universal Feast of New Kingdom of Heaven on Earth, also known as Kingdom Sunday is the first Sunday after Ecumenical Sunday. Feast of the New Kingdom of Heaven on Earth

Entrance Antiphon: Prov. 20: 28

Love and faithfulness keep a ruler safe; through mercy and justice his office is made secure.

Magisterium: Matthew Matt.13:24-35

Jesus put before them a parable, saying; Here is an image of the kingdom of heaven. There was a land owner who sowed his fields with clean seed; but while all the world was asleep, an enemy of his came and scattered a damaging weed among the wheat, and was gone. So, when the blade had sprung up and come into ear, the terrible weeds, too, came to light. The men of the land owner came to him to give account and he said to them, was it not clean seed thou did sow in thy fields? How comes it, then, that there are such damaging weed in them? The men did reply, Master an enemy has done it. Would thou then have us go and gather them up? But the land owner said No; for perhaps while you are gathering the weeds you will root up the wheat with them. Leave them to grow side by side till harvest, and when harvest-time comes I will give the word to the reapers, Gather up the weeds first, and tie them in bundles to be burned, and store the good wheat in my barn. Jesus did then put before them another parable, saying: The kingdom of heaven is like a grain of mustard seed, that a man has taken and sowed in his ground; Of all seeds, none is so little, but when it grows up it is greater than any garden herb; for it grows into a tree, so that all the birds come and settle in its branches. And he told them still another parable, saying: The kingdom of heaven is like leaven, that a woman has taken and buried away in three measures of meal, enough to leaven the whole batch. All this Jesus said to the multitude in parables, and would say it in parables so fulfilling the words that were spoken in the Psalms, I will speak my mind in parables, I will give utterance to things which have been kept secret from the beginning of the world.

Good News: Matthew

Matt. 25: 31-46

Jesus said, When the Son of Man comes in his glory, and all the united armies of Heaven with him, he shall sit upon the throne of his glory, and every nation and its leaders will be gathered in his presence, where he will divide men one from the other, as the shepherd divides the sheep from the goats. He will set the merciful, the just and the virtuous and on his right; and the wilfully ignorant, arrogant and wicked on his left. Then the King will say to those who are on his right hand, Come, you that have received a blessing from my Father, take possession of the Kingdom of Heaven upon the Earth that has been promised you since the foundation of the world. For I was hungry, and you gave me food, thirsty, and you gave me drink; I was a stranger, and you brought me home, naked, and you clothed me, sick, and you cared for me, a prisoner, and you came to me. Whereupon the just shall answer, Lord, when was it that we saw thee hungry, and fed thee, or thirsty, and gave thee drink? When was it that we saw thee a stranger, and brought thee home, or naked, and clothed thee? When was it that we saw thee sick or in prison and came to thee? And the King will answer them, Trust me, when you did it to one of the least of my brethren here, you did it to me. Then he will say to those who are on his left hand, in their turn, Go far from me, you that have condemned yourselves unto perdition, until you awaken to the truth and have truly reformed through your necessary custody and penance. For I was hungry, and you never gave me food, I was thirsty, and you never gave me drink; I was a stranger, and you did not bring me home, I was naked, and you did not clothe me, I was sick and in prison, and you did not care for me. Whereupon they, in their turn, will answer, Lord, when was it that we saw thee hungry, or thirsty, or a stranger, or naked, or sick, or in prison, and did not minister to thee? And he will answer them, Hear me, when I say unto you that if you refused it to one of the least of my brethren, you refused it to me. And these shall pass into the spiritual custody to serve their punishment, and the just to the joy of heaven.

Offertory Antiphon

O God and Divine Creator of all Heaven and Earth, who through your Holy Spirit and the Revelation of your Divine Covenant of Heaven has heralded this be the time of fulfilment of your promise of the unity of Heaven and Earth, grant us the strength and inspiration to proclaim your Divine Mission of New Evangelisation to all corners of the world and for every generation to come. Through our Lord Jesus Christ, your Son, who lives and reigns with you in the unity of the Holy Spirit, one God, for ever and ever.

Prayer over the Offerings

May God and the Divine Creator accept and sanctify these humble gifts as symbols of the genuine personal offerings we make in respect and honour of your *Holy Feast of the New Kingdom of Heaven on Earth*. Through Christ our Light and Saviour.

Communion Antiphon — Psalm 74: 12

For God is my King of every age through his mercy and salvation over all the Earth.

Prayer after Communion

Heavenly Father and God of all Heaven and Earth, we give thanks for the nourishment of your heavenly gifts of the Bread and Fruits of Eternal Spiritual Life. May our earnest participation in your *Holy Feast of the New Kingdom of Heaven on Earth* bring forth favourable blessings upon our lives, our community and your Holy Apostolic Universal Ecclesia. Through your Son our Lord Jesus Christ.

XX.IV – FEAST OF THE PROFESSIONS

1. The Universal Feast of the Professions, also known as Profession Sunday is the second Sunday after Ecumenical Sunday. — Feast of the Professions

Entrance Antiphon: — Prov. 2: 7-8

The Divine holds success in store for the upright, he is a shield to those whose walk is blameless, for he guards the course of the just and protects the way of his faithful ones.

Magisterium: Matthew — Matt.20: 1-16

Jesus said, Here is an image of the kingdom of heaven; a rich man went out at day-break to hire labourers for work in his vineyard; and when he sent them out into his vineyard he agreed with the labourers on a silver piece for the day's wages. About the third hour he came out again, and found others standing idle in the market-place; and to these also he said, Away with you to the vineyard like the others; you shall have whatever payment is fair. Away they went; and at noon, and once more at the ninth hour, he came out and did the like. Yet he found others standing there when he came out at the eleventh hour; How is it, he said to them, that you are standing here, and have done nothing all the day? They told him, It is because nobody has hired us; and he said, Away with you to the vineyard like the rest. And now it was evening, and the owner of the vineyard said to his bailiff, Send for the workmen and pay them their wages, beginning with the last comers and going back to the first. And so the men who were hired about the eleventh hour came forward, and each was paid a silver piece. So that when the others came, who were hired first, they hoped to receive more. But they were paid a silver piece each, like their fellows. And they were indignant with the rich man over their pay. Here are these late-comers, they said, who have worked but one hour, and thou hast made no difference between them and us, who have borne the day's burden and the heat. But he answered one of them thus; My friend, I am not doing thee a wrong; did we not agree on a silver piece for thy wages? Take what is thy due, and away with thee; it is my pleasure to give as much to this late-comer as thee. Am I not free to use my money as I will? Must thou give me sour looks, because I am generous? So it is that they shall be first who were last, and they shall be last who were first. Many are called, but few are chosen.

Good News: Luke Luke 6: 40 -49

Jesus said, A disciple is no better than his master; he will be fully perfect if he is as his master is. How is it that one cannot see the speck of dust in the eye of another, yet is not aware of the beam that is thy own? By what right does one say to thy brother, Brother let me rid thy eye of that speck, when thou cannot see the beam that is in thy own? You hypocrite! take the beam out of thy own eye first and so you shall have clear sight to rid thy brother of the speck in his eye. There is no sound tree that will yield withered fruit, no withered tree that will yield sound fruit. Each tree is known by its proper fruit; figs are not plucked from thorns, nor grapes gathered from brier bushes. A good man utters what is good from the knowledge of mercy, wisdom and virtue of his heart; whereas the wicked man from his closed heart can utter nothing but what is evil. For it is from the heart's overflow that the mouth speaks its truth. How is it that you call me, Master, and yet you will not do what I bid you? If anyone comes to me and listens to my commandments and carries them out, I will tell you what he is like; he is like a man that would build a house, who dug deep, and laid his foundation on rock. Then a flood came, and the river broke upon that house, but could not stir it; because of its sound foundations. But the man who listens to what I say and does not carry it out is like a man who built his house on sand without foundation; when the river broke upon it, it fell at once, and great was the ruin of such a house.

Offertory Antiphon

O God and Divine Creator of all Knowledge and Skills, grant your blessings, guidance and wisdom to all the professionals in service of our community and the world. Gently remind them of the necessary humility that all knowledge, skill and authority comes from the Divine; and to always guard against the beguiling falsities of nihilism that promise people of skill and intellect the lie that they may be gods above other people and life, or the lie that a legacy of arrogance and tyranny has any spiritual or temporal permanency. Through our Lord Jesus Christ, your Son, who lives and reigns with you in the unity of the Holy Spirit, one God, for ever and ever.

Prayer over the Offerings

May God and the Divine Creator accept and sanctify these humble gifts as symbols of the genuine personal offerings we make in respect and honour of your *Holy Feast of the Professions*. Through Christ our Light and Saviour.

Communion Antiphon — Psalm 19: 9

How plain be the duties that God enjoins unto the truth of the heart of all men and women. How clear be the commandments of God to bring forth the enlightenment of the mind of all men and women.

Prayer after Communion

Heavenly Father and God of all Knowledge and Skills, we give thanks for the nourishment of your heavenly gifts of the Bread and Fruits of Eternal Spiritual Life. May our earnest participation in your *Holy Feast of the Professions* bring forth favourable blessings upon our lives, our community and your Holy Apostolic Universal Ecclesia. Through your Son our Lord Jesus Christ.

XX.V – FEAST OF THE FIDUCIARIES

1. The Universal Feast of the Fiduciaries, also known as Fiduciary Sunday is the third Sunday after Ecumenical Sunday. Feast of the Fiduciaries

Entrance Antiphon: Prov. 10: 7

The name of the righteous is remembered in blessings, but the name of the wicked shall be struck from memory and forgotten.

Magisterium: Luke Luke 16: 1-12

And Jesus said to his disciples, There was a rich man that had a steward, and a report came to him that this steward had wasted his goods. Whereupon he sent for him, and said to him, What is this that I hear of thee? Give an account of thy stewardship, for thou cannot be my steward any longer. At this, the steward said to himself, What am I to do, now that my master is taking my stewardship away from me? I have no strength to dig; I would be ashamed to beg for alms. I see what I must do, so as to be welcomed into men's houses when I am dismissed from my stewardship. Then he summoned his master's oldest debtors one by one; and he said to the first, How much is it that thou owe my master? Thirty barrels of oil, he said; and he told him, Here is thy bill; quick, sit down and write it as twenty. Then he said to a second, And thou, how much dost thou owe? A hundred quarters of wheat, he said; and he told him, Here is thy bill, write it as eighty. And when the steward returned to his master, he was rewarded for his discernment and prudence in redeeming himself and his actions to become a wise steward. For indeed, the children of this generation can be more prudent after their own fashion than the children of rigidity and doctrine of past ages. And my counsel to you is, make use of your wealth wisely to help others and your community, and to leave a modest legacy. He who is trustworthy over a little sum is trustworthy over a greater; he who plays false over a little sum, plays false over a greater; if you, then, could not be trusted to use the base riches you had, who will put the true riches in your keeping? Who will give you property of your own, if you could not be trusted with what was only lent you?

Good News: Matthew

Matt 6:19-34

Verily, do not strive to hoard a treasure of temporal things for your self upon the Earth, where there is moth and rust to consume it; and where there are thieves to break in and steal it. Instead, strive to gain for yourself the treasures of knowledge from Heaven, that no moth or rust may consume, nor any thief may break in and steal. Behold! Where your treasure is, there will your heart be also. The light of the body is the eyes. If therefore thy eyes be as one for such truth, then thy whole body shall be full of light. Whereas if thy sight be only for ignorance and greed, then thy whole body shall be full of darkness. If therefore the light that is in thee be darkness, how great is that darkness! For no one can serve two masters: for either they will hate the one, and love the other; or else they will hold to one and despise the other. Verily, you cannot both serve God and the false god of money. Therefore, I say unto you, do not worry over the future time of your life, what you shall eat, or what you shall drink; nor be obsessed over your body and how it is clothed. Is not the presence of your life itself in this moment, a more precious gift than the future worries of food, or body or clothing? See how the birds of the air never sow, or reap, or gather grain into barns, and yet your heavenly Father feeds them. Is not human life even a greater gift? Can any one for all their worrying and anxiety, add an arm's length to their height? Why should anyone be so obsessed over superficial appearances? See how the wild flowers grow; they do not toil or spin; and yet I tell you that even Solomon in all his glory was never arrayed in such splendour like one of these. If God, then, so clothes the grasses of the field, which today are alive, then will he not be even more ready to clothe you, people of little faith? Thus, do not fret, then, asking, What are we to eat tomorrow? or What are we to drink then? or How shall we find clothing? It is for the foolish and ignorant to busy themselves over such things; as you have a Father in Heaven who knows that you need them all. Make it your first care to find the true treasures of knowledge from Heaven, and authentic Divine Law; and all these things shall be granted to you. Live therefore without fear; and leave tomorrow to fret and fear over its own needs. Verily, the troubles of today are enough.

Offertory Antiphon

O God and Divine Creator of all Rights and Authority, bless all those who hold positions of trust in our community the wisdom to act with honesty, diligence and humility. Through our Lord Jesus Christ, your Son, who lives and reigns with you in the unity of the Holy Spirit, one God, for ever and ever.

Prayer over the Offerings

May God and the Divine Creator accept and sanctify these humble gifts as symbols of the genuine personal offerings we make in respect and honour of your *Holy Feast of the Fiduciaries*. Through Christ our Light and Saviour.

Communion Antiphon — Psalm 62: 10-11

Let us trust not in power through oppression, nor to become robbers and pirates against others. For if our riches increase, then let our hearts not become beguiled by them. God has warned us against defiling his laws and all power and authority comes from God.

Prayer after Communion

Heavenly Father and God of all Rights and Authority, we give thanks for the nourishment of your heavenly gifts of the Bread and Fruits of Eternal Spiritual Life. May our earnest participation in your *Holy Feast of the Fiduciaries* bring forth favourable blessings upon our lives, our community and your Holy Apostolic Universal Ecclesia. Through your Son our Lord Jesus Christ.

XX.VI – FEAST OF THE VOCATIONS

1. The Universal Feast of the Vocations, also known as Vocation Sunday is the fourth Sunday after Ecumenical Sunday. Feast of the Vocations

Entrance Antiphon: — Prov. 19: 8

The one who gets wisdom loves life; the one who cherishes

understanding will prosper in spirit.

Magisterium: Matthew Matt. 25:14-29

Jesus spoke to them of a parable and said: So it was with a man who went on his travels; he called his trusted servants to him and committed his money to their charge. He gave five talents to one, two to another, and one to another, according to their several abilities, and with that he set out on his journey. The man who had received five talents went and traded with them, until he had made a profit of five talents more; and in the same way he who had received two made a profit of two. Whereas he who had received but one went off and made a hole in the ground, and there hid his master's money. Long afterwards, the master of those servants came back, and entered into a reckoning with them. And so the man who had received five talents came forward and brought him five talents more; Lord, he said, it was five talents thou gave me, see how I have made a profit of five talents besides. And his master said to him, Well done, my good and faithful servant; since thou hast been faithful over little things, I have great things to commit to thy charge; come and share the joy of thy Lord. Then came the man who had received two talents; Lord, he said, it was two talents thou gave me; see how I have made a profit of two talents besides. And his master said to him, Well done, my good and faithful servant; since thou hast been faithful over little things, I have great things to commit to thy charge; come and share the joy of thy Lord. But when he who had received but one talent came forward in his turn, he said, Lord, knowing thee for a hard man, that reaps where he did not sow, and gathers in from fields he never planted, I took fright, and so went off and hid thy talent in the earth; see now, thou hast received what is thine. And his lord answered him, Base and slothful servant, thou knew well that I reap where I did not sow, and gather in from fields I never planted; all the more was it thy part to lodge my money with the bankers, so that I might have recovered it with interest when I came. Take the talent away from him, and give it to him who has ten talents already. Whenever a man is rich in heroic virtue, greater gifts will be made to him, and his riches will abound; if he is poor in courage and morals, even what he accounts his own will be taken from him.

Jesus said, Hear me when I tell you that the man who climbs into the sheep-fold by some other way, instead of entering by the door, comes to steal and to plunder. Verily, it is the shepherd, who is called to tend to his flock, that enters through the proper door. At his coming the keeper of the door throws it open, and the flock are attentive to his voice; and so he calls each by name that choose to join with him, and leads them out with him. When the shepherd has brought out all that choose to be with him, he walks in front of them, and they follow him, because they recognise and trust his voice. If a stranger comes, they move away from him instead of following him; because they cannot recognise or trust the voice of a stranger. When Jesus was finished speaking, the disciples said, Master we do not understand exactly what you mean by this parable. So Jesus spoke to them and said, Behold! it is I who am the true door. Those who seek to enter and make claims against the people in an improper manner are pirates and thieves. Yet I am the door to eternal life. Verily, a man or woman will find salvation if they make their way in through me; They will come and go at will, and find pasture. The thief only comes to steal, to slaughter, to destroy; I have come so that all may have life, and have it more abundantly. I am the good shepherd. A good shepherd is a calling where one is willing to lay down his life to protect and save those entrusted to his care; whereas an agent or contractor is no shepherd and is not called to make his life a vocation. At the first sign of danger, the agent or contractor abandons his post and takes flight, scattering those entrusted to his care. The agent or contractor flees, because he cares not for those entrusted to him, nor does he trust the voice of God. Yet I am the good shepherd. Those with true faith are loved by me and know me, just as I am loved by my Heavenly Father, and to know him. And for the salvation of these souls I am willing to lay down my life. There are others that do not yet belong to this faithful fold; and it be a solemn and sacred mission of all who follow in my footsteps to be good shepherds, that they must bring them into the fold of the love and protection of God. Thus, in the fullness of time, when all is fulfilled, there will be one fold, one family and one shepherd. For no greater love does my Heavenly Father have, than for one who is willing to lay down their life for others, to protect the innocent, to remain resolute to their faith and their absolute trust in God the Father. Verily, no one can demand such heroic virtue, for it must be of one's own accord. The free will to accept or not accept such calling. This commandment have I received from my Father.

Offertory Antiphon

O God and Divine Creator of all Knowledge and Revelation, bless and guide all those in our community who have been called by you to a vocation of duty and service, especially those delegated with the task of defending our community and our borders and nations. Through our Lord Jesus Christ, your Son, who lives and reigns with you in the unity of the Holy Spirit, one God, for ever and ever.

Prayer over the Offerings

May God and the Divine Creator accept and sanctify these humble gifts as symbols of the genuine personal offerings we make in respect and honour of your *Holy Feast of the Vocations*. Through Christ our Light and Saviour.

Communion Antiphon — Psalm 23: 1-3

The Lord is my shepherd; I shall not want. He makes me lie down in green pastures. He leads me beside still waters. He restores my soul. He leads me in paths of righteousness for his name's sake.

Prayer after Communion

Heavenly Father and God of all Knowledge and Revelation, we give thanks for the nourishment of your heavenly gifts of the Bread and Fruits of Eternal Spiritual Life. May our earnest participation in your *Holy Feast of the Vocations* bring forth favourable blessings upon our lives, our community and your Holy Apostolic Universal Ecclesia. Through your Son our Lord Jesus Christ.

XX.VII – FEAST OF THE GUARDIANS

1. The Universal Feast of the Guardians, also known as Guardian Sunday is the fifth Sunday after Ecumenical Sunday. — Feast of the Guardians

Entrance Antiphon: — Prov. 11: 11

Through the blessings of the merciful and just a city is exalted. But through the unpunished offences of the wicked it is destroyed.

Magisterium: Luke

Luke 18: 1-8

And Jesus told them a parable, saying: Make earnest prayer a daily event and never become discouraged. Once in a prosperous city there lived a Judge who had no fear of God nor regard for men and women without means or a profession. Yet there was a poor widow who was wise in knowledge of the law, resolute in her conviction, but gentle and without scandal in her approach. Every year she would come before this Judge and give sound arguments for redress against those of the city that had cheated her. For years he refused, saying to himself, I have no fear of God, nor any such person of meager wealth, yet I fear her resolute integrity and her knowledge shall destroy me, unless I yield and give her the legal remedy she deserves. Thus, listen to these words and be not reckless to rise to belligerence in the face of injustice, lest you be the one who most gravely injures the law. For I tell you, no cry of injustice goes unheard by my Heavenly Father. But when the Son of Man comes, will he find such patient faith left on Earth?

Good News: Matthew

Matt. 18: 1-14

The disciples came to Jesus at this time and said, Tell us, who is greatest in the kingdom of heaven? Whereupon Jesus called to his side a little child, to whom he gave a place in the midst of them, and said, Hear me and hear my words, unless you become like little children again, you shall not easily enter the kingdom of heaven. He is greatest in the kingdom of heaven who will abase himself like this little child. He who gives welcome to such a child as this in my name, gives welcome to me. And if anyone hurts one of these little ones or corrupts the innocence of their childhood, then trust in me, it would be better that he have been drowned in the depths of the sea, with a mill-stone hung about his neck, than the punishment that awaits him in the afterlife. Woe unto the world because of such wickedness against the innocence of children! For if one hurts a little one, but confesses with genuine contrition then there is hope in redemption; but woe unto that man with no conscience or remorse who abdicates his humanity and becomes like a dangerous creature needed to be put down. If thy hand or thy foot is culpable of committing evil against children, then cut it off and cast it away from thee. Verily, it is better for thee to enter into the afterlife crippled or lame, than to have two hands or two feet when thou art cast into punishment for such depravity. And if thy eye is culpable of committing foul and depraved visions or desire to witness to such visions against children, then better for thee to enter into life with one eye, than to have two eyes when thou art cast into great punishment in the afterlife. Therefore, see to it that you do not treat even one of these little ones with contempt; I tell you solemnly, they indeed have angels of their own in heaven, that behold the face of my heavenly Father continually. Behold! The Son of Man has come to save all that was lost. Tell me this, if a man has a hundred sheep, and one of them has gone astray, does he not leave those ninety-nine others on the mountain-side, and go out to look for the one that is straying? And if, by good fortune, he finds it, he rejoices more, believe me, over that one, than over the ninety-nine which never strayed from him. So too it is not your heavenly Father's pleasure that one of these little ones should be lost.

Offertory Antiphon

O God and Divine Creator of all Rights and Authority, bless and guide all those delegated with the solemn task of protecting the most vulnerable of our community, especially against those who would still choose to do harm. Grant all Guardians who honour their duties your peace, love and healing, so they do not succumb to the scars and burdens of such a Divine Vocation. Through our Lord Jesus Christ, your Son, who lives and reigns with you in the unity of the Holy Spirit, one God, for ever and ever.

Prayer over the Offerings

May God and the Divine Creator accept and sanctify these humble gifts as symbols of the genuine personal offerings we make in respect and honour of your *Holy Feast of the Guardians*. Through Christ our Light and Saviour.

Communion Antiphon — Psalm 22:11

From the hour of my birth, thou art my guardian; since I left my mother's womb, thou art my God!

Prayer after Communion

Heavenly Father and God of all Rights and Authority, we give thanks for the nourishment of your heavenly gifts of the Bread and Fruits of Eternal Spiritual Life. May our earnest participation in your *Holy Feast of the Guardians* bring forth favourable blessings upon our lives, our community and your Holy Apostolic Universal Ecclesia. Through your Son our Lord Jesus Christ.

XX.VIII – FEAST OF DIVINE HEALING

1. The Universal Feast of Divine Healing, also known as Healing Sunday is the sixth Sunday after Ecumenical Sunday. Feast of Divine Healing

Entrance Antiphon: Prov. 10: 3

The Lord does not let the righteous go hungry, but he thwarts the craving of the wicked.

Magisterium: Mark Mark 5:21-34

So Jesus went back by boat across the sea, and a great multitude gathered about him; and while he was still by the sea, one of the rulers of the synagogue came up, Jairus by name, and fell down at his feet when he saw him, pleading for his aid. My daughter, he said, is at the point of death; come and lay thy hand on her, that so she may recover, and live. So he turned aside with him, and a great multitude followed him, and pressed close upon him. And now a woman who for twelve years had had an issue of blood, and had undergone much from many physicians, spending all she had on them, and no better for it, but rather grown worse, came up behind Jesus in the crowd (for she had been told of him), and touched his cloak; If I can even touch his cloak, she said to herself, I shall be healed. And immediately the source of the bleeding dried up, and she felt in her body that she had been cured of her affliction. Jesus thereupon, inwardly aware of the power that had proceeded from him, turned back towards the multitude and asked, Who touched my garments? His disciples said to him, Canst thou see the multitude pressing so close about thee, and ask, Who touched me? But he looked round him to catch sight of the woman who had done this. And now the woman, trembling with fear, since she recognised what had befallen her, came and fell at his feet, and told him the whole truth. Whereupon Jesus said to her, My daughter, thy faith has brought thee recovery; go in peace, and be rid of thy affliction.

Good News: John

John 8:31-47

Jesus then called out into the multitude to the zealous followers of the temple laws since the time of the Persians, saying: *Hear me when I say unto you, only if you listen to the words I reveal to you, shall you be true disciples of God; for you shall come to know the truth, and the truth will set you free.* Yet the zealots and religious fanatics responded to him and said, We are the chosen of Abraham and we can never be enslaved, for we be the only people who proclaim a divine right to enslave heathens. What then do you mean by saying you shall be free? And Jesus answered them and said, *Woe unto those who bear false witness against heaven and seek to enslave their brother. For everyone who acts so wickedly is indeed a slave of such transgressions; and such a slave of wicked perfidy shall find no rest, nor peace in their home or their heart, but does condemn themselves unto a perpetual abyss of madness. It is why then I say to you, that it is only the Son who can free you from your illness, for you have no discernment to even know of what you speak. Verily, my words be from the same Father unto Abraham yet my words find no spare room in you.* The religious fanatics then said to him: We are the sons of Abraham and Moses and we know very well the laws of God. Jesus replied, saying: *And yet you plot to murder a messenger of God. Who said unto you this is the will of God? It was certainly not a man of God who said these things to you, for this is not the way of Abraham. No, it is your real father you follow and not God.* The religious fanatics were now enraged and called out to him midst the crowd, We are no bastards! God, and he only, is the Father we recognise and his laws. Jesus then said, *Verily, if you were the chosen children of God, you would welcome me gladly; as it is from God I take my origin, and from him I have come. Why is it then that you cannot understand the words I speak? It is because you have no ear for the message I bring. You belong to your father, who is the father of lies, of confusion and of madness that you eagerly serve and defend. Alas, you have allowed all the rooms of your mind to be filled up by the lodgings of false priests, ghosts and smoke. Thus, the reason you do not trust that what I speak is the truth is not just that you have no discernment, but that you cannot hear me from the din of voices in your own heads. Can any of you truly condemn me of an offence against heaven? If not, why is it that you do not seek to atone so that you may be healed of such illness? The man who belongs to God listens to God's words. Alas, you and your future generations are lost to the abyss and so I pray for your healing.*

Offertory Antiphon

O God and Divine Creator of all Mercy, Healing and Salvation, grant us the serenity of surrendering to your Divine Mercy that we may heal our internal and external wounds. Through our Lord Jesus Christ, your Son, who lives and reigns with you in the unity of the Holy Spirit, one God, for ever and ever.

Prayer over the Offerings

May God and the Divine Creator accept and sanctify these humble gifts as symbols of the genuine personal offerings we make in respect and honour of your *Holy Feast of Divine Healing*. Through Christ our Light and Saviour.

Communion Antiphon — Psalm 30: 2

O Lord my God, I cried unto thee, and thou hast healed me.

Prayer after Communion

Heavenly Father and God of all Mercy, Healing and Salvation, we give thanks for the nourishment of your heavenly gifts of the Bread and Fruits of Eternal Spiritual Life. May our earnest participation in your *Holy Feast of Divine Healing* bring forth favourable blessings upon our lives, our community and your Holy Apostolic Universal Ecclesia. Through your Son our Lord Jesus Christ.

XX.IX – FEAST OF ELDERS

1. The Universal Feast of Elders, also known as Elders Sunday is the seventh Sunday after Ecumenical Sunday. — Feast of Elders

Entrance Antiphon: — Prov. 16: 31

Gray hair is a crown of splendour; it is attained in the way of righteousness.

Magisterium: John — John 5:1-13

Jesus and his disciples came to a sacred town renown for a miraculous healing pool, enclosed by an ancient portico, where a multitude of diseased, blind, lame and dying people from all regions would come wait for a sign in the disturbance in the water. The people had faith that from time to time an angel would come down upon the pool and the waters would be stirred up; and the first man who stepped into the pool after the stirring of the water, recovered from whatever infirmity it was that oppressed him. Among those that waited was an old and crippled man who had been waiting for nearly forty years. Jesus saw him lying there, and knew that he had waited a long time and said to him, Has thou still your faith, to recover your strength? The old man replied, Sir, I have no one to let me down into the pool when the water is stirred; and while I am on my way, somebody else steps down before me. Jesus said to him, *Rise up, take up thy bed, and give thanks to God.* And all at once the man recovered his strength, and took up his bed, and walked to the nearby temple. As the day was a customary day of rest and reverence since the time of the Persians, the local priests were outraged to see the old man in rags dragging a bed to the sanctuary of the temple, and demanded he cease. He answered them, The man who gave me back my strength told me himself, Take up thy bed, and give thanks to God. So they asked him, Who is this lawbreaker that told you to defile our doctrines? For the priests had no interest in miracles or signs from God. The old man replied, Though I do not yet know his name, I know he is truly a Man of God. For I have prayed every day for nearly forty years to God and did not abandon my faith and he answered me.

Good News: Mark

Mark 7:1-16

When the crowds had subsided and Jesus sat down with his disciples, some of the doctors of law and scribes also gathered around and began to find fault, because they had seen some of his disciples sit down to eat without first performing the ritual washing ceremony. For the doctors of law and many of the people did hold to the traditions since the time of the Persians and the first temple, not to eat without washing their hands again and again; and not sit down to meat, coming from the market, without thorough cleansing; as well as many other customs held as traditions such as purifying of cups and pitchers and pans and beds. So the doctors of law and scribes asked him, Why do you permit thy disciples eat with defiled hands, instead of following the tradition of our ancestors? But

Jesus answered, Behold! Well has Isaiah prophesied of you hypocrites, as it is written, These people honour me with their lips but their hearts are far from me. They worship me in vain, for it is upon the teachings and doctrines of men, not God. Jesus then said to them, Verily, you ignore the true commandments of God, yet hold the traditions of men, such as purifications, of garments and other superficial observances. You have rejected the very Word of God as Divine Law, to establish and keep your own traditions. For did not Moses say unto you, Honour thy father and thy mother; and who so curses thy father or mother, then dies without hope of reprieve? But you teach, practice and promote in your courts that the testament of a father or mother is nothing without your proof; and that the value of such inheritance can only be judged by your courts because it must be offering to God; and any who cheat their fathers and mothers in such a way shall be free to profit with you. So it is with this and many like observances, that you have sought to pervert the laws of God to make them ineffectual through false doctrines and traditions you have promulgated. Jesus then called the multitudes back to him and said to them, Listen to me, all of you, and grasp this; Nothing that finds its way into a man from outside can make him spiritually unclean. What makes a man unclean is what comes out of a man. If any man have ears to hear, let him hear.

Offertory Antiphon

O God and Divine Creator of all Ages, may every blessing be bestowed upon the elders of our community, so that they see and witness our respect and esteem and in turn may impart their wisdom and experience to us. Through our Lord Jesus Christ, your Son, who lives and reigns with you in the unity of the Holy Spirit, one God, for ever and ever.

Prayer over the Offerings

May God and the Divine Creator accept and sanctify these humble gifts as symbols of the genuine personal offerings we make in respect and honour of your *Holy Feast of the Elders*. Through Christ our Light and Saviour.

Communion Antiphon

Psalm 25: 6-7

Remember, O God, thy tender mercies and thy loving kindnesses; for they have been ever of old. Remember not the sins of my youth, nor my transgressions: according to thy mercy remember thou me for thy goodness' sake.

Prayer after Communion

Heavenly Father and God of all Ages, we give thanks for the nourishment of your heavenly gifts of the Bread and Fruits of Eternal Spiritual Life. May our earnest participation in your *Holy Feast of the Elders* bring forth favourable blessings upon our lives, our community and your Holy Apostolic Universal Ecclesia. Through your Son our Lord Jesus Christ.

XX.X– FEAST OF HEROES & MARTYRS

1. The Universal Feast of Heroes and Martyrs, also known as Martyrs Day is the eighth Sunday after Ecumenical Sunday. Feast of Heroes & Martyrs

Entrance Antiphon: Prov. 15: 15

Though the days of the oppressed may be wretched, the cheerful heart has a continual feast.

Magisterium: Mark Mark 2:1-12

After some days, Jesus and the disciples returned to a village they had previously visited. And as soon as word went round that he was in a house there, such a crowd gathered that there was no room left even in front of the door; and he preached the word to them. And now they came to bring a palsied man to him, four of them carrying him at once; and found they could not bring him close to, because of the multitude. So they stripped the tiles from the roof over the place where Jesus was, and made an opening; then they let down the bed on which the palsied man lay. And Jesus, seeing their faith, said to the palsied man, Son, thy sins are forgiven. But there were some of the scribes sitting there, who reasoned in their minds, Why does he speak so? He is talking blasphemously. Who can forgive sins but God, and God only? Jesus knew at once, in his spirit, of these secret thoughts of theirs, and said to them, Why do you reason thus in your minds? What command is more lightly given, to say to the palsied man, Thy sins are forgiven, or to say, Rise up, take thy bed with thee, and walk? And now, to convince you that the Son of Man has authority to forgive sins while he is on earth (here he spoke to the palsied man): I tell thee, rise up, take thy bed with thee, and go home. And he rose up at once, and took his bed, and went out in full sight of them; so that all were astonished and gave praise to God; they said, We never saw the like.

Good News: John

John 15: 18-27

Jesus said, If the world hates you, be sure that it hated me before it learned to hate you. If you belonged to the world, the world would know you for its own and love you; it is because you do not belong to the world, because I have singled you out from the midst of the world, that the world hates you. Do not forget what I said to you, No servant can be greater than his master. They will persecute you just as they have persecuted me; they will pay the same attention to your words as to mine. And they will treat you thus because you bear my name; for they have no true knowledge of him who sent me. If I had not come and given them my message, they would not have been in fault; as it is, their fault can find no excuse. To hate me is to hate my Father too. If I had not done what no one else ever did in their midst they would not have been in fault; as it is, they have hated, with open eyes, both me and my Father. And all this, in fulfilment of the saying which is written in their law, They hated me without cause. Do not fear. For when the truth-giving Spirit, who proceeds from the Father, has come to protect you, he whom I will send to you from the Father's side, he shall testify of me. And you that have been with me from the beginning also shall also have the courage to bear witness, because of the strength of the Spirit.

Offertory Antiphon

O God and Divine Creator of all Vocations and Courage, may the blessings of your beloved heroes and martyrs who showed us the power of faith and spirit to overcome any obstacle, including the temporary nature of the flesh, grant us the courage to stand by our faith when tested and not to deny your name when inconvenient or when challenged to declare our trust in you. Through our Lord Jesus Christ, your Son, who lives and reigns with you in the unity of the Holy Spirit, one God, for ever and ever.

Prayer over the Offerings

May God and the Divine Creator accept and sanctify these humble gifts as symbols of the genuine personal offerings we make in respect and honour of your *Holy Feast of*

Heroes and Martyrs. Through Christ our Light and Saviour.

Communion Antiphon — Psalm 23:4

Even though I walk through the valley of the shadow of death, I fear no evil, for you are with me; your rod and your staff, they comfort me.

Prayer after Communion

Heavenly Father and God of all Vocations and Courage, we give thanks for the nourishment of your heavenly gifts of the Bread and Fruits of Eternal Spiritual Life. May our earnest participation in your *Holy Feast of Heroes and Martyrs* bring forth favourable blessings upon our lives, our community and your Holy Apostolic Universal Ecclesia. Through your Son our Lord Jesus Christ.

XX.XI – FEAST OF UNIVERSAL PEACE

1. The Universal Feast of Universal Peace, also known as Peace Day is the ninth Sunday after Ecumenical Sunday. — Feast of Universal Peace

Entrance Antiphon: — Prov. 3: 1-2

Do not forget the teachings of Christ, but keep these commands in your heart, for they will prolong your life many years and bring you peace and prosperity.

Magisterium: Mark — Mark 5:35-43

While he was yet speaking, messengers came from a ruler's house to say, Thy daughter is dead; why dost thou trouble the Master any longer? Jesus heard the word said, and told the ruler of the local temple, No need to fear; thou hast only to believe. And now he would not let anyone follow him, except Peter and James and James' brother John; and so they came to the ruler's house, where he found a great stir, and much weeping and lamentation. And he went in and said to them, What is this stir, this weeping? The child is not dead, she is asleep. They laughed aloud at him; but he sent them all out, and, taking the child's father and mother and his own companions with him, went in to where the child lay. Then he took hold of the child's hand, and said to her, Maiden, I say to thee, rise up. And the girl stood up immediately, and began to walk; she was twelve years old. And they were beside themselves with wonder. Then he laid a strict charge on them to let nobody hear of this, and ordered that she should be given something to eat.

Good News: Matthew — Matt.10:24-42

Jesus said, Do not imagine that I have simply come to bring peace to the earth; I have come to bring the sword of heaven, before there be lasting and universal peace. I have come to see a man at variance with his father, and the daughter with her mother, and the daughter-in-law with her mother-in-law. For the enemies of a man will be the people of his own house. Verily, a man or woman is not worthy of Christ, who loves their father or mother more than God the Father. A father or mother is not worthy of Christ, who loves their son or daughter more than the Son of the Father. A son or daughter is not worthy of being called a true disciple of Christ, who does not take up his cross and follow me. Behold, anyone who seeks to secure his own life will lose it; yet it is the one who loses his life for my sake that will secure it. Those who give you welcome, gives me welcome too; and he who gives me welcome gives welcome to him that sent me. He who gives a prophet the welcome due to a prophet shall receive the reward given to prophets; and he who gives a just man the welcome due to a just man shall receive the reward given to just men. And if a man gives so much as a draught of cold water to one of the least of these here, because he is a disciple of mine, I promise you, he shall not miss his reward.

Offertory Antiphon

O God and Divine Creator of all Forces and Authority, grant your spiritual armies the mandate to occupy every place and space in their temporal world, to aid those you have called by vocation to end all forms of human conflict and war to achieve your Holy Mission. Through our Lord Jesus Christ, your Son, who lives and reigns with you in the unity of the Holy Spirit, one God, for ever and ever.

Prayer over the Offerings

May God and the Divine Creator accept and sanctify these humble gifts as symbols of the genuine personal offerings we make in respect and honour of your *Holy Feast of Universal Peace*. Through Christ our Light and Saviour.

Communion Antiphon — Psalm 29: 11

May God give strength unto his people; and bless his

people with peace and goodwill.

Prayer after Communion

Heavenly Father and God all Forces and Authority, we give thanks for the nourishment of your heavenly gifts of the Bread and Fruits of Eternal Spiritual Life. May our earnest participation in your *Holy Feast of Universal Peace* bring forth favourable blessings upon our lives, our community and your Holy Apostolic Universal Ecclesia. Through your Son our Lord Jesus Christ.

XX.XII – ALL SAINTS DAY

1st November

1. All Saints Day is the 1st November. All Saints Day

Entrance Antiphon: Prov. 4: 18-19

The path of the righteous is like the morning sun, shining ever brighter till the full light of day. But the way of the wicked is like deep darkness; for they do not know what makes them stumble.

Magisterium: Luke Luke 12: 22-31

Jesus said to his disciples, I say to you, then, do not obsess over your life, how to support it with more and more possessions; or over the looks of your body, how to keep it clothed in finer and finer garments. Life itself is a greater gift than any amount of gold; and the health of the body, than any amount of finer garments. See how the ravens never sow or reap, having neither storehouse nor barn, and yet God feeds them; have you not an excellence far beyond theirs? Can any of you, for all his fretting, add a cubit's growth to his height? And except for unjust enrichment and oppressive greed, why do you fret about the possessions of others? See how the lilies grow; they do not toil, or spin, and yet I tell you that even Solomon in all his glory was not arrayed like one of these. If God, then, so clothes the grasses which live to-day in the fields and will feed the oven to-morrow, will he not be much more ready to clothe you, men of little faith? You should not be asking, then, what you are to eat or drink, and living in suspense of mind yet to come. It is for the arrogant and wilfully ignorant that have faith in nothing to busy themselves over such things. For your Father knows well that you need them. Verily, make it your first care for others and the knowledge of the Kingdom of Heaven and all these things you need shall be provided to you.

Good News: Revelation

Rev 7: 2-17

And I saw a great Light arise from the east, having the seal of the Living God. And he cried out to the four angels of the north, south, west and east, to whom it was given to cleanse the whole earth and sea and air of all iniquity and blasphemy, saying: destroy not this wicked world, nor cleanse the whole earth or sea or air until we may protect all life and give a seal and number as a sign of forgiveness and salvation for all the People of God. Then I heard the number of them that were sealed and could not comprehend it, for came to score every tribe and people from the beginning of time as the sons and daughters of God the Divine Creator. All the sons and daughters of Adam and Eve since the time of the Elohim; and all the first tribes of Yapa of the Saltwater People, of Mandi of the Plains People, of Tia of the Mountain People, of Waiata of the Sea People, of Five Worlds of the First Nations, of Adamus of the Holly and of Mamma of the Mother Earth; and all the sons and daughters of Ebla of Abraham and Patriarchs, of Kabalaah of Moses and the Hyksos, of Revelations of the Great Prophets of Yeb and of Tara of Jeremiah and the Celts; and all the nations of Acadia of Xerxes, of Missal of Baal Mithra, of Eternal Mysteries of Isis, of Eliada of Alexander, of Self Enlightenment of Gautama, and of Heaven and Earth of Qin Shi Huang; and all the faithful of our Lord Jesus Christ and all the future tribes and nations yet to come. And then I saw the multitude assembled, beyond all counting, taken from all nations, tribes, peoples and languages. They stood clothed in white robes before the throne in the presence of the lamb, with palm-branches in their hands, and cried with a loud voice, To our God, who sits on the throne, and to the Lamb, all saving power belongs to thee. And all the angels and saints that were standing round the throne, round the elders and the living figures, fell prostrate before the throne and paid God worship; Amen, they cried, blessing and glory and wisdom and thanksgiving and honour and power and strength belong to our God through endless ages, Amen. And one like the Son of Man, stood next to me and said to me, Behold! Look at their number beyond comprehension! Do you understand how this came to be and why all are robed in white? And I said unto him, My

Lord please tell me, so that I may understand. Then he said, Verily, the People of God have survived and overcome many great tribulations, yet they have washed their robes and made them white through the blood of the lamb and the blessed martyrs and saints. And now they stand before the throne of God, honouring him in his temple and in the presence of him who is seated on the throne, who dwells among them. They shall no more hunger, nor thirst. Neither shall they suffer from the heat nor cold. For the lamb who dwells among them shall protect them and shall lead them unto the living fountains of eternal waters; and God will wipe away all tears from their eyes.

Offertory Antiphon

O God and Divine Creator of all Heaven and Earth, may all your saints in Heaven bestow every blessing upon the Earth, to inspire and help our leaders and aid in the healing and unity of different dimensions as well as different conflicts and tensions between communities within the temporal world. Through our Lord Jesus Christ, your Son, who lives and reigns with you in the unity of the Holy Spirit, one God, for ever and ever.

Prayer over the Offerings

May God and the Divine Creator accept and sanctify these humble gifts as symbols of the genuine personal offerings we make in respect and honour of your *Holy Feast of All Saints*. Through Christ our Light and Saviour.

Communion Antiphon Psalm 85: 8

We hear the truth of God when he speaks; for he speaks of peace, love and mercy unto his people through his saints and we shall not corrupt his truth.

Prayer after Communion

Heavenly Father and God of all Heaven and Earth, we give thanks for the nourishment of your heavenly gifts of the Bread and Fruits of Eternal Spiritual Life. May our earnest participation in your *Holy Feast of All Saints* bring forth favourable blessings upon our lives, our community and your Holy Apostolic Universal Ecclesia. Through your Son our Lord Jesus Christ.

XX.XIII – FEAST OF THE SACRED EARTH

1. The Universal Feast of the Sacred Earth, also known as Earth Sunday is the Sunday before Mission Sunday. Feast of the Sacred Earth

Entrance Antiphon: Prov. 21: 30

There is no wisdom, no insight, no plan that can succeed without the presence of the Divine Creator.

Magisterium: Matthew Matt. 9:14-17

Then the disciples of John the Baptist came to Jesus and asked, How is it that thy disciples do not fast, when we and even the scribes and doctors of the law fast so often? To them Jesus said, Can you expect the men of the bridegroom's company to go mourning, while the bridegroom is still with them? No, the days will come when the bridegroom is taken away from them; then they will fast. Nobody uses a piece of new cloth to patch an old cloak; that would take away from the cloak all its pattern, and make the rent in it worse than before. Nor is new wine put into old wine-skins; if that is done, the skins burst, and there is the wine spilt and the skins spoiled. If the wine is new, it is put into fresh wine-skins, and so both are kept safe.

Good News: Matthew Matt 24:1-36

As Jesus and his disciples departed through the main gate of the outer sanctuary of the Great Temple at Jerusalem, he paused and looked back, before pointing at its immensity and said: Do you not see and feel the power of such buildings? Verily, I say unto you, there shall not be left here one stone upon another, that shall not be thrown down. Later, as he sat with his disciples, they asked him saying, Master, tell us when these things shall come to pass? And what shall be the signs of its coming and the end of the world? Jesus answered them and said, Take care that you do not allow anyone to deceive you. Many will come making use of my name; they will say, I am the Risen Christ, and many will be deceived by it, for they are ignorant of the revelation of scripture and the true signs. And those that shall follow you will hear of wars, and rumours of wars and great destruction. See then that you and those that follow are not troubled by such attempts to sow the seeds of fear. Change must happen, but it shall not be in the manner and way that people expected. For until that time, nation will continue to rise in arms against nation, kingdom against kingdom, and there will be plagues and famines and earthquakes in this region or that. Yet none of these are the hand of God, nor the true signs of the new beginning. Alas, it shall be when men will give you up to persecution, and will put you to death; and when all the world will be hating you because you bear true to my name and my teachings. Whereupon many will lose heart, and will betray and hate one another. Many false prophets and teachers will arise, and many will be deceived by them; and the charity of most men will grow cold, as they see wickedness abound everywhere. Yet mankind shall be saved by those heroes who endure to the last and restore life to the vine. Verily, the gospel of the kingdom must first be preached all over the world, so that all nations may hear the truth; only after that will the end and the new beginning come. When, you and those that are to follow shall see the fulfilment of the prophecies given by Daniel, then less the wicked who have set themselves up as false gods then flee into the mountains; and let those who have raised themselves in towers above the people, not come down for fear of judgement; and neither let the plantation owner return to the fields to take his profits. Alas, it will be hard for women who are with child, or have children at the breast, in those days; and you must pray that your flight may not be in the winter nor the feast days, for there will be distress then such as has not been since the beginning of the world, and can never be again. If not for those with heroic virtue, there would not have been hope for humanity, for in those days, such madness shall reign among the elect that they shall seek to cut short the days of men as they are gods or know the true mind of the Father of all Creation. At such a time, if a man tells you, See, here is the Risen Christ, or See, he is there, do not trust him. There will be many false messiahs and false prophets, who will rise up and pretend to show great signs and wonders, so that if it they can make possible, even the chief priests, kings and leaders shall be deceived. Mark well, I have given you and all future generations warning of it. If they tell you, then, See, he is here, in the desert, do not stir abroad; if they tell you, See, he is there, in hidden places, do not trust them. When the Son of Man comes, it will be like the lightning of scripture fulfilled that springs up from the east and flashes across to the west. It shall be like the great wind and spirit of the south, that heralds the change of seasons. In those days, the sun will be darkened, and the moon will refuse her light, and the stars will fall from heaven, and the powers of heaven will rock; and then the sign of the Son of Man will be seen in heaven; then it is that all the tribes of the land will unite and they will see the Son of Man coming through a new Covenant of Heaven, with great power and glory; and he will send out his angels with a loud blast of the trumpet, to gather his elect from the four winds, from one end of heaven to the other. The fig-tree will teach you a parable; when its branch grows supple, and begins to put out leaves, you know that summer is near; so you, when you see all this come about, are to know that it is near, at your very doors. Hear me, the generations of faithful will not have passed, before all this is accomplished. Though heaven and earth should pass away, my words will stand. But as for that day and that hour you speak of, they are known to none, not even to the angels in heaven; only the Father knows them.

Offertory Antiphon

O God and Divine Creator of all Heaven and Earth, who entrusted the sancity and care of the Earth and all Life to the community of nations of people, grant us the willingness and persistence to use our skills, talents, voices and choices to end all forms of rampant destruction of the environment or species for profit or political gains; and to each act in a concrete and responsible way in our lives in reducing waste of precious food and products that damage the environment. Through our Lord Jesus Christ, your Son, who lives and reigns with you in the unity of the Holy Spirit, one God, for ever and ever.

Prayer over the Offerings

May God and the Divine Creator accept and sanctify these humble gifts as symbols of the genuine personal offerings we make in respect and honour of your *Holy Feast of the Sacred Earth*. Through Christ our Light and Saviour.

Communion Antiphon — Psalm 104: 24-25

O God, how manifold are thy works! in wisdom hast thou made them all to be cared in your name. The earth is full of thy riches for all your children; and great are the lands and waters, wherein all forms of life, small and large are granted the right of dignified existence.

Prayer after Communion

Heavenly Father and God of all Heaven and Earth, we give thanks for the nourishment of your heavenly gifts of the Bread and Fruits of Eternal Spiritual Life. May our earnest participation in your *Holy Feast of the Sacred Earth* bring forth favourable blessings upon our lives, our community and your Holy Apostolic Universal Ecclesia. Through your Son our Lord Jesus Christ.

XX.XIV – FEAST OF CHRISTIAN MISSION

1. The Universal Feast of Christian Mission, also known as Mission Sunday. Feast of Christian Mission

Entrance Antiphon: Prov. 8: 13

To love God is to resist against all evil.

Magisterium: Matthew Matt.14:13-21

When Jesus heard the news of the cruel murder of John the Baptist, he withdrew into desert country, to be alone. But the multitudes from the towns heard of it, and followed him there. So, when he arrived, he found a great multitude there, and he took pity on them, and healed those who were sick. And now it was evening, and his disciples came to him and said, This is a desolate place and the people are hungry; yet we have struggled to find enough to fill ourselves. Better it we tell the multitudes to disperse in your name so that they may fend for themselves and not cause riot against what little we have. But Jesus told them, *There is no need for them to go away. Verily, it be a mark of your faith in me, that I shall not abandon you; and it be your mission and duty to the people to give them food to eat*. They answered, We have nothing with us, except five loaves and two fishes. Jesus then said, *Bring them to me here*. He then told the multitudes to sit down, and when the five loaves and the two fishes were brought to him he looked up to heaven, blessed and broke the loaves, and gave them to his disciples; and the disciples gave them to the multitude. All ate and had enough, and when they picked up what was left of the broken pieces they filled twelve baskets with them; about five thousand men had eaten, not reckoning women and children.

Good News: John

John 17: 20–26

Jesus prayed to our Heavenly Father and said, It is not only for the change of heart of the wicked that I pray; I pray for all those who shall find faith in me through the words of you my Father and Divine Creator. That in fulfilment of scripture they may one day all be united; and that they too may be one in heart, mind and spirit with us, as you my Father am in me, and I am in thee; so that such a world may be reborne to live in peace, love and dignity. For I have given them the divine wisdom and laws that you gave unto me, so that they can all be one, as we are one, if they so choose to fulfil your mission. While you are in me O Heavenly Father, grant that I may be in them, so they may be perfectly made one in the end. Thus, the world shall then know that it is you that has sent me; and it is you Father of all Life and Creation that has bestowed your love upon them as you have bestowed it upon me. This then my Father is my Will and Testament, that all those whom thou have entrusted to me may be granted your Divine Mercy and Forgiveness and so shall be granted eternal life and therefore give and do mercy and justice in your name, as it has been given to them. Heavenly Father, thou be perfect justice, yet the world has never properly acknowledged such Divine Mercy and Justice through your Divine Law. Yet these men acknowledge thee, as I acknowledge thee. Verily, I have revealed that your true name is love, so that the love thou has bestowed upon me may dwell in them and that I too may dwell in them through your Kingdom of Heaven upon the Earth.

Offertory Antiphon

O God and Divine Creator of all Existence and Mission, bless all those who choose to read and to hear your call to bring to life your Divine Word and Divine Liturgy as your Divine Mission through your One Holy Apostolic Universal Ecclesia. Through our Lord Jesus Christ, your Son, who lives and reigns with you in the unity of the Holy Spirit, one God, for ever and ever.

Prayer over the Offerings

May God and the Divine Creator accept and sanctify these humble gifts as symbols of the genuine personal offerings we make in respect and honour of your *Holy Feast of*

Christian Mission. Through Christ our Light and Saviour.

Communion Antiphon — Psalm 27: 1

The Lord my God is my light and my salvation; whom shall I fear? the Lord is the strength of my life; of whom shall I be afraid?

Prayer after Communion

Heavenly Father and God of all Existence and Mission, we give thanks for the nourishment of your heavenly gifts of the Bread and Fruits of Eternal Spiritual Life. May our earnest participation in your *Holy Feast of Christian Mission* bring forth favourable blessings upon our lives, our community and your Holy Apostolic Universal Ecclesia. Through your Son our Lord Jesus Christ.

Title XXI – Notes

XXI.I – NOTES

1. There are no Notes associated with the Official English First Edition of *Proper of Life and Mysteries* of *Missale Christus*. Notes

Title XXII – Tables

XXII.I – TABLES

1. The following Table assists in calculating from the Spring Equinox from 2021 to 2025 the Date for Good Friday and Easter Sunday. Tables

---

2021

1. Vernal Equinox – Saturday, March 20, 2021 2021

Good Friday – Friday, March 26th

Easter Sunday – Sunday, March 28th

2022

1. Vernal Equinox – Sunday, March 20, 2022 2022

Good Friday – Friday, March 25th

Easter Sunday – Sunday, March 27th

2023

1. Vernal Equinox – Monday, March 20, 2023 2023

Good Friday – Friday, March, March 24th

Easter Sunday – Sunday, March, March 26th

2024

1. Vernal Equinox – Tuesday, March 19, 2024 2024

Good Friday – Friday, March, March 22nd

Easter Sunday – Sunday, March, March 24th

2025

1. Vernal Equinox – Thursday, March 20, 2025 2025

Good Friday – Friday, March, March 21st

Easter Sunday – Sunday, March, March 23rd

www.ingramcontent.com/pod-product-compliance
Lightning Source LLC
LaVergne TN
LVHW081250100826
845148LV00009B/1184
9781644190661